Sexual Jihad

Sexual Jihad

The Role of Islam
in Female Terrorism

Christine Sixta Rinehart

LEXINGTON BOOKS
Lanham • Boulder • New York • London

Published by Lexington Books
An imprint of The Rowman & Littlefield Publishing Group, Inc.
4501 Forbes Boulevard, Suite 200, Lanham, Maryland 20706
www.rowman.com

6 Tinworth Street, London SE11 5AL, United Kingdom

British Library Cataloguing in Publication Information Available

Library of Congress Cataloging-in-Publication Data

ISBN 978-1-4985-5751-1 (cloth)
ISBN 978-1-4985-5753-5 (paper)
ISBN 978-1-4985-5752-8 (electronic)

Table of Contents

Acknowledgments

Writing a book requires a village and my village has been very supportive and helpful. My first debt of gratitude belongs to the University of South Carolina Union Campus. The Research and Productive Scholarship grant that I received for summer 2017 to interview convicted female terrorists in an Israeli prison was immensely helpful in adding some reality to this theory. I wish to thank the campus dean for creating a scholarship grant for faculty. I also want to personally thank him for his support of my research and the time he has spent reading everything I have ever published under his tenure. In addition, I wish to thank my two undergraduate research assistants for their editing and opinions concerning the book. Dawn and Bryana, you are fabulous!

Another debt of gratitude belongs to the people who helped me with Israel. A special thanks to the man who got me into the Israeli prison in two weeks, doing what political representatives could not accomplish at all—you know who you are. I also wish to thank the Israelis who helped to set up my interviews in Israel, including the Israeli Prison Services and academics at various universities who assisted me, including the University of South Carolina. I regret that you shall remain nameless but I am grateful for all of you. I also wish to thank my editor and the staff at Lexington Books, who are excellent to work with and are highly competent. Even after three books with Lexington, and different staff each time, you are all still wonderful to work with! *Volatile Social Movements and the Origins of Terrorism: The Radicalization of Change* was first published in 2014 and *Drones and Targeted Killing in the Middle East and Africa: An Appraisal of American Counterterrorism Policies* was first published in 2016.

I also want to thank my translator in Israel, who is simply amazing in one word and I find you inspirational. I hope and pray that you fulfill every potential that you have inside you for you are certainly a diamond in the rough.

I also wish to thank my reviewer for the time and effort he put into reviewing this manuscript: I must confess that I did not take every suggestion to heart and that the errors that I make are my own responsibility.

Lastly, my largest debt of gratitude is for my husband who was my chauffeur and handler in Israel and who has always given me tremendous support in all my endeavors.

Introduction

The Concept of Sexual Jihad

One of the earliest works on female terrorism was published by Eileen Mac-Donald in 1991. *Shoot the Women First*[1] was a particularly clever title as it referred to the advice given by the German GSG 9 anti-terrorist squad, who found that female terrorists were much more savage and volatile than male terrorists; therefore, shoot the women first! Of course, the Germans were facing the German Red Army Faction that counted two women among its founders including Gudrun Ensslin and Ulrike Meinhof, who were both formidable women in their own right. However, the book had a larger agenda in that MacDonald makes the point that female terrorists are not pawns nor duped into terrorism; for the women, just like the men, terrorism is a personal choice. MacDonald conducted several interviews with infamous female terrorists, so that academics and the public could finally get some insight into these intriguing, yet perplexing women.

Taking a similar viewpoint to MacDonald, the author also asserts that women, even Muslim women in repressive countries in the Middle East and North Africa (MENA), make their own choices concerning their involvement in terrorist organizations. Women are agents in their own societies and are not portrayed as victims in this book. Too often has research on female terrorism been relegated to feminist scholarship where feminists have looked at these women as victims of their own societies as though these women are incapable of making personal decisions. Through years of research on this topic, including conducting interviews and reading autobiographies, the author has come to view these women, particularly after speaking with some of them, as masters of their own destiny. Furthermore, the author asserts that for women in terrorist groups, their roles mostly reflect their cultural/religious norms. Thus although culture and society do have an effect on the roles that women play in terrorist organizations, the choice to act and how to act is a personal decision for these women.

There is limited research on female terrorism. Scholars in this field, like Mia Bloom, have contributed their share of scholarship but the concept of the jihadist (which will be defined later in this chapter) female terrorist has been almost ignored or, more frequently, relegated to the "do not touch for fear of condemnation, accusations of prejudice or intolerance, or even for the fear of one's own safety." The overarching goal of this book is exactly that. The research question that this book attempts to answer is "What is the role of Islam in female terrorism?"

This book is not a judgement of the religion of Islam nor is it an attempt to proselytize Muslims, Christians, or any other religion. Western scholars who are often secular have failed to take religion earnestly as a motivating factor for violence. Social, economic, or political factors are taken seriously yet religion rarely receives any credence despite that the fact that jihadist groups persistently use the religion of Islam as a justification for violence. The point should also be made here that any religion can be used to justify violence under an accommodating interpretation.[2]

That being said, the author is not a scholar of Islam but an international terrorism and counterterrorism expert. The only thing that a researcher should present is unbiased data and that is the author's role in this book. The goal is to clarify what role Islam plays in the motivation and cultural designation of jihadist female terrorism. The author is simply an observer and these women will tell their story in their own words. To do so otherwise generates a Western interpretation of jihadist violence.

Considering that eight jihadist case studies are used to illustrate the theory in this book, the author could not for reasons of safety, time, and ability gather her own primary data on all these groups. Therefore, this book contains little original primary research. Chapter 6 includes primary research on convicted female terrorists in an Israeli prison to bolster the theory presented in this book. However, it was simply not possible to gather research on the eight case studies in this book so the author relies on research conducted by others to create and document theory.

The title of the book, "Sexual Jihad," might appear risqué, but it actually refers to the Islamic practice of Muslim women traveling to war zones to marry and provide sexual comfort to male jihadists. The Arabic term is "*jihad al-nikah.*" As many religious figures in Islam have forbade women to participate in jihad, sexual jihad is a societal preordained role for female jihad. "Sexual" refers to the biological sex of the woman. A Muslim woman who provides sexual comfort to a jihadist will automatically enter paradise according to some Muslim Quranic interpretation. These women may be kidnapped and forced into sexual slavery or they may willingly go to a war zone to find their own jihadists. The title corresponds to the domestic role (that will be discussed later in the book) that women in jihadist terrorist organizations fulfill. As examples of this practice, ISIS jihadists have regularly kidnapped Yazidis, selling or holding them captives as sex slaves after forcible conversion to Islam. In other situations, ISIS jihadists have married Muslim women who have come to assist ISIS.[3]

This book has been on the author's to do list since graduate school. The author's previous research indicates that female terrorists both in the past and present are different than their male counterparts. Although women have regularly played a role in combat or insurgent organizations,[4] the presence of women in jihadist terrorist groups is greatly increasing. Scholars Russell and Miller[5] and Weinberg and Eubank[6] all assert that women in terrorist organizations are usually middle class, educated, and likely to be older when they first embrace terrorism than their male counterparts. Most importantly, women serve different roles in their organization and these roles depend on the society that they are living in. Weinberg and Eubank find that Italian women terrorists from the late twentieth century tend to be supporters 27 percent of the time, regulars 66 percent of the time, and leaders only 7 percent of the time.[7] However, these statistics for female jihadists are quite different as they are never leaders and rarely regulars.

Table I.1: The Roles of Female Terrorists throughout the World[1]

Terrorist Organization	Role of Women
Al-Aqsa Martyrs' Brigade	Suicide Bombers
Al-Qaeda	Logisticians, Recruiters
Boko Haram	Suicide Bombers
Chechen Separatists	Suicide Bombers
Euskadi Ta Askatuna (ETA)(Dead)	Supporters
HAMAS	Supporters, Suicide Bombers
Hezbollah	Logistician, Recruiters, Supporters
Japanese Red Army (Dead)	Leaders
Liberation Tigers of Tamil Eelam (LTTE)	Logistician, Recruiter, Suicide Bombers
Kurdistan Workers Party (PKK)	Supporters, Operators, Suicide Bombers
Provisional IRA (PIRA) (Dead)	Supporters, Planners of Attacks
Red Army Faction (RAF) (Dead)	Leaders, Founders, and Operators
Red Brigades (Dead)	Leaders
Revolutionary Armed Forces of Colombia (FARC)	Leaders and Operators
Sendero Luminoso (Shining Path)	Leaders, Operators, and Planners of Attacks
Weatherman	Leaders, Operators, and Planners of Attacks

1. This table is based on the author's observations throughout the years of women's roles in various terrorist organizations.

As academic Karla Cunningham[8] stated in 2003 in her article in *Studies in Conflict and Terrorism*, women's involvement in terrorist activity is increasing ideologically, logistically, and regionally for reasons such as: societal control that increases women's political participation and the strategic advantage of women in terrorist organizations. In his research performed from 1974–2008, scholar Ariel Merari found that approximately 5 percent of all suicide bombings were committed by women; this included 146 out of 2,896 total suicide bombings.[9] In Table I.1: The Roles of Female Terrorists throughout the World, a cross-longitudinal and cross-cultural examination of the roles of women in terrorist organizations is provided. Women in terrorist organizations are leaders, logisticians, recruiters, suicide bombers, operators, planners of attacks, founders, and supporters. Logisticians are responsible for business operations like transporting weapons, maintaining personnel and facilities, and making sure operations run smoothly. The word "operators" describes women who are foot soldiers like women in the FARC and LTTE. In the Western organizations such as the Red Army Faction in Germany, women are leaders and founders.

In this book, the author asserts that jihadist female terrorists are placed in three roles: the disposable, the domestic, or the secretary, which will be explained in great detail in chapter 1. Jihadist female terrorists do not take leadership roles like women have in Western terrorist organizations. Women are rarely, if ever, leaders and are definitely never the founders of jihadist terrorist organizations. Women in jihadist terrorist organizations are also rarely on the front lines or fighting as foot soldiers (operators). They are relegated, even in terrorist organizations, to the societal roles that Islamic society has given them or, more specifically, Islam. Women to some degree enforce and reinforce their positions in society, despite patriarchal culture. In Muslim countries, the religion of Islam cannot be divorced from the government and society, for it is an inherent part of law and culture. This chapter will continue with a literature review concerning the motivations of female terrorists.

THE MOTIVATIONS OF FEMALE TERRORISTS: A LITERATURE REVIEW

In the following literature review, the motivations of women in terrorist organizations are investigated. Academics Chenoweth and Moore note that "the study of terrorism has been dominated by assumptions that terrorism is a fundamentally masculine activity"[10] so research on terrorist motivations has mainly focused on men. There is little research concerning the functions/roles that women play in terrorist organizations so motivations are a natural substitute to explore instead. The few sources on the roles of women are also tied in where appropriate.

Early literature on female terrorists was often sexist and accused terrorist women of being ugly and masculine to the point that only a man in a terrorist organization would want them. Their femininity and sexuality was often called into question by scholars. In his chapter in *Perspectives on Terrorism*, Dr. Daniel Georges-Abeyie found that

> women who lack the characteristics and traits that society considers appropriate—gentleness, passivity, non-violent personalities, seductiveness, physically attractive faces and figures—may seek success in some non-feminine realm, by displaying aggression, unadorned faces and bodies, toughness, or other masculine qualities.[11]

Georges-Abeyie suggested that terrorist women have "masculine body types and psychological profiles." In early female terrorist literature, many female scholars even evaluated these theories. Georges-Abeyie goes on to provide an overview of traditional and somewhat patriarchal reasons for women to resort to terrorism. He found the following reasons for women's involvement in terrorism:

> 1) Revolutionary and terrorist activity offers excitement; 2) Danger is both an attraction as well as a repellant; 3) Terrorist violence is tied to causes which initially may appear legitimate; 4) Terrorist organizations provide an opportunity for upward mobility, in leadership and in an active role formulating the groups' policies, opportunities that are absent or extremely limited in the white male-dominated world of legitimate activity; 5) Terrorist organizations offer change and a renunciation of the current male-dominated chauvinistic mores; 6) The traditional . . . stereotype of women as weak, supportive, submissive, silent, and of lower intelligence and drive is absent in the philosophies of many terrorist organizations; 7) Membership in a terrorist organization is the natural outgrowth of extreme feminist organizations; 8) Women are by nature more violent and dangerous than men, and terrorist organizations provide an outlet for this tendency; 9) Women are rejecting stereotypical roles and thus adopting traditional male roles that include revolutionary and terrorist violence; 10) Hormonal disturbances, caused by excessive sexual freedom and particularly by having sexual relations before maturity, affect these women; 11) Economic, political, familial liberation due to the trend toward greater justice and equality for women plays a role; 12) A continuation of natural selections, or the survival of the fittest has an influence; 13) Middle-class white Anglo-Saxon Protestant (WASP) restraints, in regard to mind-sets (ideas and attitudes) as well as behavior are rejected.[12]

Although Georges-Abeyies introduces numerous valid reasons why women are inclined to join a terrorist organization, many of these reasons are somewhat suspect as they apply to a small minority and in some cases are quite sexist. For example, it is doubtful that women become terrorists because of sexual promiscuity before physical maturity. One has to wonder if it has ever been speculated that men become terrorists because of sexual promiscuity at an early age. In addition, when gender is used as a predictor of crime, women rarely commit crimes in comparison to men.[13]

The following literature review section will focus on the six major categories that motivate women to join terrorist organizations. The first category, "It's a Man's World," talks about the domination of women by men in terrorist organizations and refers to patriarchal explanations for women to join terrorist organizations. Under this theory, female terrorists are the pawns of male terrorists and patriarchal societies are perpetuated. Women are forced by men to participate in terrorist organizations in one way or another. The second category, "Liberation!", discusses literature that argues that women join terrorist organizations to advance the equality of women in society. Although they may not be Western feminists per se, these women may seek to increase women's rights in a culturally acceptable or radical manner. The third category, "The Gray Areas: The Four R's and Other Motivations," talks about the various personal individual motivations that cause women to participate in terrorists organizations; this area specifically refers to Mia Bloom's[14] concepts: revenge, redemption, relationships, respect, and rape (rape is later discussed in Bloom's book *Bombshell*). The fourth category, "Hard Times," talks about financial difficulties that may cause women to join a terrorist organization or to engage in martyrdom operations to get money. The fifth category, "Cultural Explanations," identifies the culture that the women grow up in as part of their motivation for joining a terrorist organization. The sixth category, "Strategic Reasons," refers to the possible strategic benefits that terrorist organizations get from including women in their ranks. Women arouse less suspicion and are able to avoid detection and capture better than men.

It is important to note that the theories presented in the following literature review are based on different case studies throughout time and place. Although jihadist women are included, Marxist terrorist organizations, like the Tamil Tigers, also have soldiers and suicide bombers so this research is not sensitive to cultural or religious variance. The reason for this is that very little research has exclusively paid attention to religious and cultural differences as female terrorists have only been examined in one homogenous category. In addition, jihadist female terrorists have rarely been examined as a category of scholarship.

As a side note on literature review organization, scholarship on female suicide bombing is also included in the literature review since it is especially relevant to book chapters later in the book. Although one may point out that committing suicide has a different motivation than joining a terrorist organization, a woman usually joins a terrorist organization, even for a short time, first before she decides to participate in a suicide bombing or she has a previous association. Typically, someone from the organization she represents must train her how to use her weapon and how to disguise her suicide terrorist attack. This training is part of her inclusion into the group.

It's a Man's World

This section argues that terrorism is essentially a man's world and that women are let in only with the acquiescence of men or are forced into the organization by men; once part of a terrorist organization, women are still controlled by the men in the organization. Social scientist Deborah Galvin finds in an early article on female terrorism that terrorism is done on men's terms. She states:

> Female terrorism, has as yet, no autonomy. It is part of a male engineered, male dominated activity and even the most ardent feminist must recognize both the fact and the remote likelihood of it changing. Terrorism is all about power. The male terrorist struggling for power is not about to share it with the female, though he welcomes her aid and actively seeks to co-opt it. The thinking female terrorist must take terrorism on these terms—or leave it.[15]

While in terrorist organizations, other scholars have stated that women are controlled and used by men in the organization. Journalist Barbara Victor[16] asserts that Palestinian female suicide bombers are victims in her book *Army of Roses*, published in 2003, which provides personal insight into the lives of these women. Palestinian suicide bombers are used by men for political purposes. In 2006 Yoram Schweitzer, senior researcher at Israel's Institute for National Security and director of the Institute's research program, argued that "Female suicide bombers appear almost exclusively in societies that are heavily traditionalist and conservative, where women lack equal rights and their status in society in much lower than that of their male counterparts."[17] Scholars Cragin and Daly[18] state that "the main differences [between female and male terrorists] arise not in the minds of women, but in the minds of the male leadership of terrorist groups—are they willing to put women on the front lines, or not?"

Adding to this idea, in another 2016 article in *Studies in Conflict and Terrorism*, scholar Margolin finds that the "patriarchal structure of society continues to be reflected in Palestinian terrorist organizations."[19] The article examines women in Palestinian terrorism from 1965 to 1995, using quantitative analysis, concerning ninety-seven cases. During the thirty-year period, women increased their participation in terrorist attacks but contributed to mostly, low intensity attacks. Before the first period (1965–1986), women's involvement in terrorism was infrequent and women were part of high intensity attacks. During the second period (1987–1995) and including the First Intifada, women's roles grew; women would act outside of the Palestinian terrorist organizations if necessary.

Liberation!

In the author's own research, she has found that women in terrorist organizations join terrorist groups to assert their equality to men and to advance their quest for liberation. Female terrorists usually do not emerge from countries that have gender equality or strong feminist movements. By joining terrorist organizations, female terrorists "are reaching for political equality by breaking the barriers of societal ideas of proper female political participation."[20] In her master's thesis Genevieve Pierce also argues that women act "violently to gain political agency and obtain a voice."[21] For a fundamental example, Kathleen Blee advocated that American white women joined the KKK in the 1920s for "protecting women and children, asserting the rights of women relative to men, and incorporating women's political savvy into the political arena."[22] This time frame coincided with the passage of the 19th Amendment and women were asserting their political rights. Journalist Eileen MacDonald found that women in the Irish Republican Army also joined the organization to advocate for women's rights.[23] Academics Weinberg[24] and Weinberg and Eubank[25] argue that waning family and Catholic religious authority allowed feminist militant ideology to take root in Italian terrorist groups and that women mobilized in Italy in the late 1960s as a result of feminist issues.[26] Researcher Talbot[27] found that women in various terrorist organizations became involved because of feminist ideology. Academics Dalton and Asal concluded from a dataset of 395 terrorist organizations that "women's social rights, educational attainment level, and terrorist organization size and age" are all important predictors of female involvement in terrorist organizations.[28] Academics Raghavan and Balasubramaniyan in their international analysis of female terrorists argue that "most of the time, it is the male domination in societies that drives women to join the ranks of terrorists and move further as suicide bombers."[29]

This equality for women in non-Western countries does not typically take a Western form. Women want equality that is culturally specific, not necessarily Western-defined. The Western idea that women are not violent is simply incorrect. Women can be violent and can use violence, like me, to accomplish their agendas. In her book *Gender and the Political*, academic Amanda Third[30] takes the concept of feminism a bit farther and asserts that female terrorists are in fact radical feminists centered on feelings of rage and retribution. This ties to the idea that feminist organizations have encouraged women to commit acts of violence. The Militant Black Panther Aunties (Germany) and Red Zora (Germany) are good examples of extreme feminist organizations that encouraged women to commit acts of terrorism against a patriarchal society. In addition, some scholars like Third assert that social changes during the 1960s and 1970s from the feminist movement have created an environment that is conducive to female violence and terrorism.

The Gray Areas—The Four Rs and Other Motivations

Several scholars find that vengeance and personal suffering are motivations for female suicide bombers. Pedazhur[31] states that personal crisis and revenge are motivations for a female suicide bombing. In a 2008 study, Jacques and Taylor[32] coded the biographical information of thirty female suicide bombers and thirty male suicide bombers. They found that women were motivated by revenge and personal motivations in comparison to men who were motivated by religious/nationalistic factors. In a study published in 2008 by Speckhard and Ahmedova of 110 Chechen female suicide bombers, the authors found that personal trauma was involved in every case.[33] Jacques and Taylor also found that female suicide bombers were just as likely as males to be recruited through peer influence, exploitation, or self-promotion, although men were liked to be motivated by religious persuasion.

Taking this a step farther, Mia Bloom[34] argues that female terrorists are motivated by the four Rs: revenge, redemption, relationship, and respect, and in some cases rape. The "revenge" component refers to women who are motivated to alleviate the painful death of a close family member through terrorism. The "redemption" component describes women who have been in illicit relationships or have committed some type of societal sin; the purpose of this redemption is to be redeemed in the eyes of the community. In the "relationship" motivation component, women are mobilized by family, friends, or significant others. The last component, "respect," refers to women who are trying to earn the esteem of their communities; this is particularly for female suicide bombers. Bloom adds that one final motivation in some cases is "rape" in that women in Muslim societies who are raped privately bear the stigma of being a rape victim and seek to clean their slate through violence.

Raghavan and Balasubramaniyan[35] corroborate Bloom's research in their international assessment of female terrorists, stating that "women take to terrorism due to various factors like economic, political, psychological, and social issues." Academic and politician Anat Berko[36] finds that Palestinian women turn to terrorism to avenge the death of a loved one or to solve a personal problem as a result of thirteen interviews with Palestinian women. In the background for these Palestinian women are the motivations of religion, culture, society, and the national issue.

Redemption refers to the uncontrollable and societally undesirable traits in women that cause rejection in society, which provide the impetus for Islamic martyrdom in particular. For example, Thouria Khamour was a failed suicide bomber in the Tanzim unit for Fatah. Thouria volunteered for a suicide mission that later failed because she was unmarriable and an embarrassment to her family due her "tomboyish" ways. After some prison time, Thouria began to state that her motives were based on the Palestinian cause, adapting to a Palestinian religious narrative.[37] The redemption component of Bloom's research needs more examination as the individual motives vary and it is impossible to question a successful suicide bomber as they are deceased.

Regarding the relationship component, many scholars have argued that women only join terrorist organizations because of the men in their lives. Whether it be brothers or husbands, voluntary or forced, women connect with terrorist organizations because of their relationships with men. Nancy Laur[38] asserts that the ETA women joined the organization because of the men in their lives. Journalist Robin Morgan[39] argues that women join terrorist organizations because they are seduced by the violent male terrorists and they support the men's struggles, perhaps to an even greater extent than the men. In a similar vein, Weinberg and Eubank,[40] Talbot,[41] and Raghavan and Balasubramaniyan[42] found that many women join terrorist organizations because of their men as can be explained by the numerous marriages in terrorist organizations. The idea is that the husband will join the organization and his wife will therefore follow suit.

Putting this idea of male control on its side, de Catalado Neuberber and Valentini find in the Italian terrorist organizations in the late twentieth century that women with weak mothers and strong fathers or women with strong suffering mothers and strong fathers tend to pursue terrorism to advocate for social justice. Most of the women that they interviewed have this similar family dynamic. "By finding a 'weak entity' to love and save outside the family [terrorist organization cause], a woman demonstrates both to her mother as well as her father what they should have done to use their strength for a 'good' cause, sacrificing themselves constructively."[43] Most of these Italian female terrorists were not repentant for their actions while the men in the same organizations were repentant.

Other scholars state that women join terrorist organizations because friends and family within their sphere of influence join the terrorist organization first.

Donatella della Porta found in her study of the women in the Italian Red Brigades that women joined because of influence from family and friends.[44] Marc Sageman also found that al-Qaeda members are likely to have relatives or friends in an organization when they join the organization.[45] Al-Qaeda solidifies their alliances with other organizations through marriage and kin ties. Raghavan and Balasubramaniyan[46] indicate that women join terrorist groups due to peer pressure or to be in a group with family and friends.

Some other scholars have found that national insecurity has been the impetus for women to join terrorist organizations. In earlier research, Caiazza asserts that "radicalism stems from a desire to protect their homes and communities in times of economic and political insecurity"[47] as these movements promise better conditions. Academic Katerina Standish[48] finds similar conclusions in her research on Chechnya and Palestine as did Speckhard and Akhmedova concerning Chechen women.[49] Standish notes that when levels of security decrease, female suicide bombing is a response to the foreign occupation. Chechen and Palestinian women are not motivated by religion but gravitate towards terrorist organizations for basic needs when social infrastructures break down. Sociologist Skaine argues that women, like men, are motivated to become suicide bombers to fulfill their need to participate in war.[50] Marvasti and Plese argue that female suicide bombers appear in communities "under invasion or occupation by a foreign army."[51] In an occupied situation, women as well as men can use suicide bombings to try to expel a foreigner.

In yet an additional set of motivations, Grisit and Mahan point out that the human rights abuses in Sri Lanka and Indonesia motivated women to join the LTTE and the GAM respectively.[52] In another article from the same year, Miranda Alison[53] explains that nationalism is a reason that women join the LTTE. Alison also gives the women agency but states that although women's rights are somewhat important to women in the LTTE, the cause of an independent Tamil country is the primary motivation for women to join the LTTE.

Hard Times

Preeminent scholar Pedazhur claims that both male and female suicide bombers may be motivated by a financial crisis to commit a suicide bombing. Saddam Hussein and the Saudi Arabian family in addition to other Arab states have been inclined to offer money to the families of martyred suicide bombers. Mayilla Soufangi was a member of the Lebanese United Front. After running away from home, she joined the organization in desperate need of money. She received financial assistance and in turn volunteered to complete a suicide mission.[54] Pedazhur states that this is a weak motivating factor as Mayilla also wanted to kill Israelis.

Cultural Explanations

In her work on Palestinian women, Terri Toles Patkin suggests that women join terrorist organizations because it is part of their culture to do so. Patkin states, "The decision to become a suicide bomber reflects a lifetime of immersion in a culture that regards terrorism as an acceptable behavioral choice, and is voluntary as any culturally-influenced choice may be."[55] She goes to state that children in Palestinian society are dressed as mini-bombers by their parents and are brought up to imitate suicide bombers.

Adding to what Patkin states, Yoram Schweitzer found that the terrorists he interviewed did not disagree with the right of any Palestinian person "to act in defense of his or her people. To them [male leaders], however, the correct way for women to act was different—not through suicide terrorist attacks."[56] However, these interviews by Schweitzer included many men who had sent women on terrorist attacks. Schweitzer noted,

> Most prominent was the women's contradictory versions of their stories, and the general effect that collective time with fellow prisoners had on their autobiographies. This aspect emerged especially in the personal interviews but in some of the media interviews as well, conducted in the earlier stages of their imprisonment, before they were briefed by their domineering cellmates. In these personal interviews, the women expressed a strong feeling that their difficult personal situation had been exploited to lead them to volunteer for their mission, without their having fully thought through the deed they planned to commit. In contrast, personal remarks were generally absent from the media interviews conducted with them after they had already spent time in prison. The latter interviews were primarily products of an indoctrination process, formal or informal, in prison. They bore a dominant nationalistic character, and reflected the uniform dogmatic messages that the organizations wish to deliver.[57]

Schweitzer makes the important point that the stories concerning the motivations of female terrorists change once the women have spent some time in prison. The culture in prison forces the women to change their stories or outlooks in addition to the peer pressure to conform to the movement rhetoric in prison.

Strategic Reasons

Other scholars advocate that men in leadership positions within the terrorist organization make the decision to use women for tactical advantages. In a short article written for the *Canadian Institute of Strategic Studies*, Jessica Davis[58] finds that women's roles in terrorism have increased tremendously because of their tactical and strategic advantages. Women are viewed as nonthreatening and are able to gain access to places that men cannot. Women are viewed as incapable of committing violence and using weaponry. Women can move in and out of the public sphere with less notice. A female terrorist attack or suicide bombing brings great notoriety to the cause and can induce men to join out of shame or guilt. In her article on female terrorists, DOD Principal Deputy Alisa Stack-O'Connor states that "Groups overcome cultural resistance to women's involvement when tactics require it or they [the terrorist organization] face a shortage of males."[59] Stack O'Connor found that women became involved when men were difficult to find in several terrorist organizations. Women can also move about with less suspicion and could hide bombs under their loose clothing.

In her article "What's Special about Female Suicide Terrorism?" Lindsey O'Rourke[60] examines female suicide attacks between 1981 and July 2008 using the Chicago Project on Terrorism. She argues that 1) Terrorist groups use females because of their superior effectiveness and as a tactical advantage. Female suicide bombers are more destructive in their attacks versus males. This is because women generate less suspicion, can conceal more explosives, and receive more relaxed security measures. 2) O'Rourke states that organizations use women because their aim is strategic success. 3) Terrorist groups use particular rhetoric to recruit female suicide bombers even though their goals are strategic success not ideology. 4) Female attackers are motivated to commit suicide bombings as a result of deep commitment to their communities. O'Rourke also found that religious groups tend to use female suicide bombers only after secular groups in the same conflict used them.

In response to Lindsey O'Rourke's work, Krislyn Reuter[61] wrote her master's thesis on the use of female suicide bombers in jihadist terrorist organizations. Reuter finds that female suicide terrorism was a technological innovation put forth by male leaders of jihadist groups who were no longer able to use male suicide terrorism. The cultural barriers against the use of female suicide terrorism including sexism and ideology only bear entry to female suicide terrorists if the gain is great enough.

In his master's thesis concerning Afghanistan, Iraq, and Sri Lanka, Matthew Dearing[62] somewhat conversely found that tactics do not explain the use of suicide bombers. Instead structural issues such as cultural norms, institutional barriers, and the dynamics of conflict play a role in whether women are used as suicide bombers. In Iraq and Sri Lanka, women are used as suicide bombers; however, in Afghanistan, women were not suicide bombers because Afghans have freedom of mobility and resistance, Afghan culture prohibits female participation, and there is not a culture of martyrdom in Afghanistan.

After women leave a terrorist organization, they are often ostracized from society whereas men are looked upon as heroes. In a 2007 article in *Studies in Conflict and Terrorism*, Berko and Erez[63] interviewed fourteen women concerning their involvement in terrorist organizations. Although women are empowered in Palestinian society after they join a terrorist organization, the authors found that women actually lose that empowerment after they leave the organization. In particular, they were shunned by Palestinian society for not fulfilling their gender roles. In the same issue of the thirtieth volume in *Studies in Conflict and Terrorism*, Von Knop[64] found that in al-Qaeda, women are interested in gaining power only through the traditional scope of their roles in society. Von Knop asserts that there is such a concept as a female jihad. Wives influence their husbands and sons to make their jihad. The mother who is the first and only love in the son's life is also responsible for finding him a bride (most likely one that he will not love). The mother continues to fulfill her traditional roles as the provider and nurturer of male jihad. This is why the concept of male jihad committed by a woman is not socially acceptable for society.

Summation of the Literature Review

Female terrorism is a relatively newly studied phenomenon. Although there are classics like Eileen MacDonald's *Shoot the Women First* published in 1992 or more recent noteworthy publications such as Mia Bloom's *Bombshell*, there is still a tremendous amount of research to be completed. There really is no consensus as to why women join terrorist groups. All of the previous studies have merit and they provide a multifaceted explanation of female terrorist motivation but there is no consensus. Bloom asserts that women are motivated by revenge, redemption, relationship, and respect, and perhaps even rape.[65] These are five reasons, in addition to the numerous other reasons mentioned.

A few scholars have considered Islam as a possible motivation for terrorism. Zedalis in her groundbreaking short research paper pays homage to the fact that religious terrorism does exist and that the motivation for female suicide bombers is documented in the Quran. Zedalis states,

> Religious terrorism is a particularly potent from of violence . . . Devout Muslims believe, that in death, every martyr, male or female, is welcomed by a minimum of 70 apparitions *(houri-el-ein)* of unnatural beauty who wipe away the martyrs' sins, open the gates of heaven, and provide them with all the pleasures that God has given to mankind.[66]

Speckhard and Akhmedova state that actively seeking out a Wahhabi terrorist group and exposure to the Wahhabism ideology was found in nearly every case of the 110 Chechen female suicide bombers. They studied the Wahhabi message and it helped the women who were searching for meaning in life.[67]

For the most part, religion as an explanatory factor has been ignored. In the case of this book, Islam is the catalyst for women's roles in jihadist terrorist organizations. The role of Islam in female terrorism is often ignored or disregarded as religion is a thorny subject that very few scholars want to address or study. The next part of this introduction will focus on the concepts used in this book including terrorism, Islamism, jihadism, and Salafism.

CONCEPTS

The Concept of Terrorism

Vastly different definitions of terrorism have been constructed because it is a complicated phenomenon to explain. There is no agreement from an American perspective to an international perspective on the definition of terrorism. The American CIA cannot even agree with the American FBI. In all her scholarship, the author has stuck to the following definition that was created for a published paper in graduate school:

> It is important to establish that terrorism is defined by those who have power. A Western definition of terrorism will differ greatly from a definition of terrorism that may come from the Revolutionary Armed Forces of Colombia (FARC) or the Tamil Tigers (LTTE). The FARC or LTTE would not call themselves terrorists but revolutionaries, a much more positive word. Non-Western violent groups are labeled as terrorist groups by Westerners, while the non-Westerners call themselves revolutionaries in their quest to end Western domination. President Ronald Reagan (1986) made this point perfectly clear when he popularized the cliché "One man's terrorist is another man's freedom fighter" in a press conference. Directly afterwards, in the same press conference, Reagan stated that the previous quote was nonsense and that terrorists were "people who deliberately chose as a target to murder and maim innocent people who have no influence upon the things that they think of as their political goals" (May 1986).
>
> What differentiates revolutionaries from terrorists? In a book about revolutions, Jack Goldstone (2003) identifies many terrorist groups as revolutionaries, but there are differences between revolutionaries and terrorists. The people attacked are important. Terrorism is a violent tactic that is used by people who call themselves revolutionaries. These revolutionaries view themselves as oppressed. Their oppression lies in their inability to possess power and resources, and by performing public acts of violence towards people or property, they exert their power in the element of surprise and fear that they create.
>
> I define "terrorists" as follows: Terrorists are non-governmental entities that intentionally attack civilian populations that are noncombatants within their

own struggle for power. Revolutionaries who use terrorist tactics (like the White Terror who killed thousands during the French Revolution) become terrorists. One who uses terrorist tactics is a terrorist. Terrorists may subscribe to revolutionary ideology but the killing or terrorizing of noncombatants is what defines a terrorist as a terrorist, and differentiates them from a freedom fighter. Terrorism is the weapon of the weak. For the most part, terrorism needs media coverage; terrorists and the media have a symbiotic relationship. For without the media, the element of fear would not be placed in the hearts of the populace and without terrorists, the media would have less to cover and would receive lower ratings. Terrorists want citizens to lose their faith in the ability of their government to protect them; terrorism thrives on chaos.[68]

The previous definition will be used in this book to categorize the organizations used in this book. All eight of the organizations used as case studies in this book—Al Aqsa Martyrs' Brigade, Boko Haram, the Chechen Separatists, Hamas, Hezbollah, ISIS, Muslim Brotherhood, and al-Qaeda—have been defined by the United States' State Department as terrorist organizations either currently or in the past.[69] The case studies in this book will be analyzed as terrorist organizations even though a few of them like Hamas and the Muslim Brotherhood are currently political parties or some have even taken government power like the Muslim Brotherhood, Hamas, or ISIS. Al Aqsa Martyrs' Brigade is part of the Palestinian National Authority. This research is not concerned with the political party or government components of the organization but instead is concerned with the terrorist tactics that the groups have used or their terrorist components. Most terrorist organizations will return to using terrorist tactics when necessary. Therefore, this research examines these groups in their roles as terrorist organizations throughout time and space.

Islamism, Jihadism, and Salafism

A distinction needs to be made on the ideologies of Islamism, Jihadism, and Salafism and the additional terminology used in this book. In her book *Knowing the Enemy*, military historian Mary Habeck[70] from Johns Hopkins University made the important point that blaming Muslims for the September 11, 2001, terrorist attacks would be unjustified as many Muslims throughout the world were horrified by these terrorist attacks. It is also true that at the same time many Muslims throughout the world were celebrating the attacks and public opinion polls showed tremendous support in some countries for the 9-11 attacks. An underlying question throughout this book is, what classification of Islam do the case studies in this book represent? Many scholars use the term "Fundamentalism," "Islamist," or "Islamism" to describe the sect of Muslims that commit acts of terrorism using holy books such as the

Quran, Hadith, or *Sunna* as a means of justification. According to Habeck, Islamists advocate for a return of Islam to political power and for a revival of the religion. Islamists believe that Islamic values should play a central role in citizenry and should govern both the personal and the political components of life. However, this term does not clarify the issue as Islamists are not always advocates of violence; some are committed to democracy and the international system. Not all Islamists advocate violence as a means of obtaining political change. So the term "Islamist" is not specific enough (nor inherently correct) to describe the terrorist organizations examined in this book.

The term Salafism or Salafist refers to Muslims who believe that the purest form of Islam occurred in the days of the Prophet Muhammad; therefore, to be a true or pure Muslim, one must follow the traditions of Muhammad as closely as possible. Salafists believe in dressing like men in the time of Muhammad with ankle length trousers and using twig tooth brushes. Salafists, from "Salaf," believe in following the letter of the law rather than the spirit. Salafists tend to practice Islam in solitude through preaching, education, and avoidance of political authorities and running for political office. Although there are some Salafi-jihadists such as some parts of al-Qaeda or ISIS, the term "Salafi" is not specific enough to refer to all the organizations in this book.[71]

Habeck settles on the term "jihadist" to describe groups such as al-Qaeda that carried out the 9-11 attacks in the name of Islam. Jihadists have specific ideas about how to revive Islam, returning Muslims to political power, and punishment for enemies. Every detail and instruction of the Quran should be followed until the end of life. Jihadists seek to overthrow the international system and put an "all-encompassing" Islamic State in its place. Therefore, jihad is used to accomplish political goals. Jihad is obligatory for every able-bodied Muslim as political leaders are not legitimate and do not command the authority to call for justified violence. Jihadists also use suicide bombings (martyrdom operations) justified by the promises in the Quran and Hadith (as will be elaborated on later in chapter 1) as one of their major terrorist tactics of choice.

Jihadists believe that the Muslim community of believers has been humiliated by the unbelievers ruling them although the classification of "unbeliever" is subjective. Habeck believes that there are three reasons for this failure of Islam according to the jihadists. The first reason lies in early Islam after the four righteous Caliphs (*al-Rashidun*) were replaced with a hereditary monarchy under the Abbasid Empire. This led to great economic, political, and social ills for Muslims, which has continued into the present time. The second reason lies in the destruction of the Ottoman Caliphate by Mustafa Kamal Atatürk, the founder of modern Turkey. The Caliphate is responsible for the implementation of Sharia Law and leading Muslims into battle against the infidels. Since the abolishment of the Caliphate, Muslims have been adrift in a weakened religion without guidance. The third reason advocates that Muslims have lost dignity and honor as a result of unbelief or specifically the unbelievers who have humiliated and dominated Islam. The unbelievers are solely responsible for all the evil that Muslims experience around the world; unbelievers are currently defined as the West, the United States, and Israel. If Europe, the United States, and Jews are destroyed, the jihadists believe that Islam will return to its former glory. Jihadists believe that only violence can save a distraught Muslim community and can bring Islam back to its former days of glory. This book will embrace the term jihadist to describe the terrorist organizations included in this book.

CASE STUDY EXPLANATION

The following section provides a brief introduction and overview for each of the case studies included in this book. The section is not meant to provide an all-inclusive chronological history or ideological study of each terrorist organization but will give the reader some necessary preliminary background on each terrorist organization. Although these organizations have changed throughout time, this book is not a study of each organization but instead focuses on how these organizations have used women throughout time. As a side note, these case studies were chosen for three primary reasons. The first reason is that these organizations are all terrorist organizations that involve and use female terrorists. Secondly, all are jihadist terrorist organizations as will be explained in the description of each case study. As a side note, from a population perspective, these groups represent the major Muslims sects throughout the world. Seven of these organizations are Sunni and one is Shia. This statistically represents the Muslim world as approximately 85 to 90 percent of all Muslims are Sunni and 10 to 15 percent are Shia. Hezbollah is the only Shia terrorist organization in the case studies. The third reason for the use of these organizations as case studies pertains to the amount of information on each organization. Organizations such as Hamas, Hezbollah, and al-Qaeda have copious amounts of information available on them. Information on other terrorist organizations such as Fatah (Tanzim) and Palestinian Islamic Jihad, which were originally included in the book proposal, have limited information. Eight case studies is also a respectable number of terrorist organizations to examine the research questions and to create reasonable theories. The case studies throughout the book will be discussed alphabetically.

Al-Aqsa Martyrs' Brigade

The al-Aqsa Martyrs' Brigade (al Aqsa) was created by fighters from Fatah as the military wing of the organization in 2000. Although Fatah did not officially recognize it until December 18, 2003, when it asked the leaders of al-Aqsa to join the Fatah Council. One al-Aqsa member noted that the organization was created after Ariel Sharon visited the Temple Mount in 2000. Al-Aqsa was created to compete with Hamas in popularity on the streets of Palestine. The group painted Quranic symbols and slogans on the streets. Al-Aqsa and Hamas at times actually sponsored joint attacks although the primacy and popularity of Hamas made that period relatively brief. The organization was funded by Yasser Arafat himself, including a 20,000 USD payment to the organization just days after the March 21, 2002, Jerusalem bombing.[72] Several other payments have been made to al-Aqsa from Fatah and the group receives 3 percent of gross income from Palestinian Authority employee salaries.[73] However, al-Aqsa states that it does not have a formal leader or central organization with small groups of men making decisions as needed.[74]

Al-Aqsa was the first Palestinian terrorist organization to use a female suicide bomber, Wafa Idris (January 28, 2002), and has also used children suicide bombers. After al-Aqsa's use of female martyrs, other Palestinian terrorist organizations such as Hamas followed suit. Fatah leaders have implored al-Aqsa not to attack so many civilians but the organization did not comply.

It can be argued that al-Aqsa Martyrs' Brigade is a jihadist terrorist organization. Al-Aqsa states that it will not stop attacks "unless Israel withdraws from the Palestinian territories, releases Palestinian prisoners and stops assassinating Palestinian leaders."[75] Al-Aqsa Martyrs' Brigade is technically a secular group, based on Palestinian nationalism. However, the group uses jihad and Islam to justify its attacks. Prospective suicide bombers are enticed with passages from the Quran and Hadith concerning martyrdom and suicide bombings are justified through the Quran and Hadith.

In addition, we must remember that the organization came out of Fatah and is funded by Fatah so we must look at Fatah to understand the ideology of al-Aqsa Martyrs' Brigade. Fatah believes in expanding the Levant to its previous capacity and returning to the former days of the Islamic empires. Fatah also believes in an Islamic Palestine ruled by Sharia Law. Although Fatah has changed its ideology throughout history, it uses jihadist rhetoric whenever politically necessary to appeal to the Palestinian people, particularly if Hamas is a political opponent at the time.[76] Although the stretch to classify al-Aqsa Martyrs' Brigade as jihadist is the largest in all the case studies in this book, the terrorist organization is a jihadist group.

Boko Haram

The *Jamā 'at Ahl al-Sunna li-Da'wa wa-l-Jihād* (The Sunni Group for Preaching and Fighting, JASDJ) or Boko Haram was founded in 2002 by Muhammad Yusuf and Abubakar Shekau, although there is some disagreement as to that date. Yusuf was engaged in several social movements before he helped form Boko Haram. From 2002 to 2008, Boko Haram was categorized as a quietist Salafi group and in 2008, the group embraced ultra-Salafi-jihadism based on the teachings of Ibn Taymiyya. The Nigerian government assassination of the founder Ustaz Mohammed Yusuf occurred on July 30, 2009 during the Boko Haram uprising. The death of its founder helped to further radicalize the group.

Boko Haram declared itself an Islamic state in 2014 and pledged itself as the West African Province of ISIS on March 7, 2015. Boko Haram is located in three states in northeastern Nigeria including: Borno, Yobe, and Adamawa. Founder Muhammad Yusuf had the point of view that anything that cannot be attested to in the Quran or Hadith is an innovation that needs to be destroyed. Boko Haram believes in the strict application of Islamic Law, which includes the rejection of the Earth revolving around the Sun, Darwinism, and the concept that rain is produced by a condensation cycle. The group also believes that other religious denominations should be destroyed, such as Christians and Shia Muslims. Western education or any education that is not based on the Quran is forbidden. As a side note in Boko Haram, the rights of women and homosexuals, the molestation of infants, democracy, blue films, prostitution, and drinking alcohol are all illegal although several of these laws follow Nigerian laws.[77]

According to academics Abdulbasit Kassim and Michael Nwankpa, Boko Haram has gone through approximately four phases of violence. The first phase (2010–2011) was low-tech and did not have any suicide bombings. Ideological solidification and proselytization, such as "commanding the good and forbidding the evil," was the purpose during this period. The second phase (2011–2012) was also marked by low-tech strategies. The first suicide bombing occurred during summer 2011, as Boko tried to start a civil war by attacking Christians and targeting greater Nigeria. The retrenchment period (2012–2013) consisted of attacks that were contained in Borno, Yobe, and Adamawa states. In 2014–2015, Boko Haram established its Islamic State. This occurred before the Nigerian Army revitalized their campaign against the group, restricting its territory back to previously held ground.[78] Boko Haram experts all frequently state that the group has increased the level of violence in its tactics and has become more sophisticated with time.[79] Boko Haram is responsible for the deaths of over twenty thousand people and the displacement of nearly three million people.[80]

In a study conducted from April 11, 2011, to June 30, 2017, Boko Haram deployed 434 bombers to 247 different targets during 238 suicide-bombing attacks. At least 56% of these bombers were women, and at least 81 bombers were specifically identified as children or teenagers."[81] The first female suicide bomber attack for Boko Haram occurred on June 8, 2014. Boko Haram can be defined as a jihadist terrorist organization because it primarily uses suicide bombings based on Quranic interpretation as its method of attack. The group is also aligned with ISIS, a jihadist group. Boko Haram seeks to reestablish the Islamic State based on Sharia Law. It seeks to accomplish its political goals through the use of jihad.

Chechen Separatists

The Chechens are primarily an ethnic Muslim minority living in Russia's North Caucasus region, who have led various independence movements for almost one hundred years. After the fall of the Soviet Union, the Chechens created a campaign for independence from Russia. As a result, two wars occurred (1991–1996 and 1999–2009) and Russia has refused to let the region go. The First Chechen War began in 1991 after the collapse of the Soviet Union when Chechnya declared independence and Dzhokar Dudayev was elected president of Chechnya. Negotiations continued between President Yeltsin and Dudayev, as Dudayev's power within Chechnya began to decline. Eventually Moscow recognized Dudayev's government although military clashes continued. The Chechen Mafiya was enlisted from 1993–1994 in the cause to help the Chechens. The mid-1990s saw Chechnya become an international Islamic jihad as Muslims from all over the world flocked to help the Chechens. The fighting continued until Dzhokar was killed in an air strike in April 1996. His deputy Aslan Maskhadov then took over and negotiated a ceasefire with General Aleksandr Lebed.[82]

As time continued, the Chechen nationalist leadership under Aslan Maskhadov was unable to control the Chechen jihadist leadership led by Shamil Basayev. At the helm of military operations was Ibn Khattab who was responsible for training jihadist forces in Chechnya. In August 1999, jihadist forces invaded Dagestan. Although the Russian military forced them out of Dagestan, the Chechen separatists kept retaliating and began targeting Moscow citizens. The suicide bombings and attacks continued to escalate, with women committing more suicide bombings than men. Maskhadov left office in 2005 and was followed by several other emirs of the Chechen Caucus. By 2009, Russia had severely incapacitated the Chechen resistance. Grozny, which had suffered tremendous damage, was eventually rebuilt and the Russian Army left the city, leaving security up to the local police. Maskhadov's successor Akhmed Zakayev called for an end to armed resistance among Chechens on August 1, 2009, leaving office shortly thereafter.[83] The last emir was Magomed Suleimanov who died in Gimry after being ambushed by Russian security forces in 2016.

In the Chechen separatists, women are primarily suicide bombers in the group although they have helped in large scale organizations such as the Moscow Theater Hostage Crisis. The term Black Widow is used to describe the female suicide bombing unit and they are part of the Riyad-us Saliheen Brigade of Martyrs. The first female suicide bombing occurred on June 7, 2000 when Khava Barayeva and Luisa Magomadova drove a truck bomb into a Russian fort.

The Chechen separatists may be defined as a jihadist terrorist organization as the Chechen terrorists embrace Wahhabism. "Wahhabism as a belief system, although not in itself necessarily militant, is the subset of Islam that has been used to inform the terrorist ideology which is at the basis of the current worldwide salafi jihad" according to terrorist expert Anne Speckhard.[84] The Chechens use jihad based on the Quran to attack and kill nonbelievers and apostate Muslims.

Hamas

In 1937 and 1938, members of the Egyptian Muslim Brotherhood under the direction of Hasan al-Banna went to Palestine to fight the British and Jews immigrating to Palestine.[85] Before 1948 in the West Bank, several of those men stayed in Palestine and later established the first international branch of the Muslim Brotherhood. After Israel was established as a state in 1948, several of the Egyptian Muslim Brotherhood men fought alongside the weak Egyptian Army in the 1948 War. When Palestine was apportioned, the West Bank part of the Muslim Brotherhood was annexed by Jordan and those Brothers joined the Jordanian Muslim Brotherhood. When the Gaza Strip was then left under Egyptian control, those members of the Muslim Brotherhood united with the Egyptian Muslim Brotherhood.

As time progressed, the only group that really challenged the authority of Fatah was the Muslim Brotherhood in Gaza and fights would often break out between the two groups. At that point, the Muslim Brotherhood did not embrace violence as a way to attack Israel so Israel allowed the Muslim Brotherhood to carry on without much oversight, even after the Six Day War in 1967. The Muslim Brotherhood received a huge boost when their founder Ahmed Yassin was able to create the Islamic Center in 1973. The Islamic Center had health services, day care, youth activities, and food services. As Yassin continued to spread his message against Israel, his fund-raising centers, safe houses, and meeting places multiplied.

The Muslim Brotherhood grew tremendously in popularity during the 1980s because it addressed the humiliation and weakness felt by Muslims in reference to Israel and the West. "Preparing the generations" meant waiting to establish a truly educated Muslim Army who could fight the Israelis and the infidels. After the first Palestinian Intifada began on December 8, Harakat al-Muqawamma al-Islamiyya or Hamas was founded by members of the Muslim Brotherhood on December 14, 1987, as an Islamic Resistance Movement against the Israeli occupation of Palestine. The goal of Hamas is the Islamization of Palestinian society and to end Israeli occupation through violent means, particularly being responsible for the spread of violence, mosques, and Islamism during the First Intifada. Hamas also wanted to destroy the power of Fatah in the Palestinian Liberation Organization (PLO) and this rivalry has endured to present times. Hamas also believes in pan-Islamic religious ideals and Palestinian nationalism.[86] The founding members were Sheikh Ahmad Yasin, Abdul 'Aziz al-Rantisi, Salah Shehadeh, Muhamma Sham'ah, 'Isa al-Nashar, 'Abdul Fattah Dukhan, and Ibrahim al-Yazuri.[87]

In 1991, after Saddam Hussein lost the Gulf War, the hopes of the Palestinians were dashed regarding the destruction of Israel by other Arab nations. The Islamists including Hamas had hoped that the Gulf War would lead to the annihilation of Israel after Saddam Hussein sent SCUD missiles into Israel. In response to the Iraq's war loss, Hamas created the Izz ad-Din al-Qassam Brigades. Arafat was worried about the challenge that Hamas presented to the PLO. He invited them to join the PLO and Hamas agreed.

Hamas describes itself as

The Islamic Resistance Movement (Hamas) is a Palestinian national liberation movement that struggles for the liberation of the Palestinian occupied territories and for the recognition of the legitimate rights of Palestinians. Although it came into existence soon after the eruption of the first Palestinian intifadah (uprising) in December 1987 as an expression of the Palestinian people's anger against the continuation of the Israeli occupation of Palestinian land and persecution of the Palestinian people, Hamas' roots extend much deeper in history.

The movement's motivation for resistance has been expressed by its founder and leader Sheikh Ahmad Yassin: 'The movement struggles against Israel because it is the aggressing, usurping and oppressing state that day and night hoists the rifle in the face of our sons and daughters.'

Hamas considers itself to be an extension of an old tradition that goes back to the early twentieth century struggle against British and Zionist colonialism in Palestine. The fundamentals from which it derives its legitimacy are mirrored in the very name it chose for itself. Hamas, in the Islamic language, means that it derives its guiding principles from the doctrines and values of Islam. Islam is completely Hamas' ideological frame of reference. It is from the values of Islam that the movement seeks its inspiration in its mobilization effort, and particularly in seeking to address the huge difference in material resources between the Palestinian people and their supporters on the one hand and Israel and its supporters on the other. . .

The forms of resistance adopted by Hamas stems from the same justifications upon which the national Palestinian resistance movement has based its struggle for more than a quarter of a century. At least the first ten articles of the Palestinian National Charter issued by the PLO show complete compatibility with Hamas' discourse as elaborated in its Charter and other declarations. Furthermore, the same justification for resistance had, prior to the emergence of Hamas in December 1987, been recognized, or endorsed, by a variety of regional and international bodies such as the Arab League, the Islamic Conference Organization, the Non-Aligned Movement and the United Nations. It is clearly recognized that the Israeli occupation of the West Bank and Gaza in 1967 is illegal in UN Security Council Resolutions 242 and 338. . . .

In spite of the overwhelming militant image it has in the minds of many people in the West, Hamas is not a mere military faction. It is a political, cultural, and social grass roots organization that has a separate military wing specializing in armed resistance against Israeli occupation. Apart from this strategically secretive military wing, all other sections within Hamas function through overt public platforms. The military wing has its own leadership and recruiting mechanism.

Hamas's social and educational activities in the Occupied Territories have become so interwoven within the Palestinian community that neither the Israelis nor their peace partners in the Palestinian Authority have been able to extricate them one from the other. The fact of the matter is that Hamas, contrary to Israeli assessment, acts as an infrastructure to the numerous cultural, educational, and social institutions in Gaza and the West Bank that render invaluable and irreplaceable services to the public. In other words, it is Hamas that gives life to these institutions and not the reverse. The Israelis have repeatedly told the PA to close them down. The PA has tried but failed. A crackdown on these institutions amounts to a declaration of war not against Hamas but against the Palestinian community as a whole.[88]

Although Hamas wants an Islamic utopian state, this does not appear to be a realistic goal. In early Hamas documents, the land component of Palestine continued from the River Jordan to the Mediterranean Sea. However, the utopian state became trivial as Hamas tried in vain to establish firmly agreed upon boundaries. Hamas focuses on the here and now dealing with problems as they come. After winning the 2006 elections, the Hamas Party has reluctantly embraced the two-state solution to the Israeli-Palestinian conflict.

Hamas adopted the use of suicide bombing in 1994 during the Oslo Peace Process and used it successfully for three additional campaigns in the 1990s.

Article 17 of the Hamas Charter published in 1988 proclaims that "The Muslim woman has a role in the struggle for liberation that does not fall from that of a man in that she is the one who produces the men."[89] Reem Raiyshi was the first female suicide bomber for Hamas. She detonated herself inside a building on January 14, 2004. Al-Aqsa Martyrs' Brigade also participated in the planning of the attack.

Hamas can be considered a jihadist terrorist organization as it believes that violence in the form of suicide bombings justified in the Quran are a form of resistance and political change. Hamas has used suicide bombings as recently as 2016 even though at that time the group was a political party in charge of the Palestinian Authority. Hamas also believes in the strict application of Sharia Law and the establishment of the Islamic Caliphate. Hamas also came from the Muslim Brotherhood which is the foundation for most jihadist terrorist groups as will be explained further in the following paragraphs.

Hezbollah

"And verily, the party of God is sure to triumph." Founded in 1982 on the previous Quranic verse, Hezbollah is a terrorist organization located in Lebanon with approximately four thousand members. Hezbollah means "the party of God" and is a Shia Islamic terrorist organization financially backed by the Iranian government and the local Shia population, predominately in Beirut. Initially Hezbollah's goal was to oust the Israeli occupation and to rid Lebanon of Western forces. Hezbollah is constantly at war whether it be with Israel, their rival Lebanese Shia movement (Amal), the Christian South Lebanese Army, or Syrian forces. Hezbollah is interested in remaking Lebanon into an Islamic State and to ensure its followers are loyal to the Iranian theocracy.[90]

It is governed by a Consultative Council (the Lebanon Council) and is composed of Lebanese Shia clerics and three regional councils (the Biqa Valley, Beirut, and the South). Seven committees distribute the workload. Due to many people publicly speaking for the group, Hezbollah appointed an official spokesperson and created a manifesto in 1985. There are also many large Shia family clans located in Lebanon that are loyal to Hezbollah as the organization somewhat reflects the family system. Mohammad Fadlallah issued a statement approving the use of female suicide bombers in 2002.[91] Women are highly involved in Hezbollah, whether they work in the Hezbollah hospitals or teach at the schools.

Hezbollah is a jihadist terrorist organization as it has used suicide bombings on a regular basis to achieve its political goals, based on the Quran and Hadith. Although the organization has changed tactically throughout time, the organization believes in the use of Sharia Law and the establishment of a Caliphate in Lebanon. The organization wants the destruction of Israel as Jews should not live on historically Muslim lands. Hezbollah uses terrorist attacks and its military to accomplish its political agenda.

ISIS

After American forces evacuated, a power vacuum was created in Iraq. There was no stable military force to keep order in a chaotic country. Kurds, Sunnis, and Shias continued to compete for power in the failed state of Iraq. A future player in the Iraqi saga, Abu Mus'ab al-Zarqawi (Ayman al-Zarqawi), was released from prison in Jordan directly before joining al-Qaeda in Afghanistan in 1999. Al-Zarqawi fled Afghanistan (briefly stopping in Iran) for Iraq after the Taliban fell somewhere in 2001 or 2002. Zarqawi believed that the United States would eventually invade Iraq and this was his chosen location for his jihad. Inevitably, the United States invaded Iraq in March 2003.

Zarqawi pledged his oath of allegiance to the leaders of al-Qaeda, Osama bin Laden and Ayman al-Zawahiri in October 2004, creating al-Qaeda in Iraq (AQI). Despising Shia Muslims, Zarqawi refused to include them in AQI and often attacked them in Iraq. Zarqawi was too vicious for al-Qaeda as Zawahiri criticized Zarqawi for attacking Shia Muslims in Iraq.[92] Zarqawi targeted Shia Muslims in suicide bombings and al-Qaeda was not comfortable with targeting Muslims. However, problems with Zarqawi were ended when an American airstrike killed him on June 7, 2006. Shortly after his death, Zarqawi's men, led by Abu Ayyub al-Masri, declared the creation of the Islamic State in Iraq much to the surprise and chagrin of Osama bin Laden and Ayman al-Zawahiri. Bin Laden and Zawahiri had wanted Zarqawi to declare an Islamic State complete with the establishment of the Caliphate after the American forces withdrew from Iraq, not beforehand.[93]

Now that the Caliphate was established with the caliph Abu Umar al-Baghdadi (a shadowy figure that may have never existed) at its head, ISI tried to repair relations with al-Qaeda. ISI declared their oath of allegiance to al-Qaeda and relationships improved. Abu Ayyub al-Masri wanted to create his own Islamic State versus another terrorist organization like al-Qaeda. Al-Qaeda did not give any approval for the declaration of an Islamic State nor did it like the primary allegiance of all ISI members to the Islamic State and not to al-Qaeda. Nevertheless a united front of al-Qaeda and ISI was presented to the world.[94]

As time progressed, ISI became a failure. The original bounty placed on al-Masri's head by the United States was 5 million in 2007 but by May 2008, the bounty had fallen to 100,000 dollars. Al-Masri was a poor manager and commander. Believing in the forthcoming apocalypse, al-Masri ordered members to build pulpits for the *Mahdi* (end of the world redeemer of Islam).[95] In addition, he ordered his followers to take over Iraq and recalled them less than a week later. Al-Masri was labeled as a lunatic by many. Al-Masri also picked another caliph, Hamid al-Zawi, a former police officer who had joined ISI.

Al-Masri's flippant choice of a new caliph would typically require the debate and affirmation of religious clerics. The designation of the caliph should be a difficult process with divine study and worship. When these problems were mentioned, al-Masri simply killed dissenters, including members of the Islamic Army in Iraq who had refused to swear allegiance to ISI. Shia Muslims were also murdered as al-Masri believed they were infidels.[96]

ISI members came from all sectors of society and were not properly vetted when they swore allegiance to ISI. Literally anyone was admitted. Al-Masri rarely knew what was going on. Numerous complaints were sent to al-Masri as members of other terrorist organizations such as Ansar al-Sunna were tortured to death by al-Masri's men. Eventually groups like Ansar-al Sunna began working with the Americans in late 2006. Even Osama bin Laden started receiving complaints about ISI, who had initially pledged loyalty to al-Qaeda. Bin Laden refused to remove ISI and eventually both al-Masri and Abu Umar al-Baghdadi were killed by Americans in April 2010. Abu Bakr al-Baghdadi became the next caliph for ISI; he was also unknown to his followers and lacked the appropriate religious pedigree.[97]

By the time American troops departed Iraq in December 2011, ISI had been discredited and disowned by al-Qaeda but would find rebirth with the oncoming civil war in Syria. Syrian president Bashir al-Assad had been releasing jihadists into Iraq since American troops invaded. A prominent study from the Brooking Institution pointed out that as many as 90 percent of Iraqi ISI members had come through or from Syria.[98] The Syrians began protesting the al-Assad regime in 2011 because he had let jihadists out of prison, which led to the ISIS creation in Syria and their renewal in Iraq began.

It was actually Ayman al-Zawahiri that ordered the Iraqi Islamic State (ISI) to "form a group and send it to [Syria]."[99] Abu Muhammad al-Jawlani was sent to oversee the effort in Syria. Originally calling itself the Nusra Front (Jabhat al-Nusra), the group only had about two hundred members in August 2012. Al-Jawlani expanded into the North but for some reason stopped performing suicide attacks against the locals. Scholar William McCants contributes this to the presence of Abu Khalid al-Suri, a propagandist and philosopher in Syria who advocated a "hearts and minds" campaign towards the Syrian population. At this point, ISI in Iraq and the Nusra Front in Syria were at odds concerning strategy and stolen Syrian oil reserves. Al-Baghdadi, the caliph of ISI, was frustrated with al-Nusra as the men in Syria were more loyal to their leader, al-Jawlani, than him. Pulling a power play, al-Baghdadi officially announced that al-Nusra was officially part of ISI on April 9,

2013. In retaliation, al-Jawlani declared al-Nusra's independence from ISI. Al-Baghdadi then appealed to al-Zawahiri (the leader of al-Qaeda) threatening a schism if al-Nusra did not comply, as ISI was still part of al-Qaeda. Al-Zawahiri trying to solve the dilemma, publicly announced that ISI and al-Nusra were under al-Qaeda and ordered al-Suri to mediate between the two parties. Al-Suri grew appalled with ISI's conduct and could not come to any agreement. Frustrated with the poor attitudes of both parties, al-Zawahiri then disaffiliated ISI and al-Nusra from al-Qaeda in February 2013, stating that they were now both independent groups.[100]

The conflict detonated into a social media battle with jihadists and religious scholars tweeting and posting their own thoughts on the squabble. ISI, in retaliation for criticism concerning killing and abusing Muslims, sent three assassins to kill Abu Khalid al-Suri. They were successful and ISI continued to steamroll their own path of conquering Iraq. Jihadists flocked to Iraq to join the winners of the dispute or perhaps what was viewed as the new Caliphate in the Middle East. In March 2013, ISI moved into Raqqa, Syria, taking over the provincial capital. It continued to take over cities and towns throughout Syria. Thus the name ISIS was attributed to the group, the Islamic State in Iraq and Syria.[101] Meanwhile, al-Nusra returned to al-Qaeda and continued to fight against Syrian forces (under Bashir al-Assad) and American intervention in Syria. Al-Nusra currently presents itself as a milder solution to ISIS as it tries to cooperate with the civilian populations.

In June 2014, ISIS moved into Mosul, Iraq and increased its territory to the outskirts of Aleppo, Syria. ISIS caliph Abu Bakr al-Baghdadi was renamed Caliph Ibrahim al-Baghdadi on June 29, 2014, claiming authority over all Muslims. Bashir al-Assad has been content to let ISIS exist within his borders in the midst of a civil war. Al-Assad was sure that Syrians would prefer his brutal regime over the vulgar, bloodthirsty infidels who had taken over Iraq.[102] On November 10, 2014, ISIS announced that it had received oaths of allegiance from jihadists (including Boko Haram) in Egypt, Libya, Yemen, Algeria, and Saudi Arabia. Some of these groups that announced their support cannot be taken seriously.[103]

In 2014–2015, it was estimated that ISIS had between 20,000 to 30,000 members with its peak estimated at 33,000. However, recent estimates in 2016 put ISIS at 19,000 to 25,000 members and this number has remained stable.[104] Whether this is due to the fact that several thousand ISIS members were killed by American airstrikes in Kobani with losses in Bayli and Ramadi in 2015 or to desertion is unknown. Many ISIS members are leaving and heading to Libya in an effort to expand ISIS as Libya now has around 5,000 ISIS members within its borders.[105] Although ISIS has taken tremendous punishment in Syria and Iraq, it has continued to move south into Africa. ISIS has recently begun to use female suicide bombers and female police, which vastly increases the involvement of women in the organization.

ISIS is a jihadist organization as it frequently uses jihad to accomplish its political goals. ISIS reestablished the Islamic Caliphate, complete with Yazidi slaves. ISIS governed its territory using a strict interpretation of Sharia Law and has consistently attacked any people that were not Sunni Muslims, including Shia Muslims.

Muslim Brotherhood

The Muslim Brotherhood was created in 1928 by Hasan al-Banna. The Brotherhood did not attract the attention of the Egyptian government until 1936 when al-Banna wrote a letter to King Farouk, al-Nahhas Pasha, and the royalty telling them to follow the path of Islam, and to reject everything Western. He placed a program before them containing fifty provisions for complete Islamic reform, which he believed they should institute.[106]

The Muslim Brotherhood were anti-British and planned to attack the British as they still had a lot of control over Egypt after the Egyptian Revolution. The British were concerned and on October 17, 1941, al-Banna and al-Sukkari were arrested. The Brotherhood's Press was closed down and the newspapers were forbidden to mention the Brotherhood. In response, the Brotherhood gathered 11,000 signatures supporting the release of al-Banna and al-Sukkari and gave them to the royal councilor and the prime minister. At this point, the radicals in the Brotherhood could no longer remain quiet. Two hundred Brothers organized a demonstration that led to conflict with the police and over thirty Brothers were arrested.[107]

In 1945, when al-Banna ran for parliament, the election was rigged and the Brotherhood lost their seat in Ismailiya. After al-Banna's defeat, the Muslim Brotherhood assassinated Prime Minister Ahmad Mahir Pasha. Mahir had recently read his decision to join the Allies in World War II and declared war on the Axis powers. Al-Banna urged the prime minister to quicken the independence and unity of the Nile Valley. Otherwise, al-Banna warned he would call for jihad and lead it himself. Al-Nuqrashi sent this request to the British government but to no avail. The Brotherhood took to the streets in demonstration and protest.[108]

When al-Banna left for Mecca on October 27, 1946, Prime Minister al-Sidqi Pasha arrested several Brothers and confiscated their newspaper. When the Brothers began a counterattack against Sidqi Pasha, he deported Brothers and dispersed them. Al-Sidqi blamed the Brothers for attacks in Cairo and Alexandria. On December 10, 1946, al-Sidqi resigned and Prime Minister al-Nuqrashi took his place. On that day, al-Banna published a letter demanding that the new government end negotiations, respect the will of Egypt, and take up jihad. Al-Banna, complaining of how the government had imprisoned Brothers and harassed them, published many other letters. A civil war between the Brotherhood and al-Nuqrashi began shortly afterward.[109]

On May 6, 1948, al-Banna held a meeting with the founding committee. They made an important decision "to declare jihad against the Jews and to adopt all measures which would guarantee the deliverance of Palestine." In reference to Egypt they demanded the cessation of discussions and negotiations and the declaration of a newspaper war until the country's status is made clear, inasmuch as the constitution makes Islam the official religion. The Arab–Israeli War began on May 15, 1948. The Muslim Brothers fought under the Arab League. It was during the war that the Brotherhood learned how valuable their training had been and gained combat experience. Egypt paid the highest price in men, supplies, and other war costs. The loss was a tremendous blow to Egyptian pride.[110]

When Prime Minister al-Nuqrashi found out that the Brotherhood had been participating in combat units and hiding bombs in the countryside, he issued a military order on December 8, 1948. Al-Nuqrashi banned the Brotherhood and all of their publications. He also ordered that all their documents be seized. Al-Nuqrashi was then assassinated on December 28, 1948, by the Brotherhood. Al-Nuqrashi's successor Ibrahim 'Abd al-Hadi Pasha took over government and attacked the Muslim Brotherhood. He put several members in jail or in concentration camps. On February 12, 1949, al-Banna was assassinated while sitting in his car in front of the Young Men's Muslim Association. King Farouk had embarrassed Egypt in the Arab–Israeli War and he eventually lost his throne on July 26, 1952. General Abd el Nasser started a military coup overthrowing King Farouk of Egypt.[111]

Famous Brother Sayyid Qutb, espousing violence, helped to institute a ferocious radical ideology to attack apostate Muslims, apostate Muslim leaders, and the West. Qutb's ideology resonated with the Brotherhood and drove them to greater heights of violence. Sayyid Qutb's book *Milestones* is required reading for Islamist and jihadist supporters today. Qutb was tortured and executed by the Egyptian government in 1966. After Israel's victory in the 1967 war, the Muslim Brotherhood receive an increase in recruits due to Arab decimation in the Six Day War. Many of the jihadist terrorist organizations in this book were founded by Muslim Brotherhood members, have ties to the Brotherhood, or were influenced by writings from the Brotherhood. The Brotherhood has grown increasingly powerful since its inception in 1928 and has branches all over the world.[112] For many Muslim Arab countries, the Muslim Brotherhood has been banned as a political party as they cannot participate peacefully in a political process. However, running under the Freedom and Justice Party, the Muslim Brotherhood managed to get Mohamed Morsi elected to the Egyptian presidency, beginning in June 2012. When Morsi tried to grant himself unlimited power without judicial oversight, protests erupted and Morsi was removed by General Abdel Fattah el-Sisi in a military coup a little over a year later. Morsi is still sitting in an Egyptian prison, although his death sentence had been commuted. This book will mostly focus on women in the Egyptian Muslim Brotherhood.

The Muslim Brotherhood is the foundation for many jihadist terrorist organizations and is also a jihadist terrorist organization. Although the Brotherhood is a political party in many parts of the world, it still publicly clings to the writing of Hasan al-Banna, which frequently call for violent jihad to create changes. Al-Banna also stated that violent jihad was obligatory for every Muslim. The Muslim Brotherhood also believes in Sharia Law as the state legal system and the group has also used suicide bombings to accomplish its political agenda throughout time. The Muslim Brotherhood regularly returns to acts of terrorism despite political participation and most of the people affiliated with the case study terrorist organizations in this book were at one time a member or still are a member of the Muslim Brotherhood. In addition, the Muslim Brotherhood doctrine has several precepts that are listed, the fourth of which is violent jihad and martyrdom.[113] Although the Muslim Brotherhood is currently the least violent terrorist organization in the eight case studies that are used in this book, it provides the theoretical and political foundation of modern jihad.

Al-Qaeda

Founded by a fundamentalist Osama bin Laden, son of a Saudi Arabian construction tycoon and a Syrian mother (Alia Ghanem), al-Qaeda came out of the 1979 revolution in Afghanistan. Osama bin Laden was one of fifty-four children; his father Mohammed bin Awad bin Laden had twenty-two wives, but would divorce and remarry at will to keep the Islamic law of having four wives at one time. Since he was one of the younger sons, it was unlikely that bin Laden would ever make money in the family construction business. Bin Laden often stated that his father wanted one son to fight for Islam and Osama fulfilled his father's goal.[114]

After a trip to Afghanistan, bin Laden became disgusted at the Soviet invasion and became convinced he should become a martyr. Without military training, he created a military base in Jaji, close to a Soviet garrison. This base was routinely bombed by the Soviets. On September 10, 1988, al-Qaeda was created from anti-Soviet elements within Afghanistan. Osama bin Laden moved the headquarters of al-Qaeida from Afghanistan to Peshwar, Pakistan, after the Saudi Arabian royal family embraced the United States as its ally in 1991. By 1992, mujahedeen men were being driven out by the Pakistani government, who were fearful of jihadists in the population. Bin Laden fled to Sudan to headquarter al-Qaeda with many of his top advisors. After the Sudanese government expelled bin Laden from Sudan, al-Qaeda moved back to Afghanistan in 1996. On August 23, 1996, Osama bin Laden declared war on the United States, being embittered by his forced move to Afghanistan.[115]

Several infamous attacks against the United States followed the first bombing of the World Trade Center on February 26, 1993. On September 11, 2001, four hijacked planes flown by nineteen hijackers flew into the United States World Trade Center, the Pentagon, and a field in Pennsylvania. On May 2, 2011, Osama bin Laden was killed by American forces in Abbottabad, Pakistan, as he was the mastermind of 9-11. His body was buried at sea as no country was willing to take the body or bury it according to Islamic law.[116]

In 2003 Umm Osama, an al-Qaeda member, claimed to be managing the training of a squad of female mujahedeen affiliated with al-Qaeda and the Taliban. Umm Osama stated, "The idea of women Kamikazes came from the success of martyr operations carried out by young Palestinian women in the occupied territories. Our organization will be open to all women wanting to serve the (Islamic) nation, particularly in this very critical phase."[117]

Al-Qaeda is the quintessential jihadist terrorist organization. Sunni in nature, the group has created other jihadist groups including ISIS. The group believes in the reestablishment of the Caliphate and restoring the Islamic Empire to its former glory including reclaiming a lot of territory in Europe for Islam. Sharia Law is the only acceptable form of government and law. Terrorist attacks such as 9-11 are the best way to create political change and accomplish its agenda. Jihad is obligatory for all Muslims.

In Table I.2: The 8 Case Studies and the Roles of Women in Jihadist Terrorist Organizations, the roles of women in the eight case studies analyzed in this book are included. As will be explained in chapter 4, the author was unable to find any evidence that al-Aqsa Martyrs' Brigade uses women in the secretarial role. This is most likely due to a lack of available data for the organization rather than the absence of the role. One other anomaly in the study is the absence of the disposable role in the Egyptian Muslim Brotherhood, the original branch of the Muslim Brotherhood. The reasons for this will be explained in chapter 5. The last part of this chapter describes the outline of the book.

Table I.2:   The 8 Case Studies and the Roles of Women in Jihadist Terrorist
             Organizations

Terrorist Group	Sect of Islam	Domestic	Secretary	Disposable
Al-Aqsa Martyrs' Brigade	Sunni	✓	?	✓
Boko Haram	Sunni (Salafi)	✓	✓	✓
Chechen Separatists	(Sunni) Wahhabi	✓	✓	✓
Hamas	Sunni	✓	✓	✓
Hezbollah	Shia	✓	✓	✓
Isis	Sunni	✓	✓	✓
Egyptian Muslim Brotherhood	Sunni	✓	✓	NA
Al-Qaeda	Sunni (Wahhabi)	✓	✓	✓

OUTLINE OF THE BOOK

Chapter 1 of the book looks at the roles of women in Islam, the Quran, and the Hadith. The history of Islam is explained as are the religious roles and heroines of women in Islam. These women provide historical and cultural role models for women in Islamic jihadist terrorist organizations. Chapter 2 focuses on the various motivations of female jihadists and the process of female jihadist radicalization as it is evident that it occurs differently from the radicalization of men. Chapter 3 discusses the domestic role that women play in jihadist terrorist organizations and provides case study examples of women in this role. Chapter 4 discusses the secretarial role that women play in jihadist organizations. Although relatively rare, this is the only minute leadership opportunity women have in jihadist organizations. Chapter 5 concentrates on female suicide bombers and the disposable mindset that jihadist terrorist organizations have towards jihadist women and women in general. In chapter 6, the author presents the interview research that was gathered from four women in an Israeli prison in fall 2017 who were convicted of terrorism; the author ties their stories in with the theories presented in this book. Chapter 7 looks at jihadist women who have emigrated or were home grown in Western nations. The Conclusion looks at the secular counterexample of Leila Khaled, a leader of Black September and the Popular Front for the Liberation of Palestine. Although atheist, Leila worked for the PFLP, a secular group that works for the independence and liberation of Palestine. Women in jihadist terrorist groups will also be compared to women in Western terrorist organizations. The conclusion finally wraps up the book, provides policy recommendations, and provides avenues for future research on female jihadist terrorism.

NOTES

1. Eileen MacDonald, *Shoot the Women First* (New York: Random House, 1992).

2. Please see *How Violence Shapes Religion* by Ziya Meral (2018) for a good discussion of this phenomenon.

3. Mary Chastain, Women Volunteer for Sexual Jihad with Islamic State, *Breit-Bart.com*, August 27, 2014, accessed January 31, 2018, http://www.breitbart.com/national-security/2014/08/27/women-volunteer-for-sexual-jihad-with-islamic-state/.

4. David E. Jones, *Women Warriors, A History* (Lincoln, NE: Potomac Books, 2005).

5. Charles A. Russell and Bowman H. Miller, "Profile of a Terrorist," in *Perspectives on Terrorism*, eds. Lawrence Freedman and Yonah Alexander, (Wilmington, DE: Rowman & Littlefield, 1983).

6. Leonard Weinberg and W. L. Eubank, "Italian Women Terrorism," in *Terrorism: an International Journal* 9 (1987).

7. Leonard Weinberg and W. L. Eubank, "Italian Women Terrorism," in *Terrorism: an International Journal* 9 (1987): 250.

8. Karla Cunningham, "Cross-Regional Trends in Female Terrorism," *Studies in Conflict and Terrorism* 26 (3) (2003).

9. Ariel Merari, *Driven to Death* (Oxford: Oxford University Press, 2010), 62.

10. Erica Chenoweth and Pauline Moore, *The Politics of Terror* (Oxford: Oxford University Press, 2018), 340.

11. Daniel Georges-Abeyie, "Women as Terrorists," in *Perspectives on Terrorism*, eds. Lawrence Freedman and Yonah Alexander (Wilmington, DE: Rowman & Littlefield, 1983), 82.

12. Daniel Georges-Abeyie, "Women as Terrorists," in *Perspectives on Terrorism*, eds. Lawrence Freedman and Yonah Alexander (Wilmington, DE: Rowman & Littlefield, 1983), 77.

13. Scott A. Bonn, "White Females Are Rarely Murder Victims or Perpetrators," *Psychology Today*, October 12, 2015, accessed September 25, 2018, https://www.psychologytoday.com/us/blog/wicked-deeds/201510/white-females-are-rarely-murder-victims-or-perpetrators.

14. Mia Bloom, *Bombshell* (Philadelphia: Penn State University Press, 2011).

15. Deborah M. Galvin, "The Female Terrorist: A Socio-Psychological Perspective" *Behavioral Sciences and the Law* 1 (2) (1983): 30.

16. Barbara Victor, *Army of Roses* (Emmaus, PA: Rodale, 2003), 288.

17. Yoram Schweitzer, *Female Suicide Bombers: Dying for Equality* N. 84, Tel Aviv; Jaffee Center for Strategic Studies, Tel Aviv University, August 2006, 10.

18. R. Kim Cragin and Sara A. Daly, *Women as Terrorists* (Santa Barbara, CA: ABC-CLIO, 2009), 12.

19. Devorah Margolin, "A Palestinian Woman's Place in Terrorism: Organized Perpetrators or Individual Actors," *Studies in Conflict and Terrorism* 39 (10) (2016).

20. Christine Sixta, "The Illusive Third Wave: Are Female Terrorists the New "New Women" in Developing Societies," *Journal of Women, Politics, and Policy,* 29 (2) (2008).

21. Genevieve Pierce, "The Media's Gender Stereotype Framing of Chechen 'Black Widows' and Female Afghan Self-Immolators" (Master's Thesis, Central European University, 2011).

22. Kathleen M. Blee, "Women in the 1920s' Ku Klux Klan Movement," *Feminist Studies* 17 (1) (Spring 1991): 72.

23. Eileen MacDonald, *Shoot the Women First* (New York: Random House, 1992).

24. Leonard Weinberg, "The Violent Life: Left- and Right-Wing Terrorism in Italy," in *Political Violence and Terror, Motifs and Motivations*, ed. Peter Merkl (Berkeley: University of California Press, 1986).

25. William Lee Eubank and Leonard Weinberg, *The Rise and Fall of Italian Terrorism* (New York: Westview Press, 1987).

26. Leonard Weinberg and W. L. Eubank, "Italian Women Terrorism," in *Terrorism: an International Journal* 9 (1987).

27. Rhiannon Talbot, "Myths in the Representation of Women Terrorists," *Éire-Ireland* 35 (3 and 4) (2000).

28. Angela Dalton and Victor Asal, "Is it Ideology or Desperation: Why do Organizations Deploy Women in Violence Terrorist Attacks?" *Studies in Conflict and Terrorism* 34 (10) (2011): 816.

29. S. V. Raghavan and V. Balasubrmaniyan, "Evolving Role of Women in Terror Groups: Progression or Regression," *Journal of International Women's Studies* 15 (2) (2017): 206.

30. Amanda Third, *Gender and the Political, Deconstructing the Female Terrorist* (New York: Palgrave MacMillan, 2014).

31. Ami Pedahzur, *Suicide Terrorism* (Malden, MA: Polity Press, 2005), 137.

32. Karen Jacques and Paul J. Taylor, "Male and Female Suicide Bombers: Different Sexes, Different Reasons?" *Studies in Conflict and Terrorism* 31 (2008).

33. Anne Speckhard and Khapta Akhmedova, "Black Widows and Beyond, Understanding the Motivations and Life Trajectories of Chechen Female Terrorists," in *Female Terrorism and Militancy, Agency, Utility, and Organization*, ed. Cindy D. Ness, (New York: Routledge, 2008), 110.

34. Mia Bloom, *Bombshell* (Philadelphia: Penn State University Press, 2011), 234–37

35. S. V. Raghavan and V. Balasubramaniyan, "Evolving Role of Women in Terror Groups: Progression or Regression," *Journal of International Women's Studies* 15 (2) (2014): 206.

36. Anat Berko, "Women in Terrorism: A Palestinian Feminist Revolution or Gender Oppression? *International-Institute for Counter-Terrorism*, June 12, 2006, accessed February 5, 2018, https://www.ict.org.il/Article.aspx?ID=962#gsc.tab=0.

37. Yoram Schweitzer, "Palestinian Female Suicide Bombers: Reality vs. Myth," in *Female Suicide Terrorism*, ed. Yoram Schweitzer (Tel Aviv: Jaffe Center Publications, 2006), 25–41, 32.

38. Nancy Laur, "Terrorism: The Female Experience" (Masters of Philosophy Thesis, The Irish School of Ecumenics, Center for Peace Studies, Trinity College, Dublin 1992), 71.

39. Morgan Robin, *The Demon Lover: The Roots of Terrorism* (New York: W.W. Norton & Company, 2001).

40. Leonard Weinberg and W.L. Eubank, "Italian Women Terrorism," in *Terrorism: an International Journal* 9 (1987).

41. Rhiannon Talbot, "Myths in the Representation of Women Terrorists," *Éire-Ireland* 35 (3 and 4) (2000).

42. S. V. Raghavan and V. Balasubramaniyan, "Evolving Role of Women in Terror Groups: Progression or Regression," *Journal of International Women's Studies* 15 (2) (July 2014): 205.

43. Luisella de Cataldo Neuberger and Tiziana Valentini, *Women and Terrorism* (New York: St. Martin's Press, 1996), 78.

44. Donatella della Porta, "Left-wing Terrorism in Italy," in *Terrorism in Context*, ed. Martha W. Crenshaw, 105–59 (State College, PA: Penn State University Press, 1994)

45. Marc Sageman, *Understanding Terror Networks* (Philadelphia: Pennsylvania University Press, 2004).

46. S. V. Raghavan and V. Balasubramaniyan, "Evolving Role of Women in Terror Groups: Progression or Regression," *Journal of International Women's Studies* 15 (2) (2014): 205.

47. Amy Caiazza, "Why Gender Matters in Understanding September 11: Women, Militarism, and Violence," *IWPR Publication* #1908 (November 2001): 3.

48. Katerina Standish, "Human Security and Gender: Female Suicide Bombers in Palestine and Chechnya," *Peace and Conflict Review* 1 (2) (2008).

49. Anne Speckhard and Khapta Akhmedova, "Black Widows and Beyond, Understanding the Motivations and Life Trajectories of Chechen Female Terrorists," in *Female Terrorism and Militancy, Agency, Utility, and Organization*, ed. Cindy D. Ness (New York: Routledge, 2008), 110.

50. Rosemarie Skaine, *Female Suicide Bombers* (Jefferson, NC: McFarland & Company, Inc., 2006).

51. Jamshid A. Marvasti and Susan Plese, "Female Suicide Warriors/Bombers," in *Psycho-Political Aspects of Suicide Warriors, Terrorism and Martyrdom, A Critical View from "Both Sides" in Regard to Cause and Cure,* ed. Jamshid A. Marvasti (Springfield, IL: Charles C. Thomas, 2008), 273.

52. Pamala Griset and Sue Mahan, *Terrorism in Perspective* (Thousand Oaks, CA: Sage, 2003), 157.

53. Miranda Alison, "Cogs in the Wheel? Women in the Liberation Tigers of Tamil Eelam," *Civil Wars* 6 (4) (Winter 2003).

54. Ami Pedahzur, *Suicide Terrorism* (Malden, MA: Polity Press, 2005), 136.

55. Terri Toles Patkin, "Explosive Baggage: Female Palestinian Suicide Bombers and the Rhetoric of Emotion," *Women and Language* 27 (2) (2004): 86.

56. Yoram Schweitzer, "Palestinian Female Suicide Bombers: Reality vs. Myth," in *Female Suicide Terrorism*, ed. Yoram Schweitzer (Tel Aviv: Jaffe Center Publications, 2006), 25–41, 30.

57. Yoram Schweitzer, "Palestinian Female Suicide Bombers: Reality vs. Myth" in *Female Suicide Terrorism*, ed. Yoram Schweitzer (Tel Aviv: Jaffe Center Publications, 2006), 25–41, 31.

58. Jessica Davis, "Women and Radical Islamic Terrorism: Planners, Perpetrators, Patrons?" *The Canadian Institute of Strategic Studies*, May 2006, accessed June 5, 2018, https://www.researchgate.net/publication/270959680_Women_and_radical _islamic_terrorism_planners_perpetrators_patrons.

59. Alisa Stack-O'Connor, "Picked Last Women and Terrorism," *Joint Force Quarterly* 44 (1) (2007): 96.

60. Lindsey O'Rourke, "What's Special about Female Suicide Terrorism," *Security Studies,* 18 (4) (2009).

61. Krislyn Reuter, "Why Not Use Women?: An Examination of the Conditions under Which an Islamic Terrorist Organization Will Employ Female Suicide Terrorism" (MA Thesis, Georgetown University, 2011).

62. Matthew P. Dearing, "Agency and Structure as Determinants of Female Suicide Terrorism: A Comparative Study of Three Conflict Regions" (MA Thesis, Naval Postgraduate School, 2012).

63. Anat Berko and Edna Erez, "Gender, Palestinian Women, and Terrorism: Women's Liberation or Oppression?" *Studies in Conflict and Terrorism* 30 (6) (2007).

64. Katharina Von Knop, "The Female Jihad: Al Qaeda's Women," *Studies in Conflict and Terrorism* 30 (5) (2007).

65. Mia Bloom, *Bombshell* (Philadelphia: Penn State University Press, 2011), 235.

66. Debra D. Zedalis, *Female Suicide Bombers* (Honolulu: University Press of the Pacific, 2004), 19.

67. Anne Speckhard and Khapta Akhmedova, "Black Widows and Beyond, Understanding the Motivations and Life Trajectories of Chechen Female Terrorists," in *Female Terrorism and Militancy, Agency, Utility, and Organization*, ed. Cindy D. Ness (New York: Routledge, 2008), 110.

68. Christine Sixta, "The Illusive Third Wave: Are Female Terrorists the New "New Women" in Developing Societies?" *Journal of Women, Politics, and Policy* 29 (2) (2008).

69. Department of State, "Foreign Terrorist Organizations," *U.S. Department of State*, 2018, accessed June 19, 2018, https://www.state.gov/j/ct/rls/other/des/123085.htm.

70. Mary Habeck, *Knowing the Enemy, Jihadist Ideology and the War on Terror* (New Haven: Yale University Press, 2006).

71. Shadi Hamid and Rashid Dar, "Islamism, Salafism, and jihadism: A Primer," *The Brookings Institution*, July 15, 2016, accessed May 28, 2018, https://www.brookings.edu/blog/markaz/2016/07/15/islamism-salafism-and-jihadism-a-primer/.

72. Matthew Levitt, *Targeting Terror U.S.: Policy Toward Middle Eastern State Sponsors and Terrorist Organizations, Post-September 11* (Washington, DC: The Washington Institute for Near East Policy, 2002).

73. Matthew Levitt, *Targeting Terror U.S.: Policy Toward Middle Eastern State Sponsors and Terrorist Organizations, Post-September 11* (Washington, DC: The Washington Institute for Near East Policy, 2002), 107.

74. Human Rights Watch, "V. Structures and Strategies of the Perpetrator Organizations," *Human Rights Watch*, 2002, accessed June 19, 2018, https://www.hrw.org/reports/2002/isrl-pa/ISRAELPA1002-05.htm#P841_205536.
Jonathan Schanzer, *Hamas vs. Fatah* (New York: Palgrave MacMillan, 2008).

75. Human Rights Watch, "V. Structures and Strategies of the Perpetrator Organizations," *Human Rights Watch*, 2002, accessed June 19, 2018, https://www.hrw.org/reports/2002/isrl-pa/ISRAELPA1002-05.htm#P841_205536.

76. Jonathan Schanzer, *Hamas vs. Fatah* (New York: Palgrave MacMillan, 2008). Frode Løvlie, "Questioning the Secular-Religious Cleavage in Palestinian Politics: Comparing Fatah and Hamas," *Politics and Religion* 7 (2014), 100–21.

77. Virginia Comolli, *Boko Haram Nigeria's Islamist Insurgency* (London: Hurst & Company, 2015), 50.

78. Abdulbasit Kassim and Michael Nwankpa, *The Boko Haram Reader* (London: Hurst & Company, 2018).

79. Virginia Comolli, *Boko Haram Nigeria's Islamist Insurgency* (London: Hurst & Company, 2015).

80. Abdulbasit Kassim and Michael Nwankpa, *The Boko Haram Reader* (London: Hurst & Company, 2018), 7.

81. Jason Warner and Hilary Matfess, "Exploding Stereotypes: The Unexpected Operational and Demographic Characteristics of Boko Haram's Suicide Bombers," *Combating Terrorism Center at Westpoint*, August 2017, accessed August 14, 2018, from https://ctc.usma.edu/app/uploads/2017/08/Exploding-Stereotypes-1.pdf.

82. Yossef Bodansky, *Chechen Jihad* (New York: Harper Collins, 2007).

83. Yossef Bodansky, *Chechen Jihad* (New York: Harper Collins, 2007).

84. Anne Speckhard and Khapta Akhmedova, "The New Chechen Jihad: Militant Wahhabism as a Radical Movement and a Source of Suicide Terrorism in Post-War Chechen Society," *Democracy and Security* 2 (2006): 2.

85. Christine Sixta Rinehart, *Volatile Social Movements and the Origins of Terrorism* (Lanham, MD: Lexington Books, 2013), 35.

86. Yonah Alexander, *Palestinian Religious Terrorism: Hamas and Islamic Jihad* (Ardsley, New York: Transnational Publishers, Inc., 2002).

87. Khaled Hroub, *HAMAS, A Beginner's Guide*, 2nd ed. (New York: Pluto Press, 2010).

88. Khaled Hroub, *HAMAS, A Beginner's Guide*, 2nd ed. (New York: Pluto Press, 2010), 15–17.

89. Mira Tzoreff, "The Palestinian Shahida: National Patriotism, Islamic Feminism or Social Crisis," in *Female Suicide Terrorism*, ed. Yoram Schweitzer (Tel Aviv: Jaffe Center Publications, 2005), 14.

90. Martin Kramer, "The Moral Logic of Hezbollah," in *Origins of Terrorism*, ed. Walter Reich (Washington, DC: Woodrow Wilson Center Press, 1998).

91. Muhammad Daraghmeh, "In Search of Stealthier Suicide Attackers: Islamic Jihad Encourages Women," *Associated Press*, May 31, 2003.

92. Charles Lister, "Profiling the Islamic State," *Brookings Doha Center Analysis Paper*, November 12, 2014, accessed March 24, 2016, http://www.brookings.edu/~/media/Research/Files/Reports/2014/11/profiling%20islamic%20state%20lister/en_web_lister.pdf.

93. Ryan Evans, "From Iraq to Yemen: Al-Qa'ida's Shifting Strategies," *Combating Terrorism Center at Westpoint*," October 1, 2010, accessed January 12, 2016, https://www.ctc.usma.edu/posts/from-iraq-to-yemen-al-qaida%E2%80%99s-shifting-strategies.

94. William McCants, *The ISIS Apocalypse: The History, Strategy, and Doomsday Vision of the Islamic State* (New York: St. Martin's Press, 2015).

95. Michael Weiss and Hassan Hassan, *ISIS: Inside the Army of Terror* (New York: Regan Arts, 2015).

96. William McCants, *The ISIS Apocalypse: The History, Strategy, and Doomsday Vision of the Islamic State* (New York: St. Martin's Press, 2015).

97. Michael Weiss and Hassan Hassan, *ISIS: Inside the Army of Terror* (New York: Regan Arts, 2015).

98. Charles Lister, "Profiling the Islamic State," *Brookings Doha Center Analysis Paper*, November 12, 2014, accessed March 24, 2016, http://www.brookings.edu/~/media/Research/Files/Reports/2014/11/profiling%20islamic%20state%20lister/en_web_lister.pdf.

99. As cited in William McCants, *The ISIS Apocalypse: The History, Strategy, and Doomsday Vision of the Islamic State* (New York: St. Martin's Press, 2015), 85.

100. William McCants, *The ISIS Apocalypse: The History, Strategy, and Doomsday Vision of the Islamic State* (New York: St. Martin's Press, 2015). Malcolm Nance, *Defeating ISIS: Who They Are, How They Fight, What they Believe* (New York: Skyhorse Publishing, 2016).

101. William McCants, *The ISIS Apocalypse: The History, Strategy, and Doomsday Vision of the Islamic State* (New York: St. Martin's Press, 2015).

102. Michael Weiss and Hassan Hassan, *ISIS: Inside the Army of Terror* (New York: Regan Arts, 2015).

103. William McCants, *The ISIS Apocalypse: The History, Strategy, and Doomsday Vision of the Islamic State* (New York: St. Martin's Press, 2015). Malcolm Nance, *Defeating ISIS: Who They Are, How They Fight, What they Believe* (New York: Skyhorse Publishing, 2016).

104. Luis Martinez, "Number of ISIS Fighters in Iraq and Syria Drops, Increases in Libya, US Official Says," *ABC News*, February 4, 2016, accessed March 24, 2016, http://abcnews.go.com/International/number-isis-fighters-iraq-syria-drops-increases-libya/story?id=36715635.

105. Luis Martinez, "Number of ISIS Fighters in Iraq and Syria Drops, Increases in Libya, US Official Says," *ABC News*, February 4, 2016, accessed March 24, 2016,

http://abcnews.go.com/International/number-isis-fighters-iraq-syria-drops-increases
-libya/story?id=36715635.

106. Christine Sixta Rinehart, "Volatile Breeding Grounds: The Radicalization of the Egyptian Muslim Brotherhood," *Studies in Conflict and Terrorism* 32 (November 2009) 952–88.

107. Christine Sixta Rinehart, "Volatile Breeding Grounds: The Radicalization of the Egyptian Muslim Brotherhood," *Studies in Conflict and Terrorism* 32 (November 2009) 952–88.

108. Christine Sixta Rinehart, "Volatile Breeding Grounds: The Radicalization of the Egyptian Muslim Brotherhood," *Studies in Conflict and Terrorism* 32 (November 2009) 952–88.

109. Christine Sixta Rinehart, "Volatile Breeding Grounds: The Radicalization of the Egyptian Muslim Brotherhood," *Studies in Conflict and Terrorism* 32 (November 2009) 952–88.

110. Christine Sixta Rinehart, "Volatile Breeding Grounds: The Radicalization of the Egyptian Muslim Brotherhood," *Studies in Conflict and Terrorism* 32 (November 2009) 952–88.

111. Christine Sixta Rinehart, "Volatile Breeding Grounds: The Radicalization of the Egyptian Muslim Brotherhood," *Studies in Conflict and Terrorism* 32 (November 2009) 952–88.

112. Matthew Levitt, *Targeting Terror U.S.: Policy Toward Middle Eastern State Sponsors and Terrorist Organizations, Post-September 11* (Washington, DC: The Washington Institute for Near East Policy, 2002).

113. Cynthia Farahat, "The Muslim Brotherhood, Fountain of Islamist Violence," *Middle East Quarterly* (Spring 2017): 8.

114. Christine Sixta Rinehart, *Drones and Targeted Killing in the Middle East and Africa, An Appraisal of American Counterterrorism Policies* (Lanham, MD: Lexington Books, 2016), Introduction.

115. Christine Sixta Rinehart, *Drones and Targeted Killing in the Middle East and Africa, An Appraisal of American Counterterrorism Policies* (Lanham, MD: Lexington Books, 2016), Introduction. Peter L. Bergen, *The Longest War, The Enduring Conflict between America and al-Qaeda* (New York: Free Press, 2011).

116. Christine Sixta Rinehart, *Drones and Targeted Killing in the Middle East and Africa, An Appraisal of American Counterterrorism Policies* (Lanham, MD: Lexington Books, 2016), Introduction. CNN Wire Staff, "Timeline: Osama bin Laden, Over the Years," *CNN*, May 2, 2011, accessed December 30, 2015, http://www.cnn.com/2011/WORLD/asiapcf/05/02/bin.laden.timeline/.

117. Giles Foden, "Death and Maidens," *The Guardian*, July 17, 2003, accessed June 6, 2018, https://www.theguardian.com/world/2003/jul/18/gender.uk.

Chapter One

The Roles of Women in Islam, the Quran, and the Hadith

This chapter will begin with a discussion of Western feminism and how Western feminists have viewed women in Muslim society. The chapter will then look at Muslim feminists and their views of Islamic society. The responses of Muslim feminists to Western feminists concerning Muslim society will also be explored. The roles of women in jihadist terrorist groups will then be discussed, based on their historical and theological foundations.

Feminism in the West and in the MENA Region

This book would not be complete without a discussion of feminism and gender roles since gender roles are one of the primary concepts within this book. If we look at Islam, through the perspective of Western feminists (considering the few that have even bothered to critique Islam), the analysis is not complimentary, or is even somewhat offensive to Muslims and Islam. Western feminism purports that women are equal to men in its most basic and generic definition. If this is so, where are the Western feminists regarding Islamic cultural abuse such as: wife beating, female genital mutilation, honor killing, or veiling to name some of the atrocities that plague Muslim women? Why are the Western feminists silent when it comes to Muslim treatment of women? In her article in *City Journal*, journalist Kay S. Hymowitz states, "As you look at this inventory of brutality, the question bears repeating: Where are the demonstrations, the articles, the petitions, the resolutions, the vindication of the rights of Islamic women by American feminists?"[1] This question is met with resolute silence.

Perhaps the answer lies in the concept of cultural relativism. The idea of human rights and the dignity, safety, and respect for women has been overrun by the concept of cultural relativism. Cultural relativists believe that we must respect the culture in Muslim countries, even it allows the horrific abuse of women and children. The concepts of equal and human rights should never be sold out to the concept of cultural relativism. Wrong is wrong, regardless of the culture. Hymowitz solidifies this argument when she states:

> But look more deeply into the matter, and you realize that the sound of feminist silence about the savage fundamentalist Muslim oppression of women has its own perverse logic. The silence is a direct outgrowth of the way feminist theory has developed in recent years. Now mired in self-righteous sentimentalism, multicultural nonjudgmentalism, and internationalist utopianism, feminism has lost the language to make the universalist moral claims of equal dignity and individual freedom that once rendered it so compelling. No wonder that most Americans, trying to deal with the realities of a post-9/11 world, are paying feminists no mind.[2]

The vast divide between Western feminists and Muslim feminists is not quite that easy to resolve. For Muslim feminists have a very different view of feminism and this Islamic personal idea of feminism is often at odds with Western feminism. Professor Miriam Cooke defined Islamic feminism as:

> Islamic feminists are not Muslims only, although by religious practice or cultural belonging they do qualify as Muslims. "Islamic" describes speech, action, writing, or way of life engaged with questioning Islamic epistemology as an expansion of their faith position and not a rejection of it. These religiously engaged public intellectuals are struggling with and on behalf of all Muslim women and their right to enjoy full participation with men in a just community.[3]

Academic Faegheh Shirazi adds that "These women are not necessarily interested in identifying with or imitating Western feminists."[4] Dr. Cooke continues, stating that "They are highlighting women's roles and status within their religious communities while declaring common cause with Muslim women elsewhere who share the same objectives."

The concept of Muslim feminism is almost opposite of mainstream Western feminism. Muslim feminists use Islam to justify their rights based on their prescribed roles in Islam. Many Muslim feminists will state that "Islam gives me all the rights I need" and this platitude is common in my experience among Muslim feminists. The recent revitalization of Islamic fundamentalism or Islamism is in many ways a reaction to Western feminism. Indeed, Islam is a prescription for the ills of Western feminism. Even the feminists in the following paragraphs in this chapter seek a new interpretation of Islam, Islamic history, or sacred Islamic texts to improve the status and rights of women in Muslim countries. There is no concept of throwing the baby out with the bathwater. Islam for Muslim feminists is not the problem. In fact, the true interpretation of Islam, which varies tremendously from woman to woman, is the salvation of the religion. Western feminism is often an anathema to Muslim feminists as it implies that Muslim women must adopt a Western culture to identify with Western feminists.

Muslim feminists may often see Western women as sexual objects who have been exploited for profit. They believe that Western women have lost their virtue and have ignored their true calling as wives and mothers in society, where their true power lies. Muslim feminists believe that Western women are obsessed with their bodies and weight, often allowing appearances to become their first priority. Muslim feminists point to Western feminism as one reason for the dissolution of the Western family and of womanhood. There is little room for agreement between the two ideologies of Western feminism and Muslim feminism.

In the following paragraphs, Muslim feminists, including various scholars and activists, explain their views on Islam. Maryam Jameelah, who has been closely associated with Jamaat-i Islami in Pakistan, wrote, "Although I believe that every woman should be educated [to] the fullest sense of her intellectual capabilities, I certainly question the advantage of taking women out of the home (particularly those with young children) to compete in business offices and factories with men and substituting nurseries and kindergartens for a home upbringing."[5] Zaynab al-Ghazali, a former leader in the Sisters of the Muslim Brotherhood, argues that women should be educated, but their main duties should be as wife and mother. She also believes that children can be harmed psychologically if they are not raised by their mothers.[6]

Academic Muslim feminists also have varying interpretations of Islam, feminism, or women's rights. Most of these analyses rely fundamentally on interpretation of the Quran and the historical period of the Prophet Muhammad. Renowned Muslim feminist Fatima Mernissi[7] believes that Islam is no more oppressive than Judaism or Christianity. The subjugation of women is usually undertaken to make a profit or for the means of profit. Mernissi advocates that Islam and democracy are compatible. Any Muslim man who believes that women should not enjoy full human rights is ignorant of the past and present of Islamic history. Muslim tradition allows for women to have human rights and full citizenship.

Scholar Asma Barlas[8] finds that the Quran is inherently anti-patriarchal and it allows for the radical equality of the sexes. Barlas decides that a text written by men for men requires Muslim women to have a stake in challenging its patriarchal exegesis. She argues that the Quran has been misread and that women should read the text and interpret it for themselves. Quranic readings that justify the abuse and degradation of women should be questioned and the legitimacy of liberating readings need to be established. Equality is not inher-

ently a Western value but may also be an Islamic value within a specifically
Islamic framework.

Similarly, scholar Nimat Hafez Barazangi argues that

> The attempt to transplant Western secular systems of education and Western
> feminists' views into Muslim communities and societies through the academic
> institutionalization of the study of Muslim women ignores the spiritual and
> intellectual worldview of the people who identify with the Quran and will not
> lead to lasting "solutions" to the problem of the secondary status of women.[9]

Barazangi believes that Muslim women must learn to interpret and understand the Quran themselves instead of understanding the holy book through
men and Islamic clergy. She asserts that contemporary Muslim women share
a lot of similarities with the American suffragettes from the late nineteenth
and early twentieth centuries. By interpreting the Quran through a female
lens, Muslim women can modify their views of "trusteeship, morality, and
authority to participate in the interpretation of Islamic texts."[10] For Barazangi,
Muslim women cannot separate themselves from the intrinsic identity of being Muslim; their culture and religion cannot be divorced from their personal
or world views.

In a related vein, self-proclaimed feminist Kecia Ali is concerned about
"Muslims living in post-traditional contexts in the West,"[11] meaning that
Muslims living in the West have a hard time deciding whether to follow
an Islamic school of jurisprudence, the Quran, or the civil laws where they
live. Ali advocates that women must be able to interpret the Quran through a
modern visage. If slavery is no longer legal in the Muslim world, then why
are problems like wife beating allowed? The Quran is a living breathing
document that guides Muslims on how to live a holy life and there must be a
modern interpretation of the Quran to understand how to use it.

Yet there are also Muslim feminists like Anwar Hekmat that call for the
overthrow of Koran, for perhaps a new era of Islam where men and women
are equal. In his book, *Women and the Koran*,[12] Hekmat states, "The unveiling of women and her emancipation from the shackles of cruel Koranic law
should not be seen as impiety and ungodliness. Islam can only benefit from the
removal of these vestiges of a medieval past, which have blocked progress in
so many countries for too long." Hekmat literally blames Muhammed for the
subjugation and maltreatment of women and turns the verses of the Quran on
their head often stating that Muhammad is a plagiarizer and provincial fanatic.

Taking it one step further if that is possible, Somalian Muslim Ayaan Hirsi
Ali is highly critical of Islam as a religion, culture, and society. Hirsi Ali
was the narrator of the film *Submission* that led to the assassination of Dutch
director Theo van Gogh in 2004. Hirsi Ali has been threatened repeatedly

for her views of Islam and has even created a non-profit organization, the AHA Foundation to defend women's rights. She believes that we should ask questions about the fundamental principles of Islam and that Islam should be critically examined. Hirsi Ali calls for a need to humanize Islam. "Criticism of Islam does not mean that the faithful reject it. But it does mean that the faithful examine particular ideas and teaching that, when applied in real life, lead to brutal behavior with unacceptable consequences."[13] Ali believes that people must interpret Islam for themselves.

Medical doctor and feminist Wafa Sultan argues that 9-11 occurred because Muslims and their god are full of hatred, particularly towards women. When Americans asked, why do they hate us? Sultan replied, "Because Muslims hate their women, and any group who hates their women can't love anyone else. People ask: But why do Muslims hate their women? And I can only reply: Because their God does."[14] Sultan, a medical doctor and psychiatrist, is a cultural Muslim from Syria, although she does not practice Islam. She was pushed into repudiation of Islam by Muslim Brotherhood attacks on her professors in Syria and since then has been an opponent of Muslim immigration to the West. She states:

> No one can be a true Muslim and a true American simultaneously. Islam is both a religion and a state. A true Muslim does not acknowledge the U.S. Constitution, and his willingness to live under that constitution is, as far as he is concerned, nothing more than an unavoidable step on the way to that constitution's replacement by Islamic Sharia Law.[15]

Wafa argues, among other things, that the United States should assist Muslims in conversion to Christianity.

Regarding terrorism, if jihadist women have any adherence to feminism, it is mostly an afterthought. Yoram Schweitzer, senior researcher at Israel's Institute for National Security and director of the Institute's research program, "suggests that if the women themselves attribute any feminist goals to their actions, this is a rationale imposed after the fact. Far from the primary catalyst that launched them on their mission, advancing gender interests is sometimes an imported cause meant to redeem—if not glorify—the aberration of a female suicide bomber."[16] While this quote applies to female suicide bombers in general, it also appeals to female jihadists.

In her conversations with Afghanistan women, academic Lina Abirafeh found that women continuously pointed out that they were Muslim and that Muslim women should follow their roles prescribed in the Quran. An eighteen-year-old Afghan woman stated to Dr. Abirafeh that "Religion is an important part of our society. Without it, there cannot be progress."[17] Islam is a very important part, if not the most important part, of Muslim societies.

What occurs in Afghanistan is not much different than what occurs in most Muslim societies. In Islamic countries, even the law (Sharia) is based on the Quran and the Hadith. Society and gender roles are literally governed by the Quran and the stories from the Prophet Muhammad (Hadith) are a secondary source. The Quran is a holy book that is the central religious text for Islam and Muslims believe it is a revelation from God. The Hadith is a collection of statements from the Prophet and a record of his daily practices within the first two centuries of the establishment of Islam. As a side note, the Quran is much less restrictive than the Hadith towards women as the Quran was written within twenty years after the Prophet's death and allows little room for human interference. The Quran is viewed as direct divine word. The Hadith was written at least a century later and was challenged from the beginning.[18]

But what exactly are the gender roles that are prescribed for women in the Quran and the Hadith? Close deciphering reveals several roles that can be classified as the domestic, the secretary, and the disposable gender roles. The rest of the chapter looks at these aforementioned positions and views that are discussed in relation to the roles that female Muslim jihadists fulfill in a jihadist terrorist organization. As the Quran and Hadith dictate what occurs in Muslim societies, these holy books also dictate what occurs in fundamentalist jihadist terrorist organizations. The perception and roles of women in jihadist terrorist groups bear a striking similarity to how women are viewed, portrayed, and utilized in the Quran and Hadith. The reason for this similarity is most likely that these Muslim organizations consider themselves austere followers of the Quran and Hadith. In their own minds they are the strictest adherents to traditional Islam so therefore they must use the strictest interpretations of Islam.

The chapter continues with a discussion of the traditional domestic roles of wife and mother in the Quran and Hadith and will then examine how women fulfill these roles in jihadist terrorist organizations. The role of the sex slave is also discussed in the context of Muhammad's spoils of war. Next, the chapter will look at the role of the secretary where jihadist women are the bookkeepers and the secretaries; although this is a rare role for women in jihadist terrorist organizations. Lastly, the chapter will proceed with the discussion of jihad and the women who fulfill the disposable role of the suicide bomber in jihadist terrorist organizations.

The Domestic Roles of Wife, Mother, and Sex Slave

The Quran and Hadith are explicit concerning what women can and cannot do in the family. The most important roles for women are their duties as wives and mothers. Indeed, most of the women in these holy books are wives or mothers and their value lies strictly in that domestic role. Many of them are not even given names but are referred to only as "wife of so and so" or "mother of so and so." Many women in the Hadith are the wives of the Prophet Muhammad and are only personified as heroines for their role of wife. At the most, the Prophet had eleven wives although this number would change frequently as he married and divorced for political gain. The Prophet Muhammad stated: "A woman is married for four things: For her possessions and wealth, For her noble descent, For her beauty, For her sense of true religion, But gain the one with the sense of true religion!"[19] Although he lived in the fifth and sixth centuries, it is evident that Muhammad valued women for what they could give to their husbands, whether it be wealth, title, beauty, or faith. The personality, skills, or internal worth of women were not highly regarded in early Islam although historically across time, space, and other religions, this is not an uncommon perspective.

The term "domestic" is used to classify these traditional feminine gender roles of wife and mother. The Quran is mostly written for men, and by men. It is evident that women must interpret their roles in the family through the ideas and thoughts of men. The Quran states:

> Men are the maintainers of women because Allah has made some of them to excel others and because they spend out of their property; the good women are therefore obedient, guarding the unseen as Allah has guarded; and (as to) those on whose part you fear desertion, admonish them, and leave them along in the sleeping-places and beat them; then if they obey you, do not seek a way against them.[20]

In this passage which is located early on in the Quran, women are to be maintained and controlled by men. Women must guard their private or "unseen" parts at all times. Any woman who is disobedient should be beaten and imprisoned in a place where she is left to think upon her actions. If a woman corrects her behavior or apologizes for being disobedient, she is then freed. The Prophet also chastised his followers about wife beating, stating, "Not one of you should beat your wife as hard as you beat your slave, for you might have sex with her at the end of the day."[21]

The honor of the family is upheld by the chastity of the women in the family. As the bearers of honor in the family, women should veil. The concept of veiling is discussed numerous times throughout the Quran and, in fact, Muhammad was the first to prescribe this as pious women were looked upon both by men with evil intentions and by good men with pure intentions. Muhammad's solution to this problem was to veil every woman to protect her from the impure thoughts of men as he noticed that his own wives were both looked upon by good and bad men. The following Quranic passage relates how women should guard their honor: by covering their hair, dressing conservatively, and not wearing any adornment to draw attention to their person. "And say to the believing women that they cast down their looks and guard their private parts and do not display their ornaments except what appears thereof, and let them wear their head coverings over their bosoms."[22] Not only is a woman to be completely covered but she should not wear anything that adorns her or that calls attention to her femininity and beauty.

Taking this one step further, for Muslim society to function, the sexuality of women must be constrained. Muhammad appears to be obsessed with virginity and the sexual purity of women, yet the purity of men is insignificant. The check on women's sexuality is done through secluding her and veiling her before she is married. The married woman must then also be secluded and veiled. If a woman is freed from her domestic bonds, she may incite *fitna* (the frenzy that occurs when a man is attracted to a woman). If man falls prey to *fitna*, he is then inhabited by Satan. Academic Fatima Mernissi states, "When a man and a woman are isolated in the presence of each other, Satan is bound to be their third companion."[23] "The whole Muslim organization of social interactions and special configurations can be understood in terms of the woman's *qaid* power [ability to deceive men through sexual manipulation]. The social order then appears as an attempt to subjugate her power and neutralize its disruptive effects."[24] Mernissi also states that the Prophet was most likely the last Muslim man to be repudiated (rejected) by a wife as it was outlawed after his death.[25] In fact, Muhammad forbade his wives to remarry after his death including Aishah who was only eighteen when Muhammad died.

Regarding marriage men can "marry such women as seem good to you, two and three and four; but if you fear that you will not do justice (between them), then marry only one or what your right hands possess; this is more proper, that you may not deviate from the right course."[26] Men are allowed to marry up to four wives as long as they can properly maintain those wives. Each wife should be treated exactly the same and typically wealthy men have the most wives. Temporary marriages are also somewhat justified as a man must marry a woman to have intercourse with her unless the woman is a slave. However, if she becomes a devout Muslim, he can marry a slave if he is not a man of means. Although there are several similar statements in the Quran, the Prophet gives his men the right to pursue temporary marriages for the purpose of sex in the following quote.

> Abdullah said: We used to go on raids with the Prophet, and we went without women, so we complained to the Prophet: "We might as well get ourselves castrated!" He forbade this suggestion, but then gave us license for the temporary marriage of women (from our captives and so on). He then recited to us: O you of the Faithful! Do not deprive yourselves of the good things in life that have been

made lawful for you by God! But take care not to overstep the boundary between what is right and what is wrong, for truly God loves not those who do wrong.[27]

As a side note, in the Quran, there are many statements referring to "those whom your right hand possesses" as stated in the previous paragraph. Slaves are "those whom your right hand possesses out of those whom Allah has given to you as prisoners of war."[28] War refers to a holy war or the conversion of the polytheists to Islam. There are several statements in the Quran allowing for the rape of slave women, captured in holy war such as "And all married women except those who your right hands possess (this is) Allah's ordinance to you; and lawful for you are (all women) besides those, provided that you seek (them) with your property."[29] The previous statement allows for the use of and rape of female sexual slaves gained from holy war as long as those women are physically provided for. However, Muhammad did make the prostitution of one's female slaves illegal, which was previously allowed.[30]

Regarding sex, the Quran states, "Your wives are a tilth for you, so go into your tilth when you like, and do good beforehand for yourselves."[31] Women are like tilled soil, ready be implanted with seed whenever men desire them. When wives are menstruating, they cannot be touched as they are unclean. "Say: It is a discomfort, therefore keep aloof from the women during their menstrual discharge and do not go near them until they have become clean; then when they have cleansed themselves, do in to them as Allah has commanded you."[32] Men must wait until their wives are no longer menstruating and have ritually purified themselves until they are able to have sex. Women who refuse sex with their husbands make the angels (*Houri*) angry and deserve a spot in hell.

In Islam, men are the initiators of divorce and are usually the only ones who can terminate a marriage unless a woman suffers unusual cruelty from her husband or he is unable to impregnate her. The husband must state, "I divorce you" three times in a nonconsecutive manner to officially be divorced from his wife.[33] In cases of severe physical abuse from their husbands, some women will receive a divorce, although this depends on the particular application of Sharia law and the country where the couple resides. After the divorce, women cannot marry another man until they have had at least three menstrual periods to ensure that a child was not conceived.[34] If women are guilty of indecency: "And as for those who are guilty of an indecency from among your women, call to witnesses against them four (witnesses) from among you; then if they bear witness confine them to the houses until death takes them away or Allah opens some way for them."[35] If a woman commits an indecent act, and there are four witnesses (males) against her, she should then be confined to a place until she dies. A woman's testimony is worth half of a man's testimony.

Family relations are very important in the Quran. Wives are especially prized for their ability to give their husbands children, particularly sons. Muhammad even states that women must breastfeed in several places in the Quran. Regarding breastfeeding: "And the mothers should suckle their children for two whole years for him who desires to make complete the time of suckling."[36]Although a woman's power in her family relies on her relationship with her husband, her son is the most important determinant of her future familial position. "In Muslim societies, not only is the marital bond actually weakened and love for the wife discouraged, but his mother is the only woman a man is allowed to love at all, and this love is encouraged to take the form of life-long gratitude."[37] The Hadith states

> A man came to the Prophet and asked him: "Who is the most entitled to the best of my companionship?"
>
> "Your mother," came the reply.
>
> "And then who?"
>
> "Your mother," repeated the Prophet.
>
> "And then who?"
>
> "Your mother," said the Prophet for the third time.
>
> "And then who?" persisted the man.
>
> "Your father."[38]

Although the father is the official chooser of the son's wife, his mother ultimately initiates the marriage. Women in secluded societies are the only ones allowed to see other women in the community. After she marries, the young bride is often under the control of her mother-in-law, whether she lives with his family or not.

Any changes in the woman's condition in society are seen as a direct attack on the Islamic faith and order. "Muslim marriage is based on the premise that social order can only be maintained if the woman's dangerous potential for chaos is restrained by a dominating non-loving husband who has besides his wife, other females (concubines, co-wives and prostitutes) available for his sexual pleasure under equally degrading positions."[39] If the sexual purity of a woman is compromised, as in, she is raped, she is either expected to marry her rapist or should commit suicide. The literal value of a woman in society and her family is based on her sexuality.[40]

If we look to the Quran and the Hadith, there are few domestic feminine heroes provided for Muslim women to emulate. Al-Khansa was considered the best female Arabic poet and she was a contemporary of Muhammad who would often ask her to recite poetry for him. She lost four sons in battle and is known as the mother of martyrs, as she encouraged war in the name of Islam.[41] Mary or Marium, Jesus's mother, is "an example for the righteous." According to Muslims, Mary's desire to isolate herself has been confirmed as an affirmation of gender-based segregation. Mary also took it upon herself to wear the veil and came to her marriage bed as a confirmed virgin like all Muslim women should. Academic Barbara Stowasser states that "Recitation of 'her [Mary's] sura' (Sura 19) is a favorite especially with women circles throughout the Muslim world, believed to confer special blessings on reciter and listeners alike. Many women in Syria are said to pray through Mary (and Fatima) in moments of anguish, as women elsewhere pray through (other) female saints."[42] Mary has been revered by Muslim women for her status as a virgin, her obedience, her tenacity, and her roles as wife and mother to Jesus, whom Muslims consider a prophet of Allah.

Fatima, the daughter of the Prophet, was the quintessential model of a housewife and she has somewhat superhuman qualities at times. She is not "polluted" as she never menstruates nor does she ever complain. Throughout her forty years of life, she only uses words from the Quran. She does not care about beautiful clothes or trinkets as she rejects these objects. Her home is always simple and neat and she does not complain about her husband or children after she is married. Fatima serves as a model of the perfect woman, who is always obedient to her father, silent and uncomplaining, an accomplished homemaker, and a dedicated wife.[43]

The best of heroic women is most likely Muhammad's third wife Aishah, who Muhammad married at the age of six and consummated the marriage at age nine. She was the only virgin wife that the Prophet had, which gives her tremendous authority over the Sunni Muslims. Aishah was fiercely loyal and obedient to Muhammad, although she did have a jealous streak. Muhammad even died with his head in Aishah's lap. Aishah gave her entire life to Muhammad even though he married twelve other women at various times in his life.[44] She was not allowed to remarry after his death and spent the remainder of her life in celibacy.

Muslim female mystics achieved spiritual significance in the religion of Islam. In her short chapter on female mystics in Islam, Emine Gürsoy-Naskali states, "In such a relationship between mystic and the Beloved [Allah] there is no room for the distinction of sex."[45] Mystics are people who seek to unite with the divine, throwing aside all of the attractions of this world. Attar, the thirteenth-century poet and mystic, stated in his biography about saints and women and mysticism in the following passage:

The holy prophets have laid it down that "God does not look upon your outward forms". It is not the outward form that matters but the inner purpose of the heart, as the Prophet said, "The people are assembled (on the Day of Judgement) according to the purposes of their hearts" . . . so also 'Abbas of Tus said that when on the Day of Resurrection the summons goes forth, "O men", the first person to set foot in that class of men (i.e. those who are to enter Paradise will be Mary, upon whom be peace. . .The true explanation of this fact (that women count for as much as men among the saints) is that wherever these people, the Sufis are, they have no separate existence in the Unity of God. In the Unity, what remains of the existence of "I" or "thou"? So how can "man" or "woman" continue to be? So too, Abu 'Ali Farmadhi said, "Prophecy is the essence, the very being, of power and sublimity. Superiority and inferiority do not exist in it. Undoubtedly saintship is of the same type".[46]

The mystic Rabi'a al-Adawiyya was one of the first to teach the doctrine of disinterested love of God. The concept of the disinterested love of God advocated the mystic worship of God for the sole purpose of worshipping God, neither for fear of condemnation to hell, nor hope of ascension in to heaven. In the domestic roles of wife and mother, women are also teachers as teaching children the Quran or education lessons come naturally to women. In this case, Rabi'a is fulfilling the domestic role. Other infamous women such as Shuhda Bint al-Ibarī, Zaynab Bint ash-Sha'ri, and Fātima Bint Ahmed Ibn Yahyā were also some of the most learned women of their time and were also teachers. Umm Waraqa Bint Abdallāh was a popular prayer leader and was supposedly instructed how to pray by Muhammad. Unfortunately, women never founded any order of saints (for lack of a better term) in Islam and there were very few women given significant spiritual significance in Islam. The spiritual hierarchy in Islam was left to the realm of the masculine.

In every organization that is used in this book, women play the traditional role of wife, mother, or sexual slave. For those women who have chosen the role of wife and mother, Muslim women in jihadist terrorist organizations do fulfill these traditional roles in their entirety including veiling, modesty, chastity, etc. This is not a colossal theory in this argument (regarding the roles of wife and mother) as women play the role of wife and mother throughout every culture or faith around the world. However, the role of sex slave is something different and is primarily used by ISIS and Boko Haram concerning the case studies used in this book. As cited earlier in this chapter, the Quran allows for the use of women and children taken in religious war in the effort to spread Islam. Known in the Quran as "those whom your right hand possesses" these women are "those whom your right hand possesses out of those whom Allah has given to you as prisoners of war."[47] As numerous documentaries can attest with a simple search on You Tube, ISIS is consistently involved in the stealing and trading of slaves for the purpose of sex and labor. Boko Haram is also a frequent purchaser of sex slaves and participates in slavery.

In August 2014, when ISIS entered Mosul, several thousand Yazidis, some Christian, were captured by ISIS and thousands more went to Mount Sinjar where they managed to escape ISIS for dehydration and starvation.[48] Captured people were presented with the option to convert to Islam or face death. Many who refused to convert or who put up a fight were killed and placed in shallow mass graves. Women were taken to a mosque, stripped of their veils, and examined like cattle for marriage to ISIS fighters. The younger women were married in hasty ceremonies to ISIS men and older women were placed in slave roles. The forced converts were made to pray five times a day. Boys as young as five years old were made child soldiers, forced to behead people, and participate in graphic and violent acts. The child soldiers were also taught to use suicide belts.[49]

Other women, not lucky enough to be married (whether temporary or not), were often sold at slave markets where their veils would be removed and the men would walk among them, picking which one they wanted. Christian, Kurdish, and Yazidi women were sold at the slave markets. Girls as young as eight were sold to men, many of these men already married with Muslim children. When the men tired of one woman, they would sell them to other men, including women and their daughters. Some women were sold several times and raped repeatedly by various men. Several girls were sexually tortured in addition to rape, while being constantly mocked and insulted. ISIS will sell people back to their family for as much as 20,000 dollars per person. It is important to state here that a woman's previous marriage and ties are dissolved once she is made a slave by a jihadist.

Boko Haram in Nigeria was also widely publicized when they kidnapped 276 girls in a school in Chibok in 2014, which is just one incident in their kidnapping campaigns. Many of these girls are Christian as Boko Haram is trying to institute an Islamic Caliphate in northeastern Nigeria and the girls were classified as infidels by the terrorist organization. The girls were forced into sexual slavery by the terrorist organization, many of them being married to militants. In addition to this incident Boko Haram has abducted people and forced them into slavery on numerous occasions. Several international efforts have occurred and several of the girls have been returned to their families. This is another testament to the role of sex slaves that women are given in the Quran as prisoners of war and jihad.[50]

ISIS and Boko Haram, relatively new jihadist terrorist organizations, are the only two Muslim terrorist organizations to use sex slaves. They are also the only two organizations that have made great attempts at reestablishing the Islamic Caliphate. The concept of sexual slavery is justified in the Quran as roles that women may play for male jihadists. Not only does the Quran justify the capturing and use of infidel women and children, but it encourages jihadists to take what Allah has provided for them. However, women will not be raped by another man until they have had a menstrual cycle and have been purified from their menstrual cycle. The purpose of this is to verify that should there be an offspring from the rape, the jihadi would be the father. Pregnant women who are kidnapped will not be raped until they have delivered their baby; until such time they are labor slaves. The previous marriage of an infidel woman who is kidnapped is nullified after she has been captured according to the Quran.

What is particularly interesting is that sometimes these sex slaves are forced into marriages, whether temporary or long term, and at other times these women are traded from man to man at slave markets. It appears that most of the time, male jihadists will wait until the women have had a menstrual cycle before they rape her but there are also stories of women being passed from man to man in the same day. Most likely marriage is only used when men need someone to take care of the household chores and cooking in addition to providing sexual favors. Loneliness and the need for companionship most likely also play a role. There are several stories of women who have freely joined ISIS who are wives of the ISIS men and are in charge of the household. The wives of ISIS men have converted to Islam or are already Muslim when they join ISIS. The husbands of these women will often also take sex slaves and force those slave women to live in the same household as subservient to their legal Muslim wives.[51] One Yazidi woman who was a former ISIS sex slave stated when asked whether jihadist men were allowed to cheat on their wives:

> Their wives knew that the fighters took us as sex slaves, they didn't consider us equals. They were even glad. They didn't consider it as cheating, because the militants were doing everything in the name of Islamic State. They raped Yazidi girls and sold them to one another. Their wives knew about it. They knew that their husbands wouldn't keep those girls in the family for a long time or marry them. Militants never treated me as their family member. They only used me for sex. Why would their wives be jealous? I would be sold in an hour or two, and I would no longer be in their house.[52]

It is evident throughout this section that the roles of mother and wife are the most important roles for women in both the Quran and jihadist terrorist organizations. Even women who are pregnant or become pregnant are not raped until after they have given birth. The role of sex slave is also a prominent role for infidel women if they are Christian or of some other faith. Women who are naturally affirmed Muslims are not subjected to sexual slavery, yet forced converts to Islam are sex slaves and are forced into marriage on a regular basis. Even as a Muslim, these women do not receive respected status. However, even Muslim women are forced to remarry after the martyrdom of the husband within the defined grief period of four lunar months and ten days, regardless of whether the marriage was consummated. The purpose of this is to keep the jihadists happy while they are fighting on the field.

The Role of the Secretary

The Quran and Hadith do not really deliver many examples of feminine heroines. Furthermore, women who provide the secretary and logistician roles are few and far between as the roles of wife and mother are a woman's first obligation in Islam. Obviously the terms secretary and logistician are not terms that would be used in the Quran. What is meant here by these terms are the roles that women play as supporters in the Quran. Perhaps they are taking notes like a secretary would or perhaps they are getting objects and carrying them from place to place like a courier. Either way these roles are the supportive roles so that men can be successful in their duties. As Middle Eastern area specialist Barbara Stowasser perfectly phrases it, "Emphasis now lies with the women's active role as helpmates on the home front whose domesticity has a new spirit and function. Secondly, prominently featured is the women's participation in the Prophet's struggle for the Cause. The domesticity theme involves the glorification of the female in her God-given roles of wife and mother."[53] However, a few women are also glorified in Islam for their roles as "second in command" or literally the support away from the battlefield. Women also use their societal ties to spread information and recruit. Academics Eickelman and Piscatori state, "Through complex social networks of their own, women may entertain friends and kin and thereby cement social ties and serve as channels of information and communication."[54]

Khadija, Muhammad's first wife, was literally his second in command before the creation and spread of Islam and was also a spiritual confidant and inspiration to the Prophet even after her death, perhaps as a spiritual presence. She was the first convert to Islam and was the only wife to give him children. Khadija supported Muhammad when no one else in the community believed in his visions and thought he was crazy.[55] Khadija was most likely the love of the Prophet's life as he was monogamous to her for twenty-five years, until her death. She was a business woman who made her fortune from running a trading caravan. She chose Muhammad as her husband even though he had much less money than her.[56] Muhammad was allowed the luxury of studying other religions for several years due to Khadija's wealth. "Khadija is celebrated as both wife and mother, the Prophet's tender 'rest and refuge.'

She is, furthermore, his fellow struggler in his great *jihad*, which she waged as his *vizier* ('second in command') from the moment of their first meeting until the day of her death."[57]

Aishah, Muhammad's third wife, is also a good example. She was offered to the Prophet at age six or seven and had sexual relations with him at age nine. Aishah was in charge of the Prophet's books.[58] She would record the words of the Prophet and would then become the final arbitrator of his life after he was dead. Muhammad was buried under her house. Aishah passed more than two thousand ahadith down in the Muslim faith, became an advisor to Muslim leaders and Muslim women, and regularly visited the grave of Muhammad. Although Aishah was present at the Battle of the Camel urging the men to fight, she later reneged on this action and stated that she wished that war had never occurred.[59]

In the role of the secretary and logistician, women fight for the cause in a patriarchal society by providing support and nurturing, which will allow her man to fight his jihad. If the home and family life are taken care of, the man is better able to pursue his jihad. Although the historic examples of the role of the secretary are rare, regarding women in the Quran and Hadith, the few examples we have provided enough of a model to facilitate these gender roles in jihadist terrorist organizations. This role is defined in the book as any supportive role that women play in jihadist terrorist organizations. Mr. Abu Haniya, analyst of Islamic groups, stated, "While the traditional jihadists limit women's participation in jihad to supporting militant men in activities such as nursing, teaching, and moral support, the new ideologues have begun to mention female participation in armed actions in their literature recently."[60]

The Role of the Disposable

A disposable object is something that is of little use and is of little significance. This object is able to be used once, usually for insignificant purposes, then should be thrown away. One does not show great concern for the destruction or disposal of the object. The concept of the disposable in this chapter relates to a Muslim woman who fulfills her role as a suicide bomber by using her body as a bomb or a weapon. She is not worth as much as a man, nor can she do as much, therefore her body is an already prepared prototype for a human bomb.

In the Quran, the status of the martyr is highly coveted and the martyr is one of the most revered in paradise. As a martyr, her body does not need to be washed before burial; the body according to the Quran has already been purified by martyrdom.[61] Additionally her wounds will be present until the Day of Resurrection when she will appear before Allah so that everyone can see her status as a martyr. She will be granted access to paradise because of her martyrdom. Her family should not mourn her but should rejoice at her death.

Her martyrdom comes as a result of her jihad. In the Quran, the term jihad has two major uses. The first of these is known as the inner jihad or the greater jihad, which refers to quest for the true Muslim life, whereby a person follows the Quran and the five pillars of Islam. This jihad refers to the inner struggle of the individual to not fall prey to Satan and to worship Allah.

The lesser jihad or outer jihad refers to a form of warfare that is sanctioned by Allah. Believed to be defensive jihad, all Muslims are obligated to participate in the lesser/outer jihad. In the lesser or outer jihad, Muslims are obligated to do battle for exactly three reasons: The first of these reasons is whether Muslims are attacked. This is why Muslim men from all over the world went to Chechnya and Afghanistan to fight the Russians.[62]

The second reason for jihad may occur if Muslim land is attacked, particularly on the Arabian Peninsula, where the cradle of Islam is located. No other religion or state can own land on the Arabian Peninsula—this has been a problem for the United States as military bases have been attacked for this reason. Lastly, if the religion of Islam is threatened or criticized, then Muslims are obligated to fight. Problematically, since defensive jihad is obligatory for all Muslims, then the declaring of jihad by lay Muslims occurs frequently, despite the fact that these people have no religious authority or education. If jihad becomes defensive, then even women must fight according to most Islamic scholars.

Shi'ites and Sunnis have a slightly different view of jihad and martyrdom. Throughout history Shi'ites have usually been martyred at the hands of Sunnis. The first martyr for Shi'ites was al-Husayn (grandson of the Prophet) who was murdered at the hands of the Sunni government militia in Karbala in 680 AD, which is in modern day southern Iraq. Many more Shi'ites from the Prophet's family were murdered by the Sunni Umayyad or Abbasid dynasties. For Sunnis, martyrdom is about jihad and victory. For Shi'ites, martyrdom is a mournful process and any victory gained from it will be deferred until Judgement Day.[63]

In comparison to Christianity, Allah does not love his followers like God loves his people or his creation. Allah loves those who do good.[64] Allah loves those who love Allah[65] and Allah loves those that do not reject Islam.[66] However, the entire concept of inherent, never-ending, and without stipulations love that God has for his people in Christianity is not there in Islam. There is no love of people in Islam simply because they are Allah's creation; one must do or act to receive Allah's love.

To take this a step further, forgiveness from Allah is something that must be earned in Islam. Unlike Christianity where forgiveness is granted by God throughout sincere atonement for sin and a simple request; in Islam, one must act to be forgiven. In the end, Muslims must stand at the gates of eternity and their actions must be weighed. To enter paradise, the good must outweigh the bad. However, there is another way to enter paradise: "And if you are slain or die in the way of Allah, forgiveness and mercy from Allah are far better than all they could amass."[67] "The Prophet said, "The person who participates in [holy battles] in Allah's cause and nothing compels him to do so except belief in Allah and His Apostles, will be recompensed by Allah either with a reward, or booty [if he survives] or will be admitted to Paradise [if he is killed in the battle as a martyr]."[68]

The Prophet also states, regarding infidels or unbelievers, "And slay them wherever you catch them, and turn them out from where they have turned you out, for tumult and oppression are worse than slaughter."[69] "And fight them on until there is no more tumult or oppression, and let there prevail justice and faith in Allah; but if they cease, let there be no hostility except to those who practice oppression."[70] Typically people of the book, such as Jews or Muslims, are supposed to be taxed at a higher rate and respected if they do not convert to Islam. However, in Muslim practice, this does not always hold true and Sunnis will often attack even Shias. Or one just needs to look to the Yazidi Christians to see a contradiction. However, anyone who does not believe in the concept of the Jewish, Christian, or Muslim God, who is the same God for all three religions, is fair game.

For those Muslims who do not want to engage in conflict or war as most modern people are not interested in conducting war on infidels, Muhammad had other ideas. He stated, "Fighting is prescribed for you, and you dislike it. But it is possible that you dislike a thing which is good for you, and that you love a thing which is bad for you. But Allah knows and you know not."[71] To take this a step farther, the people who do not take up the lesser jihad are not equal and even unworthy of the Muslims who do take up arms. Muhammad stated, "Not equal are those believers who sit [at home] and those who strive hard and fight in the Cause of Allah with their wealth and lives."[72]

However, Muhammad was not a fan of sending women to war nor having women in leadership positions; indeed, the concept of female jihad is distasteful. In the Quran, Muhammad and his wife Aisha discussed the concept of female jihad. Aisha stated, "Apostle! We consider Jihad as the best deed. 'Should we not Fight in Allah's Cause?' He [Muhammad] said, 'The best Jihad for women is the Hajj done as I have done it."[73] Although Muhammad states his preference that women do not engage in jihad but instead pursue the holy pilgrimage to Mecca, Muhammad does not outlaw jihad for women.

There are other statements by the Prophet in the Quran that women should stay home and pursue their spiritual lives through chastity, obedience to their husbands, and motherhood.

Seldom are there historical accounts of female fighters in Islam who would often recite prose to inspire the men on the battlefield. Rare examples exist such as Nusayba bint Káb who fought in the Battle of Uhud with her husband and two sons. Nusayba was a companion of the Prophet, fighting in a surprise attack from the Meccans. Nusayba suffered eleven wounds and lost an arm in the battle. She was also a devout protector of Muhammad and follower of Islam.[74] Safiya, the aunt of the Prophet Muhammad, hid from the Jews in Medina during the Battle of Khandaq (627 AD). When the Jews attacked their place of refuge, she cut off one of their heads and threw it back at the Jews. The Prophet Muhammad's wife Aishah led the Battle of the Camel, although she was more of a strategic planner than an actual leader in the battle as she directed her forces on the back of a camel in a howdah (bed). The Prophet's granddaughter Zaynab bint Al was present during the Battle of Karbala, although her tent was looted and then burned afterwards. However, these women are rare and two are also related to the Prophet. Umm Umāra was a nurse who fought in some of the Muslim battles although her main purpose was to provide aid to the wounded.[75]

Academic David Cook states that Aliyya Mustafa Mubarak in her book *Sahabiyyat Mujahidat* found sixty-seven women who fought in the wars with the Prophet Muhammad or afterwards in the Muslim conquests. However, Cook transcribes that the actions of these women appear to be relatively minute, whether it is sailing a boat or defending themselves. Cook mentions that Syrian writer Nawaf al-Takruri in his numerous editions of *Martyrdom Operation in the Legal Balance* could not come to a decision on whether women should fight in jihad as he was worried they would have to be immodestly dressed to fight and/or carry munitions.[76] Cook also states that there is a different category of women called the *mutarajjulat* who are women who dress like men. The Prophet strongly condemned this action and these women. They might not have been lesbians but were certainly women operating in a man's world. There were several accounts of these women participating in battles in Arab folk tales.[77]

In the fifteenth century, the Islamic jurisprudence of jihad, in particular Nahhas al-Dumyati (d.1414) took an even more misogynistic view of women in that they kept a righteous Muslim man from fulfilling his duty to Allah through jihad. Ibn Nahhas wrote:

If you say [wanting to avoid jihad]: My heart is not comfortable parting from my wife and her beauty, the companionship I have close to her and my happiness in touching her—even if your wife is the most beautiful of women and the loveliest of the people of the time, her beginning is a small drop [of sperm] and her end is a filthy corpse. Between those two times, she carries excrement, her menstruation denies her to you for part of her life, and her disobedience to you is usually more than her obedience. If she does not apply kohl to her eyes, they become bleary, if she does not adorn herself she becomes ugly, if she does not comb her hair it is disheveled, if she does not anoint herself her light will be extinguished, if she does not put on perfume she will smell bad and if she does not clean her pubes she will stink. Her defects will multiply, she will become weary, when she grows old she will become depressed, when she is old she will be incapacitated—even if you treat her well, she will be contemptuous towards you.[78]

However, as previously mentioned in this section and chapter, the entire concept of jihad and martyrdom is revered in the Islamic faith and is given first preference for paradise over anything else. Therefore, Muslim women have begun to embrace martyrdom like men have and male leaders of terrorist organizations have found that Muslim women are able to get through checkpoints easier due to their gender. Muslim women are also able to strap on bombs under the pretense of being pregnant or obese. And most people do not suspect that a woman would become a suicide bomber as they are still used less frequently than male suicide bombers.

The Shi'ite tradition differs slightly from the Sunni tradition. The tenth century jurisprudent Ibn Babawayhi agrees that both men and women have a jihad. Ibn Babawayhi wrote, "The man's jihad is to sacrifice his wealth and his blood until he is killed in the path of Allah, but the jihad of the woman is to endure suffering at the hands of her husband and his jealousy [of her]."[79] The endurance of spousal abuse is the female jihad for this tenth century Islamic jurisprudent.

In traditional Islam, a dichotomy exists between historical minor examples of female fighters and Muslim society. Even if women (not including the Prophet Muhammad's family) did participate in battle or jihad, the whole concept of recruiting them was an affront to the head male in the women's family. Women were always the property of men and were never free to attach themselves to anything outside of their family. The concept of jihad for women had a completely different meaning than it did for men and it still does today.

In her book, *Beyond the Veil*, Fatima Mernissi states that

Sexual equality violates Islam's premise, actualized in its laws, that the heterosexual love is dangerous to Allah's order. Muslim marriage is based on male dominance . . . The woman should be under the authority of fathers, brothers, or husbands. Since she is considered by Allah to be a destructive element, she is to be spatially confined and excluded from matters other than those of the family.[80]

Mernissi goes on to state that "the whole system is based on the assumption that the woman is a powerful and dangerous being."[81] Sharia Law was created to restrain her power, most particularly her sexuality. Her power is thus relegated to the domestic family sphere of influence where she cannot cause any embarrassment to her family through unrestrained sexuality. The power of the woman is based on her role as mother and wife in a secluded, modest environment. In addition, the concept of suicide or martyrdom for either men or women in Islam is the most satisfying quest for termination of life. The Hadith states (9.93.519),

> Allah guarantees [to the person who carries out Jihad in His Cause and nothing compelled him to go out but Jihad in His Cause and the belief in His Word] that He will either admit him into Paradise [martyrdom] or return him with reward or booty he had earned to his residence from where he went out.[82]

Thus the concept of martyrdom for women is the ultimate romantic and pious Muslim death. She is promised entry into heaven, eternal reward, and riches beyond her imagination.

The most common weapons of choice for female jihad, suicide bombings, have some general qualities that are relatively predictable. First, suicide bombings are planned by an established organization 95 percent of the time and this organization has operated effectively over time. Secondly, the majority of places where suicide attacks occur involve territorial conflicts pertaining to the struggles of ethnic or nationalist groups opposing foreign militaries on what the group identifies as their homeland. The goal of these organizations is to remove the foreign occupiers. Third, suicide bombings rarely occur as an isolated event and are typically tied to a string of bombings or a campaign planned by an organization. Fourthly, around 70 percent of suicide attacks occur against a democracy. Lastly, the diffusion of technology that has occurred with terrorist weaponry has also occurred with suicide bombings. Like most organizations, terrorist groups learn from and use the innovations of their peers.[83]

Jihadist terrorist groups currently use women as suicide bombers on a regular basis. This is a relatively new phenomenon that jihadist terrorist groups have begun using in the last few decades, perhaps since the 1990s as Cook[84] states. Throughout Islamic history, Muslim women were not allowed to fight in war, including acts of martyrdom. However, recently in the last few decades the strategic value of women has been observed and female suicide bombers have been used frequently by Jihadist terrorist groups, although the climax in popularity of this practice occurred slowly.

The first ever female suicide bomber was Dalal Al Maghribi, according to political scientist Mia Bloom. Dalal was a Palestinian who blew up a bus going to Tel Aviv on March 11, 1978, in the Coastal Road Massacre. This attack committed by Fatah was one of several in a terrorist spree of attacks.[85] Sana'a Mehaidli was a lone suicide bomber who blew herself up on April 9, 1985, for the Syrian Social Nationalist Party. The Chechens were the first terrorist organization to use women on a regular basis. On June 9, 2000, Hawa Barayev drove into a Russian Special Unit in Alkhan Khala, killing twenty-seven Russian soldiers. Her last words were reportedly, "I know what I am doing: Paradise has its price."[86] These female Chechen terrorists become so prolific that they were dubbed the "Black Widows" as many of them lost family or husbands in the conflict with Russia in addition to the reference to the female spider that eats its mate and can kill humans with its toxin.

The martyrdom of Hawa Barayev began to stir debate in the Islamic world as to whether it was appropriate to have female suicide bombers. Psychotherapist Cindy D. Ness found that the High Islamic Council in Saudi Arabia issued a fatwa encouraging Palestinian women to become suicide bombers within a year after the first female Chechen suicide bomber.[87] The first female suicide bomber in the Israeli-Palestinian conflict is widely attributed as Palestinian Wafa Idris who detonated herself on January 27, 2002, for al-Aqsa Martyrs' Brigade. Al-Aqsa Martyrs' Brigade started a special female suicide bombers unit for women named after Wafa Idris.[88] Boko Haram began using women as suicide bombers on June 8, 2014, when a middle-aged woman on a motorcycle detonated herself near a Nigerian military barracks in Gombe, Nigeria, killing one policeman.[89] Hamas, the Palestinian terrorist group, has been using female suicide bombers since January 14, 2004, when Reem Raiyshi, a mother of two in her early twenties, blew herself up on the Israeli border with Gaza.[90] Sheik Ahmad Yassin, the spiritual founder of Hamas, was asked by journalist Barbara Victor about female suicide bombers. Victor asked him,

How do you feel, Sheik Yassin, a man of God, when you hear that a young woman has strapped on an explosive belt and blown herself up in a market, killing dozens of Israeli men, women, and children?" Sheik Yassin responded: "It is a good sign. Once women were squeamish about seeing blood or committing acts of martyrdom. Now they are willing to die for the sake of our cause. For me, it is a good sign that women are beginning to take up the fight alongside our men.[91]

Rima Fahri, a female Hezbollah leader, stated, "The list of women willing to commit suicide attacks in Hezbollah is as long as the men's."[92] The Muslim Brotherhood has not yet used female suicide bombers in 2018 when this chapter is being written nor has al-Qaeda. Scholar Cindy Ness also found that al-Qaeda has not publicly sanctioned female suicide bombers but has published anecdotal reports, threatening female suicide bombings. Published in March 2003, *Asharq al-Awsat*, a woman calling herself "Um Osama" or the mother of Osama bin Laden stated:

> We are preparing for the new strike announced by our leaders and I declare that it will make America forget . . . the September 11 attacks. The idea came from the success of martyr operations carried out by young Palestinian women in the occupied territories. Our organization is open to all Muslim women wanting to serve the [Islamic] nation . . . particularly in this very critical phase.[93]

ISIS sent an unknown female suicide bomber to the Hussienieh Ali Basha Shia Mosque in Iraq on July 5, 2013, but the first publicized and confirmed attempt by ISIS to use a female suicide bomber occurred in Libya in mid-February 2016 although she was not successful.[94] Since this time, ISIS has been using female suicide bombers all over the world.

The concept of martyrdom is well-established in the Quran, promising forgiveness, riches, and seventy-two virgins and many Muslims are inclined to chase martyrdom to pursue the rewards promised to them for dying in the name of Islam. This group also includes women. One of the major and arguably largest roles for women in jihadist terrorist organization is as the disposable, a quick and dirty bomb that can be used one time to inflict the most damage and suffering possible on others. It was argued by Victor[95] that women that were chosen for suicide bombing were frequently deficient in some way in that they are unable to fulfill the role of the traditional Muslim woman like the culture expects. The trend of the Muslim female suicide bomber will continue to grow.

CONCLUSION

The Quran creates and justifies the role of women in Islamic society. Granted, the interpretation may vary according to the Islamic scholar. However, most of Muslim society expects women to fulfill the roles designated for them in Quran. These roles including the domestic status of women, the bookkeeper or secretary, the kinswoman, and the martyr are all the same roles for women in terrorist organizations. Leadership and soldier roles for women are not present in jihadist terrorist organizations. In fact, the Prophet forbade women to be used in war. "A woman was found killed during a series of raids led by the Prophet. So the Prophet forbade the killing of women and children."[96]

However, the role of the foot soldier and leader are present in Western terrorist organizations like the Red Army Faction or the Weathermen.

In comparing East to West, there is a vast divide concerning the roles of women in terrorist organizations. The jihadist terrorist organizations reflect their views of the West and Westernization regarding women. Arab Muslims view Western society as decadent, objectifying women as sexual objects to be placed on display. The honor of the Western woman is compromised as is her soul due to her impurity. Many Muslim women feel that Allah and Islam have given them equality to men and all the rights that they need. The concept of feminism is distasteful and inherently mannish as it takes women from their primary roles as wife and mother. The concept of Western feminism is foreign and offensive.

NOTES

1. Kay S. Hymowitz, "Why Feminism is AWOL on Islam," *City Journal*, Winter 2003, accessed January 8, 2018, https://www.city-journal.org/html/why-feminism -awol-islam-12395.html.

2. Kay S. Hymowitz, "Why Feminism is AWOL on Islam," *City Journal*, Winter 2003, accessed January 8, 2018, https://www.city-journal.org/html/why-feminism -awol-islam-12395.html.

3. Miriam Cooke, "Women, Religion, and the Postcolonial Arab World," *Cultural Critique* 45 (Spring 2000): 151.

4. Faegheh Shirazi, *Velvet Jihad: Muslim Women's Quiet Resistance to Islamic Fundamentalism* (Gainesville: University of Florida Press, 2009), 5.

5. As cited in Dale F. Eickelman and James Piscatori, *Muslim Politics* (Princeton: Princeton University Press, 1996), 92.

6. Valerie Hoffman, "An Islamic Activist: Zaynab al-Ghazali," in *Women and the Family in the Middle East: New Voices of Change*, ed. Elizabeth W. Fernea (Austin: University of Texas Press, 1985), 233–54.

7. Fatima Mernissi, *The Veil and the Male Elite* (New York: Basic Books, 1991). Fatima Mernissi, *Beyond the Veil: Male-Female Dynamics in Modern Muslim Society* (New York: John Wiley and Sons, 1975).

8. Asma Barlas, *"Believing Women" in Islam: Unreading Patriarchal Interpretations of the Qur'an* (Austin: University of Texas Press, 2002.

9. Nimat Hafez Barazangi, *Women's Identity and the Qu'ran: A New Reading* (Gainesville: University of Florida Press, 2004), 8.

10. Nimat Hafez Barazangi, *Women's Identity and the Qu'ran: A New Reading* (Gainesville: University of Florida Press, 2004), 10–11.

11. Kecia Ali, *Sexual Ethics and Islam: Feminist Reflections on Qur'an, Hadith, and Jurisprudence* (Oxford: One World, 2006), xxii.

12. Anwar Hekmat, *Women and the Koran: The Status of Women in Islam* (New York: Prometheus Books, 1997).

13. Ayaan Hirsi Ali, *The Caged Virgin: An Emancipation Proclamation for Women and Islam* (New York: Free Press, 2006), 155.

14. Wafa Sultan, *A God Who Hates* (New York: St. Martin's Press, 2009), 7–8.

15. Wafa Sultan, *A God Who Hates* (New York: St. Martin's Press, 2009), 243.

16. Yoram Schweitzer, "Introduction," in *Female Suicide Bombers: Dying for Equality?*, ed. Yoram Schweitzer (Tel Aviv: *Jaffee Center for Strategic Studies*, August 2006), 10–11.

17. Lina Abirafeh, "Gendered Aid Interventions and Afghan Women: Images Versus Realities," in *Muslim Women in War and Crisis*, ed. Faegheh Shirazi (Austin: University of Texas Press, 2010), 86.

18. Wiebke Walther, *Women in Islam* (Princeton: Markus Wiener Publishing, 1992), Introduction.

19. Khan, Hadith 7:18.

20. Shakir, Quran IV: 34.

21. Khan, Hadith 7/98:100.

22. Shakir, Quran XXIV: 31.

23. As cited in Fatima Mernissi, *Beyond the Veil: Male-Female Dynamics in Modern Muslim Society* (New York: John Wiley and Sons, 1975), 12.

24. Fatima Mernissi, *Beyond the Veil: Male-Female Dynamics in Modern Muslim Society* (New York: John Wiley and Sons, 1975), 5.

25. Fatima Mernissi, *Beyond the Veil: Male-Female Dynamics in Modern Muslim Society* (New York: John Wiley and Sons, 1975), 19.

26. Shakir, Quran IV: 3.

27. Shakir, Quran V: 87.

28. Shakir, Quran XXXIII: 50.

29. Shakir, Quran IV: 24.

30. The al-Khansa ISIS female police brigade has been rumored to have their own prostitution houses for female slaves, even though prostitution of slaves taken in religious war was forbidden by Muhammad. The women of al-Khansa are rumored to be mostly British. See the following: Russell Myers, "British Female Jihadis Running ISIS 'Brothels' Allowing Killers to Rape Kidnapped Yazidi Women," *Mirror*, September 10, 2014, accessed June 23, 2017, http://www.mirror.co.uk/news/uk-news/british-female-jihadis-running-isis-4198165.

31. Shakir, Quran II: 223.

32. Shakir, Quran II: 222.

33. Shakir, Quran LXVI: 1.

34. Shakir, Quran II: 228.

35. Shakir, Quran IV: 15.

36. Shakir, Quran II: 233.

37. Fatima Mernissi, *Beyond the Veil: Male-Female Dynamics in Modern Muslim Society* (New York: John Wiley and Sons, 1975), 69.

38. Khan, Hadith 8:2.

39. Fatima Mernissi, *Beyond the Veil: Male-Female Dynamics in Modern Muslim Society* (New York: John Wiley and Sons, 1975), 100.

40. Bruce B. Lawrence, *Shattering the Myth: Islam Beyond Violence* (Princeton: Princeton University Press, 1998).

41. Frances S. Hasso, "Discursive and Political Deployments by/of the 2002 Palestinian Women Suicide Bombers/Martyrs," *Feminist Review* 81 (1) (2005): 23–51, 33.

42. Barbara Freyer Stowasser, *Women in the Qur'an, Traditions, and Interpretation* (Oxford: Oxford University Press, 1994), 81.

43. Esko Naskali, "Women of the Prophet's Family as They Feature in Popular Bazaar Literature," in *Women in Islamic Societies, Social Attitudes and Historical Perspectives*, ed. Bo Utas (London: Curzon Press Ltd, 1983).

44. Ergun Mehmet Caner and Emir Fethi Caner, *Unveiling Islam* (Grand Rapids, MI: Kregel Publications, 2002), 56–60.

45. Emine Gürsoy-Naskali, "Women Mystics in Islam," in *Women in Islamic Societies: Social Attitudes and Historical Perspectives*, ed. Bo Utas (London: Curzon Press Ltd, 1983), 238.

46. As cited in Emine Gürsoy-Naskali, "Women Mystics in Islam," in *Women in Islamic Societies: Social Attitudes and Historical Perspectives*, ed. Bo Utas (London: Curzon Press Ltd, 1983), 238–39.

47. Shakir, Quran XXXIII: 50.

48. Sam Masters, "Iraq Crisis: Starving, Desperate, but Safe from ISIS on Mount Sinjar," *Independent,* August 9, 2014, accessed June 23, 2017, http://www.independent.co.uk/news/world/middle-east/iraq-crisis-starving-desperate-but-safe-from-isis-on-mount-sinjar-9659449.html.

49. "*ISIS: Sex Slaves*," YouTube documentary, 40:31, posted by Ahlulbayt: Documentaries, June 14, 2016, https://www.youtube.com/watch?v=3A6-55TJNrI&t=148s.

50. Larisa Epatko, "Surviving Boko Haram: Kidnapped Girls Tell Their Stories," *PBS Newshour*, October 19, 2016, accessed June 23, 2016, http://www.pbs.org/newshour/updates/surviving-boko-haram-kidnapped-girls-tell-stories/.

51. Rukmini Callimach, "ISIS Enshrines a Theology of Rape," *New York Times*, August 13, 2015, accessed June 23, 2017, https://www.nytimes.com/2015/08/14/world/middleeast/isis-enshrines-a-theology-of-rape.html?_r=0.

52. Sophie Shevardnadze, "ISIS Sex Slave Survivor: They Beat Me, Raped Me, Treated Me Like an Animal," *RT*, August 19, 2016, accessed June 23, 2017, https://www.rt.com/shows/sophieco/336398-is-slave-horrors-crime/.

53. Barbara Freyer Stowasser, *Women in the Qur'an, Traditions, and Interpretation* (Oxford: Oxford University Press, 1994), 126.

54. Dale F. Eickelman and James Piscatori, *Muslim Politics* (Princeton: Princeton University Press, 1996), 98.

55. Wiebke Walther, *Women in Islam* (Princeton: Markus Wiener Publishing, 1992), Women in Islamic History Chapter.

56. Esko Naskali, "Women of the Prophet's Family as They Feature in Popular Bazaar Literature," in *Women in Islamic Societies: Social Attitudes and Historical Perspectives*, ed. Bo Utas (London: Curzon Press Ltd, 1983).

57. Barbara Freyer Stowasser, *Women in the Qur'an, Traditions, and Interpretation* (Oxford: Oxford University Press, 1994), 126.

58. Ergun Mehmet Caner and Emir Fethi Caner, *Unveiling Islam* (Grand Rapids, MI: Kregel Publications, 2002), 135.

59. Wiebke Walther, *Women in Islam* (Princeton: Markus Wiener Publishing, 1992), 107.

60. Murad Batal al-Shishani, "Is the Role of Women in al-Qaeda increasing?" *BBC News*, October 7, 2010, accessed June 27, 2017, http://www.bbc.com/news/world-middle-east-11484672.

61. David Cook and Olivia Allison, *Understanding and Addressing Suicide Attacks: The Faith and Politics of Martyrdom Operations* (Westport, CT: Praeger Security International 2007), 9–10.

62. Michael Bonner, *Jihad in Islamic History* (Princeton: Princeton University Press, 2006).

63. David Cook and Olivia Allison, *Understanding and Addressing Suicide Attacks: The Faith and Politics of Martyrdom Operations* (Westport, CT: Praeger Security International 2007), 19–21.

64. Shakir, Quran II: 195.

65. Shakir, Quran III: 31.

66. Shakir, Quran III: 32.

67. Shakir, Quran III: 157.

68. Khan, Hadith I: 35.

69. Shakir, Quran II: 191.

70. Shakir, Quran II: 193.

71. Shakir, Quran II: 216.

72. Shakir, Quran IV: 95.

73. Khan, Hadith IV: 52:43.

74. David Cook, "Women Fighting in Jihad?" in *Female Terrorism and Militancy: Agency, Utility, and Organization*, ed. Cindy D. Ness (New York: Routledge, 2008), 37–48.

75. Wiebke Walther, *Women in Islam* (Princeton: Markus Wiener Publishing, 1992), 111.

76. David Cook, "Women Fighting in Jihad?" *Studies in Conflict and Terrorism* 28 (5) (2005): 375–84.

77. David Cook, "Women Fighting in Jihad?" in *Female Terrorism and Militancy: Agency, Utility, and Organization*, ed. Cindy D. Ness (New York: Routledge, 2008), 37–48.

78. As cited in David Cook, "Women Fighting in Jihad?" in *Female Terrorism and Militancy: Agency, Utility, and Organization*, ed. Cindy D. Ness (New York: Routledge, 2008), 40.

79. As cited in David Cook, "Women Fighting in Jihad?" in *Female Terrorism and Militancy: Agency, Utility, and Organization*, ed. Cindy D. Ness (New York: Routledge, 2008), 39–40.

80. Fatima Mernissi, *Beyond the Veil: Male-Female Dynamics in Modern Muslim Society* (New York: John Wiley and Sons, 1975), xv.

81. Fatima Mernissi, *Beyond the Veil: Male-Female Dynamics in Modern Muslim Society* (New York: John Wiley and Sons, 1975), xvi.

82. As cited in Ergun Mehmet Caner and Emir Fethi Caner, *Unveiling Islam* (Grand Rapids, MI: Kregel Publications, 2002), 196.

83. Ami Pedahzur, *Suicide Terrorism* (Malden, MA: Polity Press, 2005), 12–14.

84. David Cook, "Women Fighting in Jihad?" *Studies in Conflict and Terrorism* 28 (5) (2005): 375–84.

85. Mia Bloom, *Bombshell* (Philadelphia: Penn State University Press, 2011), 23.

86. Janny Groen and Annieke Kranenberg, *Women Warriors for Allah: An Islamist Network in the Netherlands* (Philadelphia: University of Pennsylvania Press, 2010), 73.

87. Cindy D. Ness, "In the Name of the Cause: Women's Work in Secular and Religious Terrorism," in *Female Terrorism and Militancy: Agency, Utility, and Organization*, ed. Cindy D. Ness (New York: Routledge, 2008), 19–20.

88. Cindy D. Ness, "In the Name of the Cause: Women's Work in Secular and Religious Terrorism," in *Female Terrorism and Militancy: Agency, Utility, and Organization*, ed. Cindy D. Ness (New York: Routledge, 2008), 26.

89. Bill Roggio and Caleb Weiss, "Female Suicide Bombers Continue to Strike in West Africa," *FDD's Long War Journal*, December 4, 2015, accessed June 23, 2017, http://www.longwarjournal.org/archives/2015/12/female-suicide-bombers-continue -to-strike-in-west-africa.php.

90. BBC News, "Hamas Woman Bomber Kills Israelis," *BBC News*, January 14, 2004, accessed June 22, 2017, http://news.bbc.co.uk/2/hi/middle_east/3395973.stm.

91. Barbara Victor, *Army of Roses* (Emmaus, PA: Rodale, 2003), 111.

92. Mary Chastain, "List of Female Hezbollah Suicide Bombers Grows," *Breitbart,* August 18, 2013, accessed June 23, 2017, http://www.breitbart.com/national -security/2013/08/18/women-rise-in-hezbollah-still-not-equal-to-men/.

93. As cited in Cindy D. Ness, "In the Name of the Cause: Women's Work in Secular and Religious Terrorism," in *Female Terrorism and Militancy: Agency, Utility, and Organization*, ed. Cindy D. Ness (New York: Routledge, 2008), 21.

94. Samuel Osborne, "ISIS Starts Using Female Fighters and Suicide Bombers for the First Time," *Independent*, February 29, 2016, accessed June 23, 2017, http://www. independent.co.uk/news/world/africa/isis-starts-using-female-fighters-and-suicide -bombers-for-the-first-time-a6903166.html.

95. Barbara Victor, *Army of Roses: Inside the World of Palestinian Women Suicide Bombers* (Emmaus, PA: Rodale, 2003).

96. Khan, Hadith 4:159–160.

Chapter Two

Some Thoughts on Female Jihadist Motivation and Radicalization

This chapter explores the topics of female jihadist motivation and female jihadist radicalization. Both of these subjects are newly considered and have rarely been broached. Female terrorist motivations have been studied by scholars such as Mia Bloom although little attention has been paid to the category of female jihadist motivations. Motivations for female jihadists have consistently been lumped in with female terrorists as though they were the same as women in the Red Army Faction or women in the Italian Red Brigades. Female jihadists have different cultures and religions that differ from Western women in addition to many other differences. Therefore, they should be studied separately.

The subject of jihadist female radicalization has not been broached by academics at all. Even regarding literature on male jihadist radicalization and recruitment, little information is available. This chapter will begin as an analysis of female jihadist motivations and will continue with a discussion of female jihadist radicalization. Although these topics are nascent by their nature, this chapter will make an initial stab at understanding and providing a foundation for the study of female jihadist motivation and radicalization.

Female Jihadist Motivation and Levels of Analysis

In graduate school, I took numerous classes from Professor Harvey Starr at the University of South Carolina where he talked about understanding international relations by looking at several levels of analysis at the same time. In his work *Approaches, Levels, and Methods of Analysis in International Politics: Crossing Boundaries (Advances in Foreign Policy Analysis)*, Starr[1] talks about looking at international relations from several points of view including local, state, national, and international explanations. This ability to look at problems and situations through various facets was drilled into my head and has helped me to better analyze my own research.

When looking at female terrorism and motivational reasons for women joining terrorist organizations, levels of analysis can be employed. There are at least three levels of motivation for a woman to join a terrorist organization although there may in fact be several motivations, depending on the individual. The first level of motivation is the primary motivation and is the number one reason for a person to join a terrorist organization. The secondary motivation is important but not as important as the primary motivation. The third level of motivation is self-explanatory in that it is not as important as the first or second levels of motivations but it does still play a role in whether a person joins a terrorist organization. Most likely these levels of motivation help explain why there are so many various reasons for women to join a terrorist organization whether it be nationalism, strategic reasons, revenge, etc. which was elaborated upon in the introduction. Reasons may be categorized as political, social, religious, economic, military, or personal, etc. In fact, it is logical that female terrorists or terrorists in general may have several levels of motivation or reasons for what they do if we assume they are rational beings. As a side note, the author has always argued that terrorists are rational entities and make decisions that best serve their own interests, whatever those interests may be. The media has often described terrorists as crazy or involving some degree of brainwashing; this stereotype is completely incorrect as terrorists function quite well in normal society. The hierarchical ranking of these motivations may not be apparent to the women themselves through introspection but when questioned, they will usually state their reasons honestly. As a researcher, the author takes these statements at face value. When women are questioned about their reasons for joining a terrorist organization, their responses are typically honest and a researcher can take their statements as true. In an environment where comfort with the investigator is maintained and there are no repercussions for honest conversation, most women will be truthful. Figure 2.1: Levels of Terrorists' Motivations is a diagram of the levels of female terrorist motivations. All of these motivations play an important role, depending upon the individual and organization.

For jihadist female terrorists, regardless of the terrorist organization they belong to, the primary motivation is most likely religion or Islam, although this is not always true. Since these organizations rely on fundamentalist interpretations of Islam, purists are typically attracted to an organization that strictly follows the Quran. This can be seen in Figure 2.2: Levels of Female Jihadist Terrorist Motivations. The motivations for jihadist female terrorists are specific, with Islam most likely playing the primary role. Unlike men in Muslim societies, Muslim women typically do not need to join a terrorist

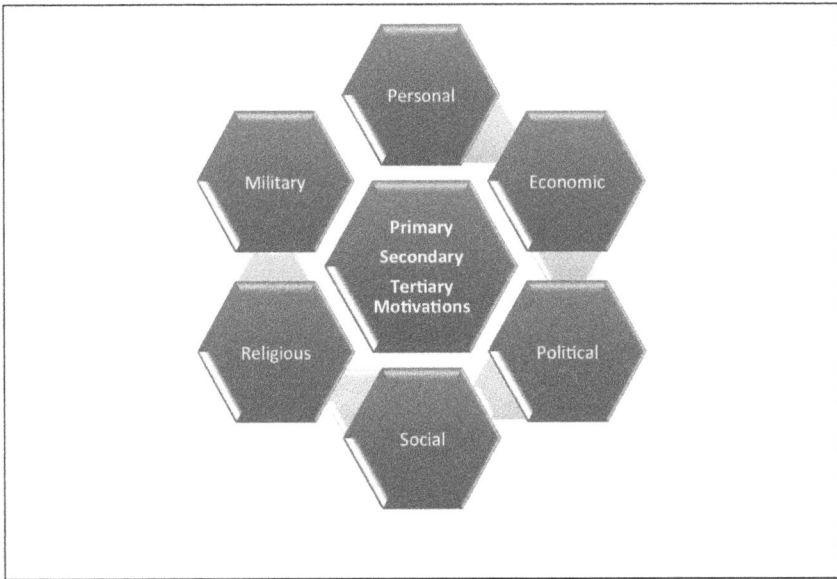

Figure 2.1.   Levels of Terrorists' Motivations. *Source*: Author

organization for any type of job or material item so economic reasons are not primary. In fact, women who join these jihadist terrorist organizations may be looked down upon (depending on where they are at) even if they are just meeting in a women's group. The men in their family are supposed to financially provide for them. Women are not supposed to have careers or spend much time outside the home and family private sphere in these fundamentalist Islamic societies. Muslim women that join terrorist organizations are not career women, although they may have careers; if they have a career it will maintain a dire existence next to the needs of their husbands and families. A woman who has a career without a husband or family in this society is an embarrassment to her Islamic faith and her family. The only thing greater than the home and family is Allah and Islam.

Women will leave their homes, often in secret from family and friends, to join a jihadist terrorist organization. From the author's experiences in interviewing these women, reading their biographies, and performing research, Islam is the first explanation that they give when questioned about their motivations. The second or third levels of motivation may include several other reasons such as: revenge against Israel if they are Palestinian or the quest to live under an Islamic state governed by Sharia Law, etc. Second and third level motivations will vary across jihadist female terrorists, depending on the woman and the group.

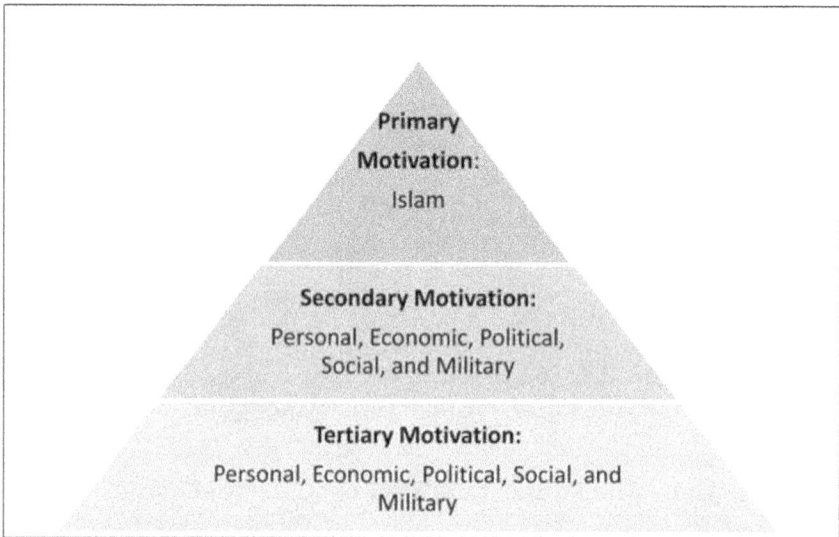

Figure 2.2.   **Levels of Female Jihadist Terrorist Motivations.** *Source*: Author

The primary motivation for female jihadist suicide bombers is religion (Islam), or more specifically paradise. If one could question every jihadist female terrorist, the primary motivation of Islam would likely be higher prioritized among jihadist female suicide bombers than jihadist female terrorists. There are various quotes that demonstrate this in addition to the evidence that is presented throughout the book. Maaka, a 19-year-old Chechen woman whose sister Aminat (suicide bomber) was a Black Widow, stated:

> I think that she did that in the name of Allah to stop the war and to save her Muslim brothers, because we are sick and tired of not being able to live in peace. Yes, I wear the scarf tied under my chin. So what? It is not a reason to treat me like a Wahhabi (Islamic fundamentalist)! Yes, I wear a long tunic because, according to my reading of Koran, the crowned book requires me to wear it, but in what does it matter to anyone else? Aminat [her sister] wanted quite simply to live as a good Muslim woman and they wouldn't let her. And me—I am extreme case because I do not have any other recourse. If the situation does not chance, if they don't let us live as we want, I would gladly join her in paradise.[2]

As the best friend of Aminat, Tamara read her final letter from Aminat that stated,

> Tamara, I left by the will of Allah—you know where. I very much wanted to see you, but that was not possible. Tamara, I stopped crying, and believe me I

could not swallow anything or even speak to anyone until had'th (account of Mahomet's words, counsels, and behaviors from the Koran in which the prophet prohibited mourning more than three days). Then only, with the greatest difficulty in the world, I calmed myself, and also because I know that, soon, Insh Allah, I will find your brother in paradise. Tamara, all that belongs to me is at your disposal. Do not be sad. The difficulties and the strength come from God. Insh Allah, we will find ourselves together in paradise.[3]

In the last two instances, Allah and paradise, which are important components of Islamic beliefs, are the primary motivations for Aminat to have become a suicide bomber.

In another example, as one failed suicide bomber Fatima (Tanzim (Fatah)) recounts, "the real reason I did it was because of the verses in the Quran that call for jihad, Jerusalem, the pictures of Palestinian children who were hurt."[4] In this statement, the Quran is the first motivation and the Palestinian children were the second motivation. Another failed suicide bomber, Yusra from an unknown Palestinian group, stated, "I wanted to be a *shaheeda* to get revenge on the Jews, because of my religion and my love of paradise [heaven]."[5] Again paradise or martyrdom is the primary motivation and revenge is the secondary. Huda, another failed suicide bomber, stated,

Paradise is the same for men and women. Women aren't promised 72 virgins because women are respected, and they don't want women to feel that they're being looked at as just wanting sex. But women have men for sex! If you fell in love with something in this world and didn't marry him, even if it happened at a different time, 20 or 40 years, or even 200 years earlier, he will be in paradise and you will marry him there. If you don't marry him, you can have him for 'that' [sex]. But you can't talk about 'that' because you don't really know what paradise is . . . The men talk about it, but for women it's something different, as far as I know 'that' remains respectable. I don't think that people only think about 'that.' . . . If they do, it makes us less respectable.[6]

It is hard to believe that a woman would commit suicide unless she was looking forward to a better life after death, since suicide is the final solution. Martyrdom for one's religion is the highest form of faith and sacrifice possible for Muslims. In Western society, people who commit suicide are inherently selfish and do not examine the needs of others before they commit suicide but again Islam views martyrdom as a gift and an honor. In Western society, suicide is a way out from a horrible life. In Islam, the personal quest to end this life and sail into paradise rarely takes the feelings of anyone else into account. Islam justifies this selfishness in that it is a sin to mourn a martyr or grieve a martyr. If a woman is martyred for her faith, she will automatically gain entrance to paradise. She will also be able to bring seventy people of her choice into paradise and will get to be one of the seventy-two virgins where she will serve the martyred men like she serves men on earth. Serving family is yet again the sole priority for a woman even in paradise. She will be one of the most beautiful women in paradise. These rewards are an incentive for some people, particularly for jihadist women.

The secondary motivation for a female terrorist or female suicide bomber may be any variety of issues discussed in the literature review in the Introduction chapter. This is where Mia Bloom's four Rs including: revenge, redemption, relationship, and respect may come into place. The secondary motivations are usually the personal issues that will most likely never be known and vary from woman to woman.

The tertiary level of motivation is typically the terrorist organization's cause. Whether it be an independent Chechnya or an independent Palestine, the main purpose of the terrorist organization will always be a motivation for women. These motivations may be somewhat in line with Islam or at least documented and justified by Islam. In the previous example with Chechnya and Palestine, Muslims will typically state that infidels such as the Jews or Russian Orthodox Christians should not control or govern Muslims as is justified in the Quran. Muslims should live under a government ruled by Sharia Law.

In addition, the motivations of members of a jihadist terrorist organization vary according to the roles that the person plays in the organization. For example, for leaders of jihadist terrorist organizations, personal power and the "cause" is the primary motivation. For someone like Osama bin Laden, his power over al-Qaeda and his quest against the Great Satan (United States) are his primary motivators. Bin Laden justified this using Islam. However, the cause is usually lip service used to unite and glorify the terrorist organization although bin Laden probably did support these things.

For the recruiters in the organization, control over recruits and personal power are the primary motivations. The author had the experience of interviewing a few recruiters and has found them to be confident, silver tongued individuals. Recruiters have a level of deviance to them that is subconsciously apparent. They may humble themselves with self-deprecating humor or a dismissive attitude but these people are the most understudied roles in terrorist organizations. They are also the most dangerous people in a terrorist organization. Recruiters are the ones who find and bring in recruits or more specifically suicide bombers. The level of manipulation that it takes for a person to use a religion to justify suicide and get a person to commit suicide cannot be underestimated. Recruiters are extremely talented and often work in the shadows. Rarely are they captured or held accountable for their crimes unlike leadership or foot soldiers within the organizations. For the foot soldiers and members, primary motivations are more likely to be ideological or religious. When these people are questioned, particularly for jihadist terrorist organizations, Islam is the primary motivation. Islam is the reason that the Muslim jihadists flocked from all over the world to Afghanistan, Chechnya, Bosnia, or any other place where Muslim people were in danger or were being attacked. They were protecting Muslim people and Muslim land, which are two reasons to make the lesser/outer jihad.

Female Jihadist Radicalization

Female jihadist radicalization is a tricky topic to tackle. The author can only address it by reviewing similarities among jihadist female terrorists that the author has found through years of studying these women. The Chechens and Boko Haram have tied women to their deaths and detonated them from afar so this does not apply to those women who were forced. Before radicalization occurs for jihadist female terrorists, these women are usually part of a conservative Muslim family although this is not always the case. There are also cases of women who convert to Islam or are weak Muslims who become jihadists. Typically converts are influenced by someone who is close to them like a husband, sibling, or best friend. Regarding their previous lives, the weak Muslims are more likely to embrace jihadist Islam if they have lived a life of sin including extra or premarital affairs, alcoholism, drug abuse, or infertility in addition to numerous other un-Islamic transgressions. As a side note, the author personally advocates that martyrdom can be used for forgiveness of sins and automatic entry into paradise as is discussed in a few chapters in the book. The next section will be divided between female jihadists and suicide bombers, beginning with female jihadists.

Women who join jihadist groups are usually practicing Muslims. Typically, these women are pulled into groups by family or friends and they join of their own volition. In some cases, husbands are a major incentive to join a jihadist terrorist organization. Regardless, the people who recruit these women tend to have very close personal relationships to them and trust is an important function of recruitment. Since family and friends are used as the number one recruiting mechanism and means of support in jihadist groups, family is a major incentive to get involved. Typically, recruitment occurs through someone who the woman looks up to or thinks highly of. When women join the organization, they are usually given "female" things to do, like visiting members in prison, joining the women's club, working in the social ministries, taking care of children, protesting, or distributing newsletters, etc. for the group. This is known as the secretarial role in this book. Most women who join a jihadist terrorist organization will typically become more conservative in their dress and speech in order to appease the organization and become a more "devout"

Muslim. They will also frequently quote the Quran as religious indoctrination and Quran recitation and study is required when joining a jihadist terrorist organization. There are rarely any other substantial roles other than support for these women who join jihadist organizations.

If a woman wants to become a suicide bomber, she will usually find the correct recruiter to accommodate her. She may be sent to a recruiter by family, friends, or even her husband. The recruiter must be someone that she highly respects and looks up to or someone that a deeply respected close friend, etc., looks up to. Typically suicide bombers are women who are the downtrodden. The author believes that the recruiter will build up the woman's self-esteem and give her personal value. After she completely trusts and submits herself to the recruiter, the game begins where the recruiter must persuade her to become a suicide bomber. If she is already willing, this is not a long process as long as she is a devout Muslim or becomes a devout Muslim. After all, who can disagree with Allah and scripture? As a side note, some women are ready to be suicide bombers and seek out the recruiters, already knowing that they wish to become a jihadist martyr.

After a period of gauging whether she is serious, will not betray the organization, and is not a security risk to the terrorist organization, the suicide bombing training will begin. It seems that the training only lasts a few weeks to a month at most; rarely do these women receive much training. During the training women may continue to live at home or they may leave their family completely and live with an older woman who will care for the martyr during her training. If they are still living at home, they are typically lying to their family about what they are actually doing. The family in all of the personal accounts rarely have any clue of what their daughter is doing which points to a somewhat laxer Muslim family or a very trustful family since women hold the honor of the family in their chastity and actions. This older woman (if the woman leaves home) also acts a chaperone for the woman so that her honor is not called into question when she is training with men. This is interesting as the sins of a martyr are wiped clean by her martyrdom according to the Quran so the attention to detail concerning her virtue seems rather redundant. However, these female handlers play a mother-figure role for these potential female suicide bombers whether she is a disciplinarian or a loving mother-figure. Women rarely train anyone for suicide bombings so the female chaperone will likely be in the background during the training. Women who are training will typically begin to wear hijab (if they have never done so) and dress more conservatively and they will also begin to quote the Quran in daily conversation. In many cases, religious training is also part of readying these women for martyrdom.

During suicide bomber training, the woman is usually alone with one or a few men. Operations are kept extremely small in number so that secrecy is maintained. The training appears to occur on private property or houses as training camps do not exist for female martyrs. Women will be trained about how to detonate their belt or how to walk normally with explosives attached to their body. The wiring of the bomb might be explained to her by her male handlers, yet it appears that the trainers do not want the woman to be too enlightened about the weapon she must wear. If a woman is doing a car bombing, she will be taught where to detonate the bomb so she can kill the most people. She will also be taught where to drive the vehicle so she can create the largest explosion, again to kill the most people possible. The training is usually concerned with how to inflict the most damage and kill the most people. It appears that these male handlers are usually respectful towards the future suicide bomber. There have been reports of threatened blackmail if the woman gets cold feet but for the most part, the training appears to be quite respectful in most of these groups. The author has never read reports or heard of women who were beaten or raped for refusing to go through with the bombing. Most of the time women who get cold feet bear the brunt of some anger but this appears to be short-term and she is never murdered for her indecision although most groups will try to push her to carry out her mission, somewhat forcefully.

Once the training is finished and the male handlers are confident that the woman can detonate her bomb and will not get cold feet, the woman is many times treated to sumptuous meals and shopping. Sometimes this shopping might be for her disguise or for fun but a woman may be given a credit card and is allowed to spend freely. The meals seem to be similar to a series of last meals where these women will go on shopping sprees and have excellent food typically in restaurants. The shopping spree and abundant lifestyle might only last a week until she is called to perform her mission, typically in the same area where her bomb is expected to detonate. This shopping spree and lavish lifestyle is most likely used to help the woman become comfortable with the neighborhood she is set to bomb. It is also the ritual of last rites and last meals.

Concerning her family, the family is always regretful that their daughter, etc., chose to become a suicide bomber. However, they are usually proud of her (particularly among the Palestinians). Frequently, the family criticizes her decision and they always regret her death. There are also times, particularly among the Palestinian cult of martyrdom, where the woman's death will be justified by her family. For example, they will publicly state that she had chosen to make poor decisions throughout her life and so she has chosen the path of the martyr to redeem herself. However, if her sins are egregious, her past is usually kept a secret so as not to embarrass the family.

The previous observations concerning female jihadist terrorists and female jihadist suicide bombers consist of similarities that the author has made through years of studying terrorism, reading terrorist autobiographies, and speaking with these women about their experiences. These explanations are not always true; however, the cycle of radicalization is apparent and enough information exists to create a theory on how women are recruited and radicalized into a jihadist terrorist organization as either a member or as a suicide bomber.

CONCLUSION

In conclusion, these preliminary observations concerning female jihadist terrorists and suicide bombers have been shared in order to provide a foundation for future scholars who wish to pursue this avenue of research. Policy makers in general have ignored or completely disregarded the threat of female terrorists, let alone female terrorists in jihadist terrorist organizations. Unfortunately, this attitude is dangerous and it will come to haunt the West and their intelligence agencies, although some would argue that the haunting is already occurring, particularly pertaining to ISIS. Female terrorists are the wave of the future as this book has shown that jihadist terrorist organizations have begun using female suicide bombers in particular and the number of female suicide bombers has increased tremendously in the last few decades. Until the West takes the strategic use of female bombers seriously, they will continue to be successful. Groups such as Boko Haram or the Chechen separatists use female suicide bombers more than male suicide bombers. The future is here and the military and intelligence agencies must face innovations in terrorist attacks.

NOTES

1. Harvey Starr, *Approaches, Levels, and Methods of Analysis in International Politics: Crossing Boundaries (Advances in Foreign Policy Analysis)* (London: Palgrave MacMillan, 2006).

2. Anne Nivat, "The Black Widows: Chechen Women Join the Fight for Independence-and Allah," in *Female Terrorism and Militancy: Agency, Utility, and Organization* ed. Cindy D. Ness (New York: Routledge, 2008), 125–26.

3. Anne Nivat, "The Black Widows: Chechen Women Join the Fight for Independence-and Allah," in *Female Terrorism and Militancy: Agency, Utility, and Organization* ed. Cindy D. Ness (New York: Routledge, 2008), 126.

4. Anat Berko, *The Path to Paradise: The Inner World of Suicide Bombers and Their Dispatchers* (Westport, CT: Praeger Security International, 2007), 104.

5. Anat Berko, *The Path to Paradise: The Inner World of Suicide Bombers and Their Dispatchers* (Westport, CT: Praeger Security International, 2007), 109.

6. Anat Berko, *The Path to Paradise: The Inner World of Suicide Bombers and Their Dispatchers* (Westport, CT: Praeger Security International, 2007), 162.

Chapter Three

The Domestics

The domestic roles of women in jihadist terrorist organizations consist of mother, wife, slave, sex slave, and recruiter. Many women in these organizations fulfill several of these capacities at one time. The roles of wife and mother are the traditional roles that women fulfill in most societies and need little explanation. General slaves will perform unwanted household or farming tasks. The sex slave fulfills the sexual needs of men, which a typical wife would do. In addition, the component of the sex slave is unique to jihadist terrorist organizations. However, the role of recruiter needs a bit more explanation. In their personal stories female jihadists typically point to a female recruiter who brought them into the organization or women mention friends and family who talked them into committing a suicide bombing. These are the kin and social roles that women tend to play in society.

In all of the case studies represented in this book—al-Aqsa Martyrs' Brigade, Boko Haram, Chechen Separatists (Black Widows), Hamas, Hezbollah, ISIS, Muslim Brotherhood, and al-Qaeda—women primarily fulfill domestic roles. This chapter will discuss and provide examples of the domestic roles that women have in jihadist terrorist organizations in the following sections: The Pious Mothers of the Martyrs and The Wives of the Prophet, The Recruiters of *Shaheed*, and The Sex Slaves of ISIS and Boko Haram.

THE PIOUS MOTHERS OF THE MARTYRS
AND THE WIVES OF THE PROPHET

The most understudied components of jihadist Islam are the roles of the mother and wife, which are multifaceted in Islamic society in general. We will first look at the role of the mother and then continue with the role of the wife. The last part of this section will use the eight case studies to validate the theories presented.

In Islam, the role of mother demands tremendous respect and is one of the few areas in Muslim society where women are idolized and actually have power. The Islamist feminist Fatima Mernissi wrote that "The close link between the mother and son is probably the key factor in the dynamics of Muslim marriage. Sons too involved with their mothers are particularly anxious about their masculinity and wary about their femininity."[1] In a culture and society with weak marital bonds, the mother is the only woman that the son is allowed to love as love for his wife is discouraged. He is applauded for showing affection to the one woman that he cannot sexually have, his mother.[2]

The mother typically plays a major role in picking the son's bride through arranged marriage. She is also the only one who can see the bride before her son is married. In Moroccan society, the mother can see her son's future bride in a public bath and can ascertain whether the woman is healthy or has any physical abnormalities. This is not uncommon in other countries. Whatever she says goes and it is not unusual for a young woman to be socially scarred by a loose tongue. Female kin to the son are also responsible for watching the prospective bride and knowing her actions through gossip and observation. Mothers will watch over the bride of their son if she is too young to have intercourse with him, even moving into their house, or having the bride live with her mother-in-law until she is sexually mature. It is ironic that the sexually inactive aged women are responsible for determining the lives of the sexually active young women.

In general, mothers will often live in their son's houses, watching over their wives and children and controlling food distribution, particularly if she is a widow. If the son buys a gift for his wife, he must buy several for his mother and sisters and then let the mother and sisters choose first, often not even giving his wife the gift he originally chose for her. The son must show gratitude to his mother his entire life. She is his confidant and his marriage actually strengthens his bond to his mother. Even though the role of mother is highly respected in Muslim society, mothers do not escape the curse that is cast upon all females as agents of the devil in Islam. A woman's power lies in her relationship with her son.[3] Mernissi states, "The triangle of mother, son and wife is the trump card in the Muslim pack of legal, ideological and physical barriers which subordinate the wife to the husband and condemn the heterosexual relation to mistrust, violence and deceit."[4]

As the primary woman and love in a man's life, mothers are highly respected by society when they become the mother of a *Shaheed* (martyr).

Although they are not always members of a jihadist terrorist organization (sometimes just supporters), the mothers of the martyrs bear a unique and important role in Islamic society. She must be proud that her son or daughter martyred themselves and she must not grieve. It is shameful to grieve for a *Shaheed*. One grieving mother was told by a Sheik that she was making her son restless in his grave because of her constant crying and that she "would be the reason for his exclusion from an event in heaven."[5] The Sheikh also stated that she should start eating or "God will not allow my son to eat with the rest of the martyrs and my son will be sitting alone in heaven without taking part in any thing that the other martyrs take part in."[6] Muslims do not view martyrdom as the end but instead as a new beginning in paradise. Unlike the West who views suicide as a tragedy, Muslims view martyrdom as a celebration and entrance into a better existence.

The mother of a martyr automatically increases her status in Muslim society after she has lost a child. She receives profound respect and income for the rest of her life if her son was martyred. This income will most likely come from the terrorist organization he was affiliated with but can also come from other Muslim governments (Saudi Arabia or Saddam Hussein in Iraq) or other Muslim Arab associations. Some Palestinian mothers have been accused of forcing their sons to commit martyrdom to receive financial gain, although there is some dispute to this. It does appear to occur infrequently.

In an article published in *Arab Studies Quarterly*, academic Nahed Habiballah interviewed sixteen mothers of martyrs from the Second Intifada or the al-Aqsa Intifada, which was primarily run by the al-Aqsa Martyrs' Brigade from 2001–2002. The male martyrs are characterized as bridegrooms on their wedding day after their deaths. Martyred sons are always portrayed as the best child in the family whether he actually was or not. He is the smartest, handsomest, and kindest, etc. Mothers of the martyrs use Islam to cope and find comfort that their son is now in paradise and Allah is caring for him, fulfilling his every wish. *Lallulations* or celebrations are used at martyrs' funerals.

Um-Nabil, the mother of a *Shaheed* stated:

I have special status with Allah. I get a lot of respect from people. I get money, not just for my studies, but for travel, for research, for everything I do. People help me a lot when they hear I'm a *shaheed's* mother.

"We *shaheeds'* mothers are invited to all kinds of social functions and we are always honored guests. Those functions are like ceremonies. For example, at school everyone tells me, You lost one son, but all of us here are your sons and daughters. Even the lecturers [Al-Quds University] tell me that. The women's societies call me and invite me to all their events and ceremonies."[7]

In an interview with the mother of martyr Mahammed al Daoud, who was martyred in fall 2000, Munabrahim Daoud stated,

> I am a believer. I believe God wanted him [Mohammed] to die in this way. We believe in fate. It was written that Mohammed should die young. But I wish I could have made the sacrifice instead of him.[8]

Another mother stated, "Praise to Allah! I hold my head high. The honor is mine I have a son who is a *shahid* and not only is my son a *shahids*, but all the *shahids* are my children, Praise Allah. The honor is mine; the pride is mine.[9] Yet another stated, "The best Mother's Day present I got this year was the death as a *shahid* of Abbas [her son]."[10]

As an interesting side note, academic Rajan finds that Palestinian mothers of the martyred are often interviewed by media using questions that portray their relationships, primarily as a mother. Their experiences concerning their relationships to their martyred sons are often exploited. In addition, names are changed to reflect that the woman is a mother of a *Shaheed*. For example, the mother of a martyr becomes um-martyr's name when introduced on television instead of by her actual name. She is portrayed only as a mother of the martyr and that is her only function in society and life.[11] Particularly in Palestinian society, there are numerous celebrations and cults honoring the martyrs where their mothers are often featured.

When the mothers of female martyrs are interviewed, Rajan[12] argues that the cases are not treated equally to the sons. Mothers have often publicly regretted the decisions of their daughters to martyr themselves. In contrast, Hamas has exploited the stories of female martyrs and their relationships with their mothers, trying to incite more female martyrdom. Videos have even surfaced of Hamas using children's television shows to encourage small children to become future martyrs under the watchful eyes of their mothers. In addition to television shows, parades of children wearing martyrdom costumes with fake Israeli blood on their hands has also been used to incite children to commit violence or become future martyrs.

Women can also use their power as a mother to recruit their children to join a terrorist organization or become a suicide bomber. Mothers raise their sons and daughters in the concept of revolutionary martyrdom in many Islamic cultures, particularly the Palestinians so in a sense they are the initial recruiters. Martyrdom may not be the initial goal when joining a terrorist organization but is always the aspired end result. One mother when she talked about whether she knew that her son went to confront the IDF stated:

> Yes, I did. Honestly, I did not want him to go, I wanted him to live longer. But it was his blood, to fight for his country for the Al-Aqsa mosque. We use to tell

him that if he wanted to do something, he should do something big, he is going to die anyways so at least he should harm the Jews, like the martyrs who bomb themselves (suicide bombers). If one Israeli died in return for my son's death then that would have made it easier.[13]

In another example, in a conversation with Fatima, who was a failed suicide bomber (unidentified Palestinian terrorist group), she states the following concerning her three-year-old nephew, which is like a son to her. "He used to ask about paradise of the *shaheeds* all the time. In the beginning I wasn't afraid he would want to be a *shaheed* [because] he was still a baby. I could make him want to be a *shaheed* and I could make him not want to be one . . ."[14] Another mother of a *Shaheed*, Mohammed al Daoud, used her power as the mother of a martyr to incite rage and violence against the Israelis as vengeance for the death of her son. She stated:

There are two paths we can take—the intifada or peace. We had ten years of negotiation and what did they bring? In the end, we had negotiations over nothing. The other people were just bidding their time. The intifada at least brought about recognition that there should be a Palestinian state. We have rights and they have to give us our rights.[15]

Another woman from Boko Haram stated, "It's OK to be a suicide bomber. It's normal."[16]

The concept of the mother is also used to propagandize. An example of this included Palestinian groups who portray women as the "mothers of a nation." In the beginning of the First Intifada, the leadership of the Palestinian National Movement called up women to take a strong role in the struggle by becoming "mothers of the nation." Women are described as *manabit* or literally plant nurseries. The terms "male baby producing factories" and "military womb" are also used to describe the reproductive organs of these women.[17] Official slogans stated, "We salute the Mother of the *Shaheed* and we stand at attention to the sound of the joyful ululation (*zaghalit*) emitted from her mouth which she will ululate twice: one on the day that her son leaves to fight and to fall and become a *Shaheed*, and the day on which the [Palestinian] state will be declared.[18]

The ideal wife for the Muslim believer according to the preeminent Sunni prophet, al-Ghazali, is "Beautiful, non-temperamental, with black pupils, and long hair, big eyes, white skin, and in love with her husband, and looking at no one but him."[19] A Muslim wife cannot demand love and respect from her husband so she is gifted with a miracle if she does receive this treatment. If a man loves a woman, it is socially unacceptable to say the least. Marriage is a partnership for procreation in Islam, not a love match. The all-encompassing love that a Muslim man must show for Allah does not have room for a wife. Polygamy and repudiation (man stating "I divorce you" three nonconsecutive times) are looked at as tools to prevent a man from loving his wife and endangering his relationship with Allah. Polygamy will not let a man have any emotional attachment to a particular woman as he must spend sexual time with his wives equally. Repudiation is final, even if the husband says it during a bout of anger.

Stereotypically in Islam, women are entitled to the following from their husbands: financial support, basic needs, the right to equal treatment with co-wives, the right to visit her parents at will, and the right to dispose and do with her possessions what she will. Wives, however must: be obedient, be faithful, breastfeed, manage the household, and defer to the family of her husband. Wives must subvert themselves to the control of their husbands and must answer with obedience. Rarely do women get a divorce and divorce only happens in cases of extreme violence or cruelty or infertility according to Sharia Law. Husbands can correct their wives through physical beatings although these are not supposed to be too harsh so that the husband can copulate with his wife at the end of the day. The woman's family will typically prefer that she stays close to home to protect her as it is natural to fear for her treatment in this kind of culture/religion.

There are several examples of mothers and wives who belong to terrorist organizations in the case studies. Beginning with al-Aqsa Martyrs' Brigade, there are few examples of mothers and wives in the group. Al-Aqsa is quite secretive and little research has been performed concerning the organization. Al-Aqsa has traditionally used very young women for suicide bombings. Kaha'ira Sa'adi from al-Aqsa Martyrs' Brigade lived in A Ram. She is a married mother of four, who along with another woman, Sna'a Shadeh, from the Kalandyia refugee camp transported a male suicide bomber to his attack on King George Street in Jerusalem on March 21, 2002. Three Israeli civilians were killed and dozens were wounded.[20]

Boko Haram has several women that are part of its group. Boko Haram kidnapped 276 women and girls (known as the Chibok girls) on April 14, 2014, and have since conducted several kidnappings of young girls and women, primarily for sex slaves and wives of fighters.[21] Several of these girls were impregnated by the fighters who became their husbands. The Chibok girls, once inducted into Boko Haram, give Islam lessons to other women in the camp, whipping the women if they do not learn the Quran in Arabic to their satisfaction.[22] Some women who are mothers have joined of their own accord, also bringing their children with them as their husbands became fighters or the women simply wanted to join Boko Haram. In the book *Stolen Girls*, Bauer mentions the married women who lived in the back of the camp who had willingly joined Boko Haram and its fighters.[23]

Other articles have been written about the loyal wives of Boko Haram fighters. The Nigerian Military has rescued several of these women who are now receiving psychosocial treatment to help rehabilitate them back to society as many Boko Haram fighters have fled leaving women and children behind. One woman, Amira, stated "My husband has a gun. If my husband is coming back from traveling, he'll call me on my phone and say, 'Sweety, I'm coming home.' So I'll go put on makeup, body spray, and I'll cook food. When he comes home, I'll collect his gun, magazine, bombs."[24]

A social worker at the safe house for former women of Boko Haram stated, "Many of these women are supporting jihad. They say it is God that helps them to do the jihad and it is God who helps them capture a place." The sole clinical psychologist stated, "Some of these women are hardened. Nobody coerced them to join Boko Haram. They voluntarily joined because they believe in their ideology. If given the chance some would go back."[25] It has been suggested that many of these women have Stockholm Syndrome in that they now defend the men that abducted and raped them, claiming that these men have been good husbands. However, Stockholm Syndrome is questionable considering that these women have not changed their support for Boko Haram even after being "rehabilitated" for several months. They cannot be placed back into society as their husbands have killed many of the loved ones in the neighborhoods they are returning to. There are rampant abuse and assassination attempts on Boko Haram and/or former members as vigilante justice is part of the culture in Nigeria.

For Chechen female terrorists, marriage and motherhood are the primary roles for women. Scholar Banner notes that women in Chechnya preserved extremely high birth rates in order to resist Soviet (later Russian) oppression, even with massive deportation and the forced influx of Russian citizens. Children can only come after marriage in Chechen society. In Chechnya, motherhood is not a choice like it is in the West but instead a woman's body is used for war as she is the producer of soldiers. Indeed, motherhood is a civic responsibility. Women are also the nurses or caregivers on the fields of battle and they provide safe houses. Women are also the keepers of Chechen cultural morality responsible for educating their children in Islam. In a strange dichotomy, Chechnya has also sponsored beauty contests for these women such as Zamira Jabrailova who won Miss Chechen Beauty in 2006. The purpose of the pageant was to make a political show of how Chechen women had laid down their guns. President Kadyrov then tried to pass a law legalizing polygamy and has forced women to wear headscarves or they will be publicly banned and not allowed to attend universities. In an even stranger turn of events, he also proposed to Mrs. Kenya during the Mrs. World beauty pageant, offering her the traditional Chechen dowry consisting of horses, a white goat, and a few hens.[26]

In a study using the psychological autopsy method to interview the family members and friends of sixty-four Chechen female suicide bombers, academics Speckhard and Akhmedova[27] found that 3 percent of the women in their study had been married. Chechen militant Wahhabis believe that is better to martyr oneself after having fulfilled life's obligations such as having children although the use of unmarried women belies this observation.[28] In addition veiling is not part of Muslim Chechen culture but was introduced by Wahhabis as part of the traditional role of women.

> Traditional Muslim garb has never been a feature of Chechen Islam and society. Rather many women in Chechnya adopted Middle Eastern dress and habits of covering with the introduction of military jihadist ideology into Chechen society, both during and after the two recent wars (1994–1996 and 1999–2000). This form of dress, used by militant Wahhabi adherents to express religious values, was also embraced by some Chechen women as an outward sign of having taken on a new identity. By do so, the women demarcated themselves as "true believers" and separated themselves from the rest of mainstream Chechen culture.[29]

In Moscow, during the Dubrovka hostage-taking in 2002, the Black Widows were wandering around calming the hostages, even playing motherly roles. The Black Widows would make sure that people had water, blankets, and chewing gum. They shared food and candy with the hostages while the men were securing the perimeter.[30] "One hostage reported that the women acted more like nuns ministering to the sick than terrorists."[31] Mia Bloom mentions that the women might have had Stockholm Syndrome, identifying with the terrorists and their plight. Some might even have been drugged, mentally ill, or pregnant; most of them were emotionally fragile.[32] When the hostages asked to use the restroom, the Black Widows would ask the men for permission, having absolutely no authority in the group.

Conversely to the Chechen Separatists, Hamas has sent many women who are mothers and wives on suicide bombing missions such as Reem al-Riyashi who was a mother of a son and a daughter.[33] Hamas is more likely to have mothers as suicide bombers than the Chechens. Women in Hamas also believe it is their duty to support children in their quest for jihad. In January 2013, the wife of a Hamas member of parliament, Khalil al-Hayya, stated that,

> Women in Palestine play a great role in raising their children and in encouraging them to wage Jihad for the sake of Allah. This is absolutely the most glorious thing a woman can do. Women play their role and are not inferior to men. When a man goes to wage Jihad, his wife does not say "Don't go" or try to stop him. She encourages and supports him. She is the one who prepares his equipment,

bids him farewell, and welcomes [his Jihad]. The mother instills in her children the love of Jihad and martyrdom for the sake of Allah. If every mother were to prevent her son from waging Jihad for the sake of Allah, who would wage Jihad? Who would support Palestine? Palestine is dear to us, and its price is paid with our body remains and our lifeblood. Is not Allah's reward precious? Allah's reward is Paradise. Paradise requires from us our blood, our body remains, and our efforts for its sake.[34]

In a similar fashion, the mother of Darine Abu Aisha, a Hamas suicide bomber, stated, "It is the duty of every Palestinian mother to encourage her sons and daughters to become martyrs. I adore my children, but if I help them achieve martyrdom, it only means that Allah has chosen them because he loves them more than I do."[35] Yet another mother, Mariam Farhat, who ran for Hamas in parliament has become the poster mother for preparing one's children for *Shaheed*. She said the following concerning her son's martyrdom and her role in his preparation of attacking an Israeli settlement:

I never saw Mahmoud happier. After we made the [martyr] video, he set out for the operation with cold nerves, calm and confident that it would succeed. But still, I was worried that he would be arrested. I prayed for him when he left the house and asked Allah to make his operation a success and give him martyrdom. Then I got a call from his brothers in the Hamas who told me that they had heard from him and he had managed to get inside the settlement. He had cut the barbed-wire fence and killed two giants, Israeli guards. I began to pray from the depths of my heart that Allah should give me ten Israelis for Mahmoud, and Allah granted my request, and his dream came true when he killed more than ten Israelis. I began to utter cries of joy.[36]

Hezbollah is the only Shiite case study in this book and the mother/wife role of women does not vary from the Sunni organizations. The Shiite people in Lebanon view Hezbollah both as an army that protects Shiites from both ISIS and al-Qaeda, as well as the Shia people. ISIS was known to slaughter Shia for pleasure under Zarqawi; however, al-Qaeda does not purposefully attack Shia. Al-Qaeda views the Shia as apostates whose ignorance can be forgiven.[37] In Hezbollah, "Other than committing suicide the women are not allowed to fight. They collect money and must prepare the fighters before a battle and take care of him if he is injured."[38]

In 2014, Hezbollah sent an aid flotilla to the Palestinians full of women called the *Mavi Marmara*, led by the vessel *Miriam*, entirely staffed by women. The Israelis had a rather difficult time turning away an aid flotilla in Gaza staffed by women. These women were required to have proper attire including veiling. Lebanese diva Haifa Wehbe was turned away from the media ploy as Hezbollah did not want to ruin the reputation of the other women on the boats. Taking it one step further, Hezbollah has engaged in several veiling campaigns to secure the morality of society. Billboards are featured in Lebanon stating things like, "Your Hijab my sister is more precious than my blood" or in reference to Ayatollah Khomeini, the veil is called a "fortress of chastity" with a picture of a veiled woman on the billboard.[39]

The mother figure role takes on an even greater significance when mothers play the role of the recruiter where they recruit their sons or daughters to martyr themselves for Hezbollah. Kendall Bianchi makes the point that Hezbollah promotes the culture of martyrdom by showcasing mothers who have lost their children, hoping to get more men for martyrdom operations. "Mothers, therefore, represent a crucial demographic for Hezbollah, serving as a bridge between the party leadership and the community from which it draws its fighters."[40] Women have a high status in Hezbollah as the leadership views them as excellent recruiting tools. Mothers are the spokeswomen for martyrs; they craft and promote the martyr narrative. However, in Hezbollah, there appears to be some trouble on the horizon as some mothers have found that the cost of their son is often not worth the price and some have spoken out against the leadership particularly concerning the conflict in Syria that Hezbollah has joined to support the Shia. UN program officer Thomas Selegny makes a similar point, stating that in Hezbollah,

> With a smile she encourages her son to become a fighter, with a smile she educates her son to hide behind women and children during battles, with a smile she and her son serve as a defensive shield for Hezbollah fighters, and all while expecting no prestige at all for her role. In a nutshell, Hezbollah women seem to be depicted as utterly subjected to their men, risking everything but gaining nothing.[41]

Hezbollah also keeps a pool of young widows for fighters to marry. Typically, these fighters are coming back from war and might be hurt or disabled due to battle injuries. "He [Hezbollah fighter] got a congratulation letter from Hasan Nasrallah himself, some money to rent and furnish a small apartment in Dahiyeh, and an additional sum as compensation for his wounds."[42] Hezbollah has also allowed for temporary marriages so that wealthy elite male members are able to engage in temporary sex with young widows. "A fatwa was issued a few years ago allowing married men to practice muta'a marriage, and another more recent one allows women to practice muta'a without having to wait forty days (Al-Edda) between one man and another—the time period usually required to make sure the woman is not pregnant."[43] However, the forty day rule does not allow any penetration so men and women are not able to satisfy their sexual desires through intercourse. Women can then marry immediately after although it is doubtful that women would participate in this act if they were not getting some type of needed compensation. This type of Islamic prostitution is perpetuated and sanctified by Hezbollah.

In the next case study, ISIS, women are recruited so that they can have children to grow the Islamic State. In a recent story published in June 2018, 560 women of ISIS were given family jail time or even the death penalty for their role in ISIS. These women have approximately 1,100 children in tow with them. That is around two children for each woman. These women have come from Russia, Turkey, Azerbaijan, Tajikistan, Germany, or France. Many of these women came voluntarily or were pushed by their husbands to live under the Islamic Caliphate in Iraq. They received 50 dollars per month from ISIS for living expenses and many of their husbands had multiple wives and/or sex slaves. Many of the women had lived in the homes of the people that ISIS had displaced.[44]

Veryan Khan, editorial director of the *Terrorism Research and Analysis Consortium* (TRAC), stated, "There's a priority for the Islamic State to attract females because it offers stability. If you want people to see you as a nation, a legitimate state, it's important to attract females and have them start families. It's not like women are an afterthought. This is a strategic move."[45] Women in ISIS are responsible for cooking, cleaning and giving birth to tiny mujahedeen.[46] Even Yazidi slave women, whom ISIS had often kidnapped, are used as household slaves and wives (only if they convert to Islam).[47] ISIS is a bit different than other jihadist terrorist organizations as it is trying to build an Islamic State composed of Muslim families and it actively recruits families. There is even an ISIS marriage bureau to help set up jihad fighters and single women (including women whose fighter husbands were recently killed). Honeymoons including a bus tour of the caliphate are included.[48]

Additionally, in ISIS, women have been assigned the role of police officers in the *Al-Khansaa* brigade or the *Hisba*. These women police not only the general public concerning what female attire is sold in retail stores, but also the women in ISIS. While this role sounds impressive, women in this brigade fulfill the role of the monitors of dress and conduct, like a strict mother figure. Women are responsible for regulating other women concerning whether or not they are wearing high heels in public or fingernail polish under their gloves. Women are not allowed to take off their niqab even while shopping in a store nor are women allowed to go outside without a close male relative.[49] This police role is honestly not outside of the domestic role of women in Islam. Women are given lashes for most infractions of Islamic law, but considering the brutality of ISIS, this is not really that surprising that the group would engage in this type of behavior.[50] Just like the female terrorists in prison who could not function without some type of authority over them, telling them how to act, the women in ISIS appear to be subjugated to the same kind of authoritative structure in their society. It is understandable that women would fulfill this role as men are not allowed to speak to or look at other women, unless they are a close family relative.

The Muslim Brotherhood is literally the theological basis for every jihadist terrorism organization. In the initial creation of the Muslim Brotherhood (1928), the founder of the organization Hasan al-Banna made it clear that the role of women was essential in Islamic Reformation. "The mother was the prime instrument of reformation."[51] Al-Banna even created a woman's branch called "The Institute for the Mothers of the Believers" in Isma´iliyya in April 1933 but it did not see the growth that the male branches had. In 1948, the Muslim Sisters claimed five thousand members. In recent years with the ousting of President Morsi, the Muslim Sisters who are three thousand strong[52] have taken a greater role in taking up for their arrested men by protesting in the streets. Problematically Morsi's Islamic constitution that he tried to force on the country of Egypt took away many rights from women and removed the marriage age. Women were also repeatedly defined as "caregivers" in his constitution. Women such as Hager El Saway, a Muslim Sister, will continue to protest until the reincarnation of the Muslim Brotherhood movement dies or the part returns to power. The Muslim Brothers will send the women back home when they return. [53]

In al-Qaeda, women play the traditional role of the wife and mother for their men. Many women whose husbands are in al-Qaeda do legitimately not know what their husbands are doing. This is true for terrorist organizations across the board; the fear of being found out is so great that many people do not even tell their spouse what they are doing. Other women in al-Qaeda are fully aware of what their husbands are doing and provide support for them. In an al-Qaeda magazine, *Beituki* or Your Home, the following advice is given to the wives of the male jihadists: "Greet your husband with a smile when he comes and a smile when he goes. Don't dabble in his work. Can you imagine all the bloodshed and bones he sees every day? Your fussing only increases the pressure."[54]

From the cases studies included in this book, it is evident that women play the supportive roles of wife and mother in jihadist terrorist organizations. This traditional role for women is included and praised in the Quran and Hadith. Women must get married, must have children, and must raise their children to have a strong Islamic faith. She will also recruit her children many times for martyrdom to become little *Shaheed*. The Muslim woman will support her husband and be obedient to him. To do anything otherwise will ostracize a woman in Islamic society most of the time. When she is ostracized in society for fertility, divorce, shame or any other number of reasons, she becomes a target for recruiters of *Shaheed*. She becomes the lonely, disposable soul that can be used to glorify Islam and jihadist goals. Indeed, it can be said that a woman's life may be in danger if she strays from the traditional roles that she is prescribed in the Quran.

The Recruiters of *Shaheed*

Recruitment is also part of the domestic female role in jihadist terrorist organizations and terrorist organizations subsist on the close personal networks that develop between people. In his work on Salafi groups (which characterize several case studies in this book), Marc Sageman emphasizes the personal relationships that are built in terrorist organizations and recruitment occurs through family and friend, stating that

> Social bonds are the critical element in this process [Salafi terrorist network recruitment] and precede ideological commitment. These bonds facilitate the process of joking the jihad through mutual emotional support and social support, development of a common identity, and encouragement to adopt a new faith. All these factors are internal to the group. They are more important and relevant to the transformation of potential candidates into global mujahedin than postulated external factors, such as a common hatred for an outside group. To an outsider, these invectives stand out. But for an insider, they are not what keeps the group together. As in all intimate relationships, this glue, in-group love, is found inside the group. It may be more accurate to blame global Salafi terrorist activity on in-group love than out-group hate.[55]

Female recruiters are fulfilling the family cultural role of mother-figure and support system. Even when mothers are not available for whatever reason, women play mother-like roles to encourage other women to join in a terrorist organization or commit a suicide bombing. In her book on suicide terrorism, Anat Berko states that "The mother is the most significant figure for both the dispatchers (recruiters) and the suicide bombers. Any conversation about their mothers causes a great rush of emotion and usually makes them cry." [56]

Female friends or relatives are often used to recruit women either for a suicide bombing or to join an organization. For Palestinian terrorist groups, scholar Anat Berko states,

> Generally, older women or friends are involved in recruiting and escorting female suicide bombers, and they keep the secret. They play a dominant role in the preparations, and one of their functions is to present the potential suicide bomber from having second thoughts, by force if necessary.[57]

In fact, for religious and cultural reasons, it appears as though women are mostly recruited by other women. In the Muslim religion and culture, women are only allowed to be around men who are immediate family members although husbands, brothers, grandfathers, or uncles, etc. may recruit women to get involved in jihadist terrorism. Male friends are relatively rare, and women and men cannot be in a secluded environment where recruitment to a terrorist organization could occur. Therefore, female family members or friends typically recruit women as they are usually the only other people that have access to women. The following case studies will illustrate the common role as women who are recruiters of the *Shaheed*.

Nazima talks about her experience in the al-Aqsa Martyrs' Brigade where she was recruited by her friend to be a suicide bomber. Nazima was looking for the excitement of a military adventure and a life that held a lot more excitement than her dreary household. What she found was a dispatcher who forced her to pursue martyrdom as she was threatened with dishonoring her family for being alone in the presence of men. Al-Aqsa made sure that Nazima had a female in the car when they picked Nazima up for training and when they dropped her off; the female was usually her female recruiter friend.[58]

In the Black Widows, older women are responsible for recruiting young women to be suicide bombers, caring for the women if they are frightened or missed their mothers during their training. Since women are not allowed to speak with unrelated men, women are the best sources to bring other women into the organization. The term "Black Widow" was based on the creepy story of Black Fatima, an older woman, fully garbed in black Muslim attire, who was the sole recruiter for female suicide bombers. Fatima was deemed the mastermind of Chechen female suicide bombers. She was the most wanted woman in Russia although it is possible she is a myth as Reuter[59] states she was fabricated by Zarema Muzhikoyeva. Fatima apparently has a crooked nose and she employs her bombers under the influence of narcotics mixed with orange juice to do her bidding. However, since many people have seen Black Fatima, she may indeed be a real person. There is also the concept of the Black Widow female spider, which kills and eats the male spider after mating so that she may have nourishment for her children.[60]

In one example, Nivat talks about the mother of Zareta Bairakova, who died in the Dubroka Theater at age twenty-six. Her mother stated,

> That Sunday at midday she was in her room praying when a woman I didn't know knocked on our door and asked to see Zareta. "Your daughter knows me well," she claimed. They left the house together. Zareta wanted to accompany her friend to the road. She never returned.[61]

Speckhard and Akhmedova found through the psychological autopsy method of 110 Chechen female suicide bombers that family members and close ties were used for recruitment. Two men Rustam Ganiev recruited five female suicide bombers and Arbi Baraev recruited at least two. In four of the cases, the women had married into Wahhabi families.[62]

In Boko Haram, recruitment of women by women has become a lot more common, particularly as there is a female wing of the organization used for suicide bombings. In July 2014, three women were arrested for recruiting widows and young girls to join.[63] The suspects, identified as Hafsat Usman Bako, Zainab Idris, and Aisha Abubakar, were arrested while traveling to the town of Madagali to get a debriefing from a commander.[64] Aisha, the wife of the commander, "recalled that, 'as *amira*, I went door to door to give gifts to the group's members. The gifts she gave were typically food or few thousand naira. This presence was important to cultivating the loyalty of Boko Haram members and submissives [slaves]"[65] Even at the UN refugee camp where she was stationed, Aisha was able to silence other women with just a look or cluck of her tongue.

In Hamas women are responsible for recruitment.

> Women play an essential role in Hamas both in terms of encouraging other women to support the movement or carrying out social tasks such as paying visits to citizens' houses and spreading Hamas' concepts among female workers and university students via the female wing of Hamas' student arm, the Islamic Bloc.[66]

Article 17 of the 1988 Hamas Covenant stipulates that women must educate the children and support men in the quest to liberate Palestine from the Israeli occupiers. Women are not allowed to be trained by men nor are they allowed to be away from home for long hours.

In schools controlled by Hamas, female teachers proudly talk about the young girls in the classroom who want to be martyrs. Barbara Victor, a journalist, interviewed several six-year-old girls who wanted to be martyrs. One girl stated that she wanted to be a martyr "To kill the Jewish and to live near God."[67] A twelve-year-old stated, "I will be a martyr and I have already talked to the people that will train me."[68] The female teacher of these young women watched in pride as her pupils talked of their dreams to become future *mujahedeen*.

In ISIS, women will often recruit women through social networking sites from other countries throughout the world to come and join ISIS in the Middle East, promising the woman a jihadi husband. Young Western girls are also recruited by ISIS men through chat rooms and Facebook.[69] Family members and friends will also recruit one another to join ISIS. Since the women of ISIS are often confined to their homes, the Internet is the major way for women to socialize and, inevitably, get other women to join them. Marriage plays an important role in recruitment as most young women are incentivized by the prospect of a handsome, young, physically fit jihadist. Media propaganda is the mouth of ISIS and is what keeps together all the ISIS cells around the world. Simon Cottee states, "Potential recruits actively seek out the message and the messenger and that the decisive factor in radicalization is typically not an anonymous predatory online recruiter but a trusted friend or family member."[70]

In the Muslim Brotherhood, the women of the group primarily belonged to the Muslim Sisterhood, a female component of the group, which was created by Hasan al-Banna. Muslim Brotherhood expert Barbara H. E. Zollner states that the "wives and sisters of Brothers played an important role in maintaining communication links. They were the backbone of a network which was built on personal bonds."[71] Many of these women knew one another and belonged to the Muslim Sisterhood. Kandil adds, "They [Muslim Sisters] do not perform the oath of allegiance or participate in battalion trainings and camps, but they do meet on the level of family and fieldtrips, and devote the rest of their time to mosque activities (recruiting women and indoctrinating children) and charity work."[72]

> Sisterhood activities included recruitment and charity, but one of the valuable functions was marrying Brothers to Sisters. The cultivation curriculum instructs Brothers to color their homes with an Islamic character: wives must uphold religious customs in dress, tone, nurturing habits; children must be shielded from non-Islamist media and familiarized with sacred history and revelation; Islamic anniversaries must be celebrated and secular ones (including birthdays) shunned. To help Brothers meet this goal, they are strongly advised to marry Sisters.[73]

Those brothers who did not do as they were told were warned that the Brotherhood would affect their lives. Wives were encouraged to inform on their husbands. "What the Brotherhood wants is for a Brother to marry a Sister to conceive Islamists "by birth," and for all these families to come together in a large Islamist community capable of engulfing the nation."[74]

Osama bin Laden stated the following about the women in al-Qaeda. "Our women had set a tremendous example for generosity in the cause of Allah; they motivate and encourage their sons, brothers, and husbands to fight for the cause of Allah in Afghanistan, Bosnia-Herzegovina, Chechnya, and in other countries . . . Our women encourage jihad."[75] In al-Qaeda, Mastors and Deffenbaugh talk about how women in al-Qaeda are expected to recruit others to the group. The secretive nature of jihadist groups like al-Qaeda allow them to survive in a somewhat tribal-like society. "Senior members of the network will offer their sisters or other relatives to new recruits."[76] Expert Farhana Qazi from the Counter-Terrorism Center states, "Militant women in al-Qaeda and its affiliated groups are often related to terrorists. This personal connection is key to identifying women. They are wives, daughters, sisters, and even mothers of militant men."[77] In one example, Sajida al-Rishawi was part of the first husband and wife suicide bombing team for al-Qaeda. Sajida was highly connected as "She is the sister of Mubarak Atrous al-Rishawi, an al-Qaeda member killed in Iraq by American forces; Her husband, Ali Hussein al-Shumari, was a committed AQ member . . . She had other relatives killed by U.S. forces in Anbar Province."[78]

In the previous eight case studies, women are the key recruiters of women for jihadist terrorist organizations. This is not to state that men do not recruit; however, women play a key role in finding women to marry male jihadists, recruiting females to work for the terrorist organization, and even in recruiting their own children for martyrdom operations as was extrapolated on in the earlier section. Female recruiters are rarely, if ever, questioned as most experts ignore the role of women in terrorist organizations. Female terrorists need to be taken earnestly as the most pertinent issue in destroying terrorism and terrorist organizations is the recruiters. If the recruiters are destroyed or imprisoned, then the numbers of every terrorist organization should decline.

The Sex Slaves of ISIS and Boko Haram

Boko Haram and ISIS are the only two jihadist terrorist organizations that use sex slaves and/or slavery in general. Slaves may be used for sex, work, or both. In these two organizations, women are kidnapped from various areas and are forced into marriage or temporary marriages, often moving from camp to camp to satisfy various fighters. Young boys and men may also be slaves, although men are usually killed by ISIS or Boko Haram if they are considered a threat. Older men may be allowed to remain farmers but are still considered slaves. In many cases, women are sold at a slave market, particularly in ISIS, similar to the American South pre-Civil War era. There is a very thin line between wife of a soldier and a submissive or slave and women can move between the two categories quite easily. Aisha, the commander's wife, stated, "If you are praying before you are caught then you are a wife; if you are not praying, you are taken as a slave but you can be made into a wife."[79] Although this may appear to be based on whether a person is Muslim or not, Boko Haram converts every person to their own brand of Islam. If she is a slave, when a woman becomes pregnant, she is usually married off to a fighter, not usually knowing who the father is. As soon as she has delivered her child, the rape begins again. As elaborated upon in the first chapter, the role of the sex slave is seen in the Quran and even justified by Muhammad for his battle weary men as rightful booty in war.

The sex slaves from Boko Haram are kidnapped girls and women as the group kidnaps people on a regular basis including work slaves. It is estimated that over a thousand women have been kidnapped by the organization. In April 2014, Abubakar Shekau, the current leader of Boko Haram, stated:

> My brothers, you should take slaves. I kidnapped girls from a school, and you are irritated. I say, we must stop the spread of Western education. I kidnapped the girls. I will sell them on the market where one can sell humans. Allah has told me to sell them. He commanded me to sell them. I will sell women. I sell women.[80]

The first large kidnapping occurred on April 14, 2014, with 276 girls and several subsequent kidnappings have occurred since then. One sex slave, Asabe, stated, "I was abducted six months ago in Delsak when our village was overrun by Boko Haram. First I had traveled from my village to a forest close to Cameroon. They turned me into a sex machine. They took turns to sleep with me. Now, I am pregnant and I cannot identify the father."[81]

Another woman who goes by the pseudonym Amina was married to three different men who raped her and physically beat her. Her first husband dislocated her arm during one of her regular beatings. She also had a child with each of the men and was forcibly married off to another fighter after each man died. Her baby of twenty-eight days died in her arms in the forest as Amina was escaping.[82]

The women are taken to various camps where they are converted to Islam (even if they are already Muslim), made submissive, and are forced to study Islam. Their headquarters are the Sambisa forest that was once a national park until Boko Haram attacked and killed two forest rangers while the other rangers fled. The forest is very isolated and surrounded by swamps.

Women who do not comply are whipped or murdered if the infraction is that serious, such as trying to escape. As one sex slave stated, "I knew a woman who refused to have sex with the man she was forced to marry. She said she wanted a proper wedding, not that pitiful ritual in the forest. I watched as they brought this woman to Shekau's hut, and as, a little later, they dragged away her corpse."[83] What makes situations like this even worse is that women in the Islamic culture who are raped are ostracized from society after they return to their homes. They are not able to find a husband and hence become financially vulnerable. They are also ostracized and endangered if the community finds out that they were members of Boko Haram.

The women who did not become wives were made into "'slaves' or 'submissives' by the insurgents. 'I was used as a slave; I cooked food when they had it and cleaned' . . . In some of the insurgency's cells, enslaved women are not married off but are systematically sexually assaulted . . . 'I was not a wife but the men forced themselves on me frequently,' Kaka reported."[84] Typically only the commanders or powerful men and their wives in Boko Haram have slaves. Most of the foot soldiers were not allowed this privilege.

In addition, rape is rampant in ISIS, particularly for non-Muslims. This started on August 3, 2014, according to one article, when ISIS kidnapped thirteen hundred Yazidi Christian women and shot all the men and boys.[85] Several thousand of Yazidis were abducted in 2017 and over three thousand are still enslaved. These people are typically of a Christian minority religion in Iraq and were targeted for their polytheism. It has been proven that ISIS extensively planned this mass kidnapping for months. They are known as "Sabaya" or slaves. There is a network of warehouses where the women are held and are inspected for purchase. They are photographed and their pictures are displayed online to prospective buyers. When buyers are present, the women are presented with no coverings and are asked about their last menstrual cycle to make sure they are not pregnant. There is a fleet of buses used to transport these women throughout the Middle East with curtains overs the windows to protect their chastity. ISIS has created their own court system to ensure the legality of the sales of these women.[86]

In an October 2014 article titled "The Revival of Slavery before the Hour," ISIS argues that Yazidi women:

> Could be enslaved unlike female apostates [the Shia], who the majority of the *fuqahā* [experts in Islamic jurisprudence] say cannot be enslaved and can only be given an ultimatum to repent or face the sword . . . After capture, the Yazidi women and children were then divided according to the *Sharīah* [Islamic law] amongst the fighters of the Islamic State who participated in the Sinjar operations, after one fifth of the slaves were transferred to the Islamic State's authority to be dived as *khums* [the one-fifth of booty or spoils that goes to the state].[87]

When this news of sexual slavery broke to ISIS supporters throughout the world, some Muslims disagreed with the practice. On the attack, one female journalist in support of ISIS stated, "What really alarmed me was that some of the Islamic State's supporters started denying the matter as if the soldiers of the Khilafah had committed a mistake or evil. I write this while the letters drip of pride. We have indeed raided and captured the kafirah [infidel] women and drove them like sheep by the edge of the sword."[88]

"A large section of ISIS members suffer from sexual anomalies and brutal instinctive desire for sex."[89] "It is permissible to have intercourse with a female slave who hasn't reached puberty, if she is fit for intercourse."[90] One thirty-four-year-old woman who was raped every day fared better after her captor bought a twelve-year-old girl. The older woman stated concerning her captor:

> He destroyed her body. She was badly infected. The fighter kept coming and asking me, 'Why does she smell so bad?' And I said, she has an infection on the inside, you need to take care of her. . . . I said to him, 'She's just a little girl.' And he answered: 'No. She's not a little girl. She's a slave. And she knows exactly how to have sex.' 'And having sex with her pleases God,' he said.[91]

The fighter continued to rape the girl, praying to Allah before each rape.

Terrorists from ISIS have also resorted to buying Viagra to make their rapes last longer and to be able to rape more women at a time. Many of these men have also bought kinky lingerie for their reluctant wives to wear.[92] It is very important that a woman is not pregnant when a man receives or buys a sex slave. Sex is the constant currency between men and women in ISIS and society of the terrorist organization is built around sex and Islam. Women who have martyred husbands are expected to remarry immediately despite the four month and ten day stipulation in Islamic law that forbids women from remarrying too quickly.[93]

If a slave owner frees his slave, he is promised a heavenly reward for doing so. In one case, an ISIS sex slave was freed from her captor. "He explained that he had finished his training as a suicide bomber and was planning to blow himself up, and was therefore setting her free." She was given a laminated "Certificate of Emancipation."[94] Women who try to escape are often raped or must provide sex in exchange for freedom.[95]

Women who have been raped by members of ISIS have recalled stories about how their abusers would pray before raping the women. One ISIS member explained to the twelve-year-old girl he was about to rape that he was allowed to rape in Islam and that raping her was not a sin as she was from a religion other than Islam. The twelve-year-old victim stated, "I kept telling him it hurts—please stop. . . . He told me that according to Islam he is allowed to rape an unbeliever. He said that by raping me, he is drawing closer to God."[96] Another victim who was fifteen and raped by an ISIS member stated, "He kept telling me that this is ibadah [or worship]. . . . He said that raping me is his prayer to God. I said to him, 'What you're doing to me is wrong, and it will not bring you closer to God.' And he said, 'No, it's allowed. It's halal.'"[97]

CONCLUSION

In conclusion of this chapter, there are several things that need to be discussed. In review, it is evident that women play domestic roles of wife and mother in all of the case studies presented in this book. Female identity in Muslim society is based on the roles that women played in the Quran, the wife and mother being the primary roles. Women are also recruiters for jihad both for other women and their own children. As the title of *Shaheed* is one of the most honorable roles in Islamic society and promises automatic entry into paradise, wives and mothers are often responsible for selecting others to go that route. The mothers and wives do not view this recruitment as evil but as an honor that Allah has chosen a person to die in their jihad. Lastly, the concept of the sex slave occurs in both Boko Haram and ISIS. What is interesting is that ISIS members may pray before they rape a woman. The author did not find that issue with Boko Haram, although this may be a local culture issue. It is evident that both groups base their logic concerning the sale and collection of sex slaves on the Quran. The idea of having sex slaves from war is well-documented in the Quran as was discussed in chapter 1.

One component of the domestic role that was difficult to document (but is still important) is that women are the celebrators and reporters of the prowess and achievements of men in these jihadist groups. The Khansa Brigade in ISIS (as was discussed previously) is named after al-Khansa who was a famous poet in the sixth and early seventh centuries who wrote poetry about her martyred brothers. This is similar to a mother or wife who is responsible for gloating over and advertising the accomplishments of her son or husband. This concept of the man and the woman struggling together, fulfilling gendered roles in the accomplishment of the same goals solidifies the two as fighters. It is obvious, however, that the man is the first and that woman is the second, existing to glorify him.

The concept of free will of these women in jihadist terrorist organizations is important to discuss. Although some women such as those in Boko Haram or ISIS are forced into joining these organizations, many women join of their own free will. In addition, many women who have been forced into joining remain with their husbands after the conflict is over. In most studies of terrorist women, women are considered victims or are not agents of their own destiny. This is not true in jihadist terrorist organizations; for the most part, women make the decision to join and remain in these jihadist terrorist organizations.

When comparing the case studies to one another, it is obvious that Chechen women have more education than their Arab sisters. Many of these women have attended a university and have pursued jobs outside of the home. The Muslim Brotherhood and Hamas also appear to be more inclusive of women as they are allowed to run for parliament in small numbers and these women have been out protesting in the streets. However, this is most likely a show to give women the idea that they are gaining rights and that these jihadist organizations are pro-women's rights. Women are still not allowed to run for higher positions in parliament so this is not much of a gain. Also, women must be home in the early evening to care for the household, husbands, and their children so the stereotype of the good Muslim women is never shed.

The future of women in jihadist groups may not be reflected by the past of women in jihadist groups. In some cases, there is simply a need to do more for these women. After the death of Wafa Idris in February 2002, journalist Samiya Sa'ad al-Din wrote in an Egyptian newspaper:

> Palestinian women have torn the gender classification out of their birth certificates, declaring that sacrifice for the Palestinian homeland would not be for men alone; on the contrary, all Palestinian women will write the history of the liberation with their blood, and will become time bombs in the face of the Israeli enemy. They will not settle for being mothers of martyrs.[98]

The author does not believe that men will push women to do more in jihadist terrorist organizations unless the gain is greater for doing so. Jihadist groups consist of fundamentalist Muslims and the Quran and Hadith are very clear about women's roles. Therefore, it is unlikely that women's roles will change. It may be that a few women will go rogue and will start doing more in jihadist terrorist organizations but their efforts will be few and futile. Most men and women in these organizations are simply not ready both on a cultural and religious level to give women more access. Most women fear going outside the box that society has designated for them. Islam is a strong persuader of what should occur in Islamic society. After all, who can argue with Allah?

One universal theme throughout this chapter is that the jihadist groups believe that their ideology should be bred into future generations. In fact, this concept of breeding the ideology into children solidifies the very survival of the movement. Women are brought in as sex slaves and wives to ensure the production of babies who will become future jihadists. Their wombs are literally the war production factories. Multiple wives are used to ensure more production and strengthen the masculinity of the Muslim male. Groups such as Boko Haram, ISIS, and the Muslim Brotherhood "have a certain spiritual conviction that any child they father will grow to inherit their ideology."[99]

Aisha, the wife of a Boko Haram fighter, stated, "There was an expectation in her marriage to the commander that they would have 'lots of kids', and that he was going to 'breed them to be Boko Haram.'"[100]

Another point that should be made is that the women in the terrorist organizations turned a blind eye to the violence that was committed against others, justified it, or believed that it did not happen. The women in Boko Haram were particularly immune to any suggestions that their husbands, often in forced marriages, engaged in violence. Many of these women enjoyed the fact that they only had to cook or clean in their Boko Haram marriages instead of working in the fields or as food producers. Women would also talk about the money and gifts they frequently received from their husbands in addition to social status they may have never had. Scholar Matfess makes the point that many women in Boko Haram had better lives in the organization than they did outside of it as domestic violence and abject poverty are widespread in Nigeria.[101]

Building from this last point, women are "kept women" in Islam and similarly in jihadist terrorist organizations. The notion of "purdah" segregates women and keeps them secluded in their homes, far away from friends and family. This concept of the "kept" women allows men to have complete control of the household, forces women to be financially dependent on their husbands, does not embrace female education or economic independence, and literally forces a wife to completely rely on her husband for everything. Women are often forced to have numerous children that they cannot feed or provide for, or may not be healthy enough to have in the first place. Birth control is generally illegal in Muslim countries or is difficult to access. Granted women may make this choice to be a "kept woman" but Islam embraces this concept. The value of a women in Islam is based on her chastity, beauty, dowry, and dependence on her husband.

Western women who marry Muslim men will talk about how the Muslim man treated them like a queen, showering gifts and affection on them. When these women return with their husbands to Muslim countries, they are often imprisoned in their house, with the acquiescence of government that legally secures the complete control of men. They cannot even go to the airport in many countries without their husband or his permission; children will remain with their fathers. It has gotten so bad that the United States Department of State regularly warns Western women from marrying Muslim men in numerous Arab countries.[102] There is no value in the intelligence or wit of women in Islamic society. For most, they are simply pretty things to be adored and sheltered. Of course this adoration is based on obedience and submissiveness.

NOTES

1. Fatima Mernissi, *Beyond the Veil: Male-Female Dynamics in a Modern Muslim Society* (New York: John Wiley and Sons, 1975), 69.

2. Fatima Mernissi, *Beyond the Veil: Male-Female Dynamics in a Modern Muslim Society* (New York: John Wiley and Sons, 1975), Chapter 7.

3. Fatima Mernissi, *Beyond the Veil: Male-Female Dynamics in a Modern Muslim Society* (New York: John Wiley and Sons, 1975), Chapter 7.

4. Fatima Mernissi, *Beyond the Veil: Male-Female Dynamics in a Modern Muslim Society* (New York: John Wiley and Sons, 1975), 79.

5. Nahed Habiballah, "Interviews with Mothers of Martyrs of the Aqsa Intifada," *Arab Studies Quarterly* 26 (1) (Winter 2004): 20.

6. Nahed Habiballah, "Interviews with Mothers of Martyrs of the Aqsa Intifada," *Arab Studies Quarterly* 26:1, (Winter 2004), 30.

7. Anat Berko, *The Path to Paradise: The Inner World of Suicide Bombers and Their Dispatchers* (Westport, CT: Praeger Security International, 2007), 144.

8. Joyce M. Davis, *Martyrs: Innocence, Vengeance, and Despair in the Middle East* (New York: Palgrave Macmillan, 2003), 123.

9. As cited in V. G. Rajan, *Women Suicide Bombers: Narratives of Violence* (New York: Routledge, 2011), 254.

10. As cited in V. G. Rajan, *Women Suicide Bombers: Narratives of Violence* (New York: Routledge, 2011), 254.

11. V. G. Rajan, *Women Suicide Bombers: Narratives of Violence* (New York: Routledge, 2011), Chapter 5.

12. V. G. Rajan, *Women Suicide Bombers: Narratives of Violence* (New York: Routledge, 2011), Chapter 5.

13. Nahed Habiballah, "Interviews with Mothers of Martyrs of the Aqsa Intifada," *Arab Studies Quarterly* 26 (1) (Winter 2004): 20.

14. Anat Berko, *The Path to Paradise: The Inner World of Suicide Bombers and Their Dispatchers* (Westport, CT: Praeger Security International, 2007), 98.

15. Joyce M. Davis, *Martyrs: Innocence, Vengeance, and Despair in the Middle East* (New York: Palgrave Macmillan, 2003), 122.

16. Chika Oduah, "The Women Who Love Boko Haram," *Aljazeera*, September 22, 2016, accessed July 19, 2018, https://www.aljazeera.com/indepth/features/2016/08/women-love-loved-boko-haram-160823120617834.html.

17. Mira Tzoroff, "The Palestinian Shahida: National Patriotism, Islamic Feminism, or Social Crisis," in *Female Suicide Bombers: Dying for Equality*, ed. Yoram Schweitzer (Tel Aviv: Jaffee Center for Strategic Studies, August 2006), 13–23, 13–14.

18. Mira Tzoroff, "The Palestinian Shahida: National Patriotism, Islamic Feminism, or Social Crisis," in *Female Suicide Bombers: Dying for Equality*, ed. Yoram Schweitzer (Tel Aviv: Jaffee Center for Strategic Studies, August 2006), 13–23, 14.

19. As cited in Fatima Mernissi, *Beyond the Veil: Male-Female Dynamics in a Modern Muslim Society* (New York: John Wiley and Sons, 1975), 59.

20. Israel Ministry of Foreign Affairs, "Attack by Female Suicide Bomber Thwarted at Erez Crossing," *Israel Ministry of Foreign Affairs*, June 20, 2005, accessed July 18, 2018, http://www.mfa.gov.il/mfa/foreignpolicy/terrorism/palestinian/pages/attack%20by%20female%20suicide%20bomber%20thwarted%20at%20 erez%20crossing%2020-jun-2005.aspx.

21. Jason Warner and Hilary Matfess, "Exploding Stereotypes: The Unexpected Operational and Demographic Characteristics of Boko Haram's Suicide Bombers," *Combating Terrorism at West Point,* August 17, 2017, accessed July 18, 2018, https:// ctc.usma.edu/app/uploads/2017/08/Exploding-Stereotypes-1.pdf.

22. Wolfgang Bauer, *Stolen Girls: Survivors of Boko Haram Tell Their Story* (New York: The New Press, 2016), 42.

23. Wolfgang Bauer, *Stolen Girls: Survivors of Boko Haram Tell Their Story* (New York: The New Press, 2016), 41.

24. Chika Oduah, "The Women Who Love Boko Haram," *Aljazeera*, September 22, 2016, accessed July 19, 2018, https://www.aljazeera.com/indepth/features/2016/08/ women-love-loved-boko-haram-160823120617834.html.

25. Chika Oduah, "The Women Who Love Boko Haram," *Aljazeera*, September 22, 2016, accessed July 19, 2018, https://www.aljazeera.com/indepth/features/2016/08/women-love-loved-boko-haram-160823120617834.html.

26. Francine Banner, "Mothers, Bombers, Beauty Queens: Chechen Women's Roles in the Russo-Chechen Conflict," *Georgetown Journal of International Affairs* 9 (2) (Summer 2008): 77–88.

27. Anne Speckhard and Khapta Akhmedova, "Black Widows: The Chechen Female Suicide Terrorists," in *Female Suicide Bombers: Dying for Equality*, ed. Yoram Schweitzer (Tel Aviv: Jaffee Center for Strategic Studies, August 2006).

28. This is in contrast to Palestinian and Lebanese terrorist groups who usually send unmarried and childless men and women to perform jihad according to Speckhard and Akhmedova, page 107.

29. Anne Speckhard and Khapta Akhmedova, "Black Widows and Beyond: Understanding the Motivations and Life Trajectories of Chechen Female Terrorists," in *Female Terrorism and Militancy, Agency, Utility, and Organization*, ed. Cindy D. Ness (New York: Routledge, 2008), 107.

30. Viv Groskop, "Women at Heart of the Terror Cells," *The Guardian*, September 4, 2004, accessed July 25, 2018, https://www.theguardian.com/world/2004/sep/05/ russia.chechnya1.

31. Mia Bloom, *Bombshell* (Philadelphia: Penn State University Press, 2011), 53.

32. Mia Bloom, *Bombshell* (Philadelphia: Penn State University Press, 2011).

33. Toby Harnden, "Hamas Mother's Suicide Bombing Kills 4," *The Telegraph*, January 15, 2004, accessed July 30, 2018, https://www.telegraph.co.uk/news/world news/middleeast/israel/1451737/Hamas-mothers-suicide-bombing-kills-4.html.

34. Toi Staff, "Encouraging Our Children to Kill Themselves for Palestine is a Mother's Most Glorious Duty, Says Wife of Hamas MP," *Times of Israel*, January 8, 2013, accessed July 30, 2018, http://www.timesofisrael.com/encouraging-our-children -to-kill-themselves-for-palestine-is-a-mothers-most-glorious-duty-says-wife-of -hamas-mp/?fb_comment_id=128360617328786_170884#f3acb71d4e376aa.

35. Barbara Victor, *Army of Roses* (Emmaus, PA: Rodale, 2003), 102.

36. Barbara Victor, *Army of Roses* (Emmaus, PA: Rodale, 2003), 167–68.

37. Daniel L. Byman and Jennifer R. Williams, "ISIS vs. Al Qaeda: Jihadism's Global Civil War," The Brookings Institution, February 24, 2015, accessed July 31, 2018, https://www.brookings.edu/articles/isis-vs-al-qaeda-jihadisms-global-civil -war/.

38. Mary Chastain, "List of Female Hezbollah Suicide Bombers Grows," *Breitbart*, August 18, 2013, accessed September 15, 2016, http://www.breitbart.com/national -security/2013/08/18/women-rise-in-hezbollah-still-not-equal-to-men/.

39. David Schenker, "The Women of Hezbollah," *The New Republic*, August 9, 2010, accessed July 31, 2018, https://newrepublic.com/article/76826/the-women -hezbollah.

40. Kendall Bianchi, "Letters from Home: Hezbollah Mothers and the Culture of Martyrdom," *Combating Terrorism Center at Westpoint* 11 (2) (February 2018), accessed July 31, 2018, https://ctc.usma.edu/letters-home-hezbollah-mothers-culture -martyrdom/.

41. Thomas Selegny, "Developments in the Modern Middle East: Gender & Revolutions: Re-thinking the "Woman Question" in the Modern Middle East," *Research-Gate*, May 2014, accessed July 31, 2018, https://www.researchgate.net/public ation/303285448_Hezbollah_women%27s_motherhood.

42. Hanin Ghaddar, "Hezbollah's Women Aren't Happy," *Tablet*, October 12, 2016, accessed August 27, 2018, https://www.tabletmag.com/jewish-news-and -politics/215483/hezbollah-women.

43. Hanin Ghaddar, "Hezbollah's Women Aren't Happy," *Tablet*, October 12, 2016, accessed August 27, 2018, https://www.tabletmag.com/jewish-news-and-pol itics/215483/hezbollah-women.

44. Jane Arraf, "ISIS Wives, With Children In Tow, Are Handed Long Jail Sentences Or Death Penalty," *National Public Radio*, June 9, 2018, accessed August 1, 2018, https://www.npr.org/2018/06/09/613067263/isis-wives-with-children-in-tow -are-handed-long-jail-sentences-or-death-penalty.

45. Kate Storey, "How Women Join ISIS: Women and Girls in Terrorism," *Maire Claire*, April 22, 2016, accessed September 8, 2016, http://www.marieclaire. com/politics/a20011/western-women-who-join-isis/.

46. Tiffany Ap, "What ISIS Wants from Women," *CNN*, November 20, 2015, accessed September 8, 2016, http://www.cnn.com/2015/11/20/europe/isis-role-of- women/.

47. David Williams, Matthew Blake, Martin Robison, and David Martosko, "Yazidi 'Slave' Women Captured by ISIS Fanatics in Iraq," *Daily Mail*, August 8, 2014, accessed September 8, 2016, http://www.dailymail.co.uk/news/article-2719698/Pres ident-Obama-authorises-airstrikes-Iraq-defend-civilians-Islamic-militants-swarming -country.html.

48. David J. Wasserstein, *Black Banners of ISIS* (New Haven, CT: Yale University Press, 2017), 130.

49. David J. Wasserstein, *Black Banners of ISIS* (New Haven, CT: Yale University Press, 2017).

50. Kate Storey, "How Women Join ISIS: Women and Girls in Terrorism," *Maire Claire*, April 22, 2016, accessed September 8, 2016, http://www.marieclaire.com/politics/a20011/western-women-who-join-isis/.

51. Richard P. Mitchell, *The Society of the Muslim Brothers* (New York: Oxford University Press, 1969), 175.

52. Janine Di Giovanni, "Enter the Muslim Sisterhood," *Newsweek*, December 19, 2013, accessed August 9, 2018, https://www.newsweek.com/2013/12/20/enter-muslim-sisterhood-244958.html.

53. Sophia Jones, "The Sisters of the Muslim Brotherhood," *The Daily Beast*, July 9, 2013, accessed August 9, 2018, https://www.thedailybeast.com/the-sisters-of-the-muslim-brotherhood?ref=scroll.

54. Biography in Context, "How to Please Your Holy Warrior; Jihadist Chick Lit," *The Economist*, February 3, 2018, accessed September 26, 2018, http://link.galegroup.com/apps/doc/A525895090/BIC?u=usclibs&sid=BIC&xid=24292283.

55. Marc Sageman, *Understanding Terrorist Networks* (Philadelphia: University of Pennsylvania Press, 2004), 135.

56. Anat Berko, *The Path to Paradise: The Inner World of Suicide Bombers and Their Dispatchers* (Westport, CT: Praeger Security International, 2007), 7.

57. Anat Berko, *The Path to Paradise: The Inner World of Suicide Bombers and Their Dispatchers* (Westport, CT: Praeger Security International, 2007), 114.

58. Anat Berko, *The Path to Paradise: The Inner World of Suicide Bombers and Their Dispatchers* (Westport, CT: Praeger Security International, 2007), Chapter 1.

59. John Reuter, "Chechnya's Suicide Bombers: Desperate, Devout, or Deceived?" *The Jamestown Foundation*, August 23, 2004, accessed July 25, 2018, https://jamestown.org/report/chechnyas-suicide-bombers-desperate-devout-or-deceived/.

60. Amanda Alcott, "Gendered Narratives of "Black Widow" Terrorism in Russia's Northern Caucasus Region" (Master's Thesis, Central European University, 2012).

61. Anne Nivat, "The Black Widows: Chechen Women Join the Fight for Independence—and Allah," in *Female Terrorism and Militancy: Agency, Utility, and Organization*, ed. Cindy D. Ness (New York: Routledge, 2008), 125.

62. Anne Speckhard and Khapta Akhmedova, "Black Widows and Beyond: Understanding the Motivations and Life Trajectories of Chechen Female Terrorists," in *Female Terrorism and Militancy: Agency, Utility, and Organization*, ed. Cindy D. Ness (New York: Routledge, 2008), 112.

63. Africa, "Boko Haram Crisis: Nigeria Arrests 'Female Recruiters,'" *BBC News*, July 4, 2014, accessed August 8, 2018, https://www.bbc.com/news/world-africa-28168003.

64. Radina Gigova, "Nigeria: Arrested Women Recruited for Boko Haram," *CNN*, July 5, 2014, accessed August 8, 2018, https://www.cnn.com/2014/07/04/world/africa/nigeria-women-suspected-boko-haram/index.html.

65. Hilary Matfess, *Women and the War on Boko Haram: Wives, Weapons, Witnesses* (London: Zed Books, 2017), 137.

66. Adnan Abu Amer, "Women's Roles in Hamas Slowly Evolve," *al-Monitor*, March 2, 2015, accessed September 15, 2016, http://www.al-monitor.com/pulse/originals/2015/02/women--role-hamas-gaza-leadership-social-mobilization.html.

67. Barbara Victor, *Army of Roses* (Emmaus, PA: Rodale, 2003), 185.

68. Barbara Victor, *Army of Roses* (Emmaus, PA: Rodale, 2003), 189.

69. Simon Cottee, "What ISIS Women Want," *Foreign Policy*, May 17, 2016, accessed September 9, 2016, http://foreignpolicy.com/2016/05/17/what-isis-women -want-gendered-jihad/.

70. Simon Cottee, "What ISIS Women Want," *Foreign Policy*, May 17, 2016, accessed September 9, 2016, http://foreignpolicy.com/2016/05/17/what-isis-women -want-gendered-jihad/.

71. Barbara H. E. Zollner, *The Muslim Brotherhood: Hasan al-Hudaybi and Ideology*, (London: Routledge, 2009), 41.

72. Hazem Kandil, *Inside the Brotherhood* (Malden, MA: Polity Press, 2015), 8.

73. Hazem Kandil, *Inside the Brotherhood* (Malden, MA: Polity Press, 2015), 74.

74. Hazem Kandil, *Inside the Brotherhood* (Malden, MA: Polity Press, 2015), 74.

75. Farhana Qazi, "A Close Look at the Women in Al-Qaeda and ISIS," *Farhana-Qazi.com*, January 31, 2015, accessed August 9, 2018, http://farhanaqazi.com/ a-close-look-at-the-women-in-al-qaeda-and-isis/.

76. Elena Mastors and Alyssa Deffenbaugh, *The Lesser Jihad: Recruits and the Al-Qaida Network* (Lanham: Rowman & Littlefield Publishers, Inc., 2007), 55.

77. Farhana Qazi, "A Close Look at the Women in Al-Qaeda and ISIS," *Farhana-Qazi.com*, January 31, 2015, accessed August 9, 2018, http://farhanaqazi.com/ a-close-look-at-the-women-in-al-qaeda-and-isis/.

78. Farhana Qazi, "A Close Look at the Women in Al-Qaeda and ISIS," *Farhana-Qazi.com*, January 31, 2015, accessed August 9, 2018, http://farhanaqazi.com/ a-close-look-at-the-women-in-al-qaeda-and-isis/.

79. Hilary Matfess, *Women and the War on Boko Haram: Wives, Weapons, Witnesses* (London: Zed Books, 2017), 139.

80. Wolfgang Bauer, *Stolen Girls: Survivors of Boko Haram Tell Their Story* (New York: The New Press, 2016), 49.

81. Philip Obaji, "Boko Haram's Rescued Sex Slaves Tell Their Horror Stories," *The Daily Beast*, May 6, 2015, accessed July 19, 2018, https://www.thedailybeast. com/boko-harams-rescued-sex-slaves-tell-their-horror-stories?ref=scroll.

82. Samuel Smith, "Girl Impregnated by 3 Boko Haram Fighters Details Horrors of Sex Slavery," *Christian Post*, January 7, 2017, accessed July 19, 2018, https:// www.christianpost.com/news/girl-impregnated-by-3-boko-haram-fighters-details -horrors-of-sex-slavery-172653/page1.html.

83. Wolfgang Bauer, *Stolen Girls: Survivors of Boko Haram Tell Their Story* (New York: The New Press, 2016), 43–44.

84. Hilary Matfess, *Women and the War on Boko Haram: Wives, Weapons, Witnesses* (London: Zed Books, 2017), 92.

85. Bruce Golding, "Female ISIS Captives Endure 'Brutal and Abnormal' Sex," *New York Post*, February 18, 2015, accessed September 9, 2016, https://nypost. com/2015/02/18/female-isis-captives-endure-brutal-and-abnormal-sex/.

86. Rukmini Callimachi, "Isis Enshrines a Theology of Rape," *The New York Times*, August 13, 2015, accessed June 23, 2017, https://www.nytimes. com/2015/08/14/world/middleeast/isis-enshrines-a-theology-of-rape.html.

87. As cited in Fawaz A. Gerges, *ISIS: A History* (Princeton: Princeton University Press, 2016), 32.

88. Rukmini Callimachi, "Isis Enshrines a Theology of Rape," *The New York Times*, August 13, 2015, accessed June 23, 2017, https://www.nytimes.com/2015/08/14/world/middleeast/isis-enshrines-a-theology-of-rape.html.

89. Bruce Golding, "Female ISIS Captives Endure 'Brutal and Abnormal' Sex," *New York Post*, February 18, 2015, accessed September 9, 2016, https://nypost.com/2015/02/18/female-isis-captives-endure-brutal-and-abnormal-sex/.

90. Rukmini Callimachi, "Isis Enshrines a Theology of Rape," *The New York Times*, August 13, 2015, accessed June 23, 2017, https://www.nytimes.com/2015/08/14/world/middleeast/isis-enshrines-a-theology-of-rape.html.

91. Rukmini Callimachi, "Isis Enshrines a Theology of Rape," *The New York Times*, August 13, 2015, accessed June 23, 2017, https://www.nytimes.com/2015/08/14/world/middleeast/isis-enshrines-a-theology-of-rape.html.

92. Bruce Golding, "Female ISIS Captives Endure 'Brutal and Abnormal' Sex," *New York Post*, February 18, 2015, accessed September 9, 2016, https://nypost.com/2015/02/18/female-isis-captives-endure-brutal-and-abnormal-sex/.

93. Kate Storey, "How Women Join ISIS: Women and Girls in Terrorism," *Maire Claire*, April 22, 2016, accessed September 8, 2016, http://www.marieclaire.com/politics/a20011/western-women-who-join-isis/.

94. Rukmini Callimachi, "Isis Enshrines a Theology of Rape," *The New York Times*, August 13, 2015, accessed June 23, 2017, https://www.nytimes.com/2015/08/14/world/middleeast/isis-enshrines-a-theology-of-rape.html.

95. Kate Storey, "How Women Join ISIS: Women and Girls in Terrorism," *Maire Claire*, April 22, 2016, accessed September 8, 2016, http://www.marieclaire.com/politics/a20011/western-women-who-join-isis/.

96. Rukmini Callimachi, "Isis Enshrines a Theology of Rape," *The New York Times*, August 13, 2015, accessed June 23, 2017, https://www.nytimes.com/2015/08/14/world/middleeast/isis-enshrines-a-theology-of-rape.html.

97. Rukmini Callimachi, "Isis Enshrines a Theology of Rape," *The New York Times*, August 13, 2015, accessed June 23, 2017, https://www.nytimes.com/2015/08/14/world/middleeast/isis-enshrines-a-theology-of-rape.html.

98. As cited in V. G. Rajan, *Women Suicide Bombers: Narratives of Violence* (New York: Routledge, 2011), 253.

99. Hilary Matfess, *Women and the War on Boko Haram: Wives, Weapons, Witnesses* (London: Zed Books, 2017), 124.

100. Hilary Matfess, *Women and the War on Boko Haram: Wives, Weapons, Witnesses* (London: Zed Books, 2017), 125.

101. Hilary Matfess, *Women and the War on Boko Haram: Wives, Weapons, Witnesses* (London: Zed Books, 2017).

102. Middle Eastern Forum, "U.S. Department of State: Marriage to Saudis," 2003, accessed August 7, 2018, https://www.meforum.org/articles/other/u-s-department-of-state-marriage-to-saudis.

Chapter Four

The Secretaries

The role of the secretary encompasses bookkeeping, logistics, and the transfer of arms and information. Other menial supportive duties are also included in the secretarial role. This role is the most significant in regards to women having any power in a jihadist organization. It requires a lot of trust and confidence in women. However, this role is somewhat rare in jihadist terrorist organizations and even rarer in the Quran. The wife of Muhammad, Aishah, was the Prophet's bookkeeper but she is one of very few women to hold a substantial role like this in historical Islam. Women rarely hold positions of power in society or organizations as it is not part of their traditional role in Islam. This chapter will explore women in these secretarial type roles in the eight case studies that are used in this book.

Beginning with the first case study, there is very little information concerning women in the al-Aqsa Martyrs' Brigade. This lack of literature trend continues with the secretarial role of women in the organization. Little to no information is available and part of this problem lies in the secrecy of the group. As stated in the Introduction, al-Aqsa Martyrs' Brigade is composed of a few secretive cells and is controlled by Fatah. Although women may have a secretarial type role in the group in some obscure cases, this information has not been found.

In Boko Haram, the wives of the soldiers, in addition to keeping house and rearing children, were often "responsible for carrying their husband's weapons."[1] Many times these so-called weapons were sticks or garden hoes etc. as the men did not have any guns. The women who toted these weapons were some of the poorest women in Boko Haram and they were also of the lowest class in the organization. Wealthy women who are married to commanders would not carry anything when the organization would move. The ability to carry their men's weapons while on the move was the closest that women in Boko Haram came to any type of secretarial role. Boko Haram is a strict Salafi group as was discussed in the Introduction chapter and women should only fulfill sexual roles or domestic roles such as wife and mother.

In Chechnya, the Black Widows are primarily known for suicide bombings and there is little literature on other roles that women play in the Chechen rebels. The whole concept of "Black Widow" refers to women who martyr themselves for Islam so there is not much else expected of women who join the Chechen rebels. Speckhard and Akhmedova mention that "three female bombers did break out of these defined roles: one learned to shoot guns and drive, and another set of sisters learned to explode grenades, plant landmines, and shoot guns."[2] Yet another woman, Larissa, was engaged to a Chechen Wahhabi. She later married a Chechen fighter she did not love. She stated, "I will continue to help the *boyviki* [Russian resistance] as best I can. In the city, I made bread and delivered arms, and sometimes my husband permitted me to shoot."[3]

Two hostage situations occurred on behalf of the Chechen terrorists where women played a role slightly outside of the disposable suicide bomber although they were martyred in the end. The Dubrovka Theater was the scene of a hostage crisis where twenty-two Chechen men and nineteen Chechen women took control over the theater on October 23, 2002. They had 25 bomb belts/vests, 2-88lb bombs in metal cylinders, 39 mines and booby-traps, 114 hand grenades, 15 AKSU-74 assault rifles, and 11 handguns. At least 170 people died in the siege when knock-out gas was pumped by the Russians throughout the theater and most people died as a result of complications from the gas.[4]

Two women played the secretarial-type roles for the Moscow hostage crisis in regards to planning the operation. Yassira Vataliyeva helped to rent safe-house apartments using fake documents and searched for targets through reconnaissance.[5] Zura Bitziyeva was the leader of the women involved, including two sixteen-year-old girls who were part of the hostage crisis. Zura was a trained business executive assistant or secretary and she had a role in planning the siege. However, the Chechen women were under the complete control of the men, asking when to use the bathroom and having suicide belts strapped onto them that the men could detonate also from remote control.[6] Some of the teenage girls did not want to be there although the other women did not appear to be forced. "The women and men had different roles: the men took care of the explosives and intimidation, while the women distributed medical supplies, blankets, water, chewing gum and chocolate . . . Sometimes, though, the women toyed threateningly with their two-kilo bomb belts."[7] In the Moscow hostage crisis, the Chechen women still played a helper type secretarial role in addition to the caretaker role of providing food and supplies. They also died in their roles as disposables having suicide belts strapped to them. The Chechen men did not appear to be wearing suicide belts, yet they had control of the women's suicide belts. The Chechen rebel women were not leaders, foot soldiers, or bomb makers; they were still relegated to traditional female roles in Islamic society.

On September 1, 2004, the Beslan School hostage crisis occurred when thirty-two terrorists took over a school and held over twelve hundred people hostage in Beslan, Russia. Two Chechen women were among the international group of terrorists whose purpose was to start an Islamic jihad war across the Caucasus. The hostages were held in a stifling hot gym without food or water for three days and were forced to drink their own sweat and urine, stripping down to their underwear to stay cool. The predominately Russian teenage girls were taken into a room and were repeatedly raped by the male terrorists. The room used for raping was next to the gym so everyone could hear the girls screaming in anguish. The planner and leader of the operation, Ruslan Khuchbarov, later detonated the suicide belts on the two Chechen women when they refused to take children as hostages and kill children after booby-trapped bombs began to detonate in a shootout. Over 330 people died in the pandemonium that occurred.[8] It is evident in the Chechen resistance that women rarely play the role of the secretary and in the end are still viewed and used as disposables.

Although Hamas grew to power during the First Intifada from 1987–1993, it was not until the Second Intifada (2000–2005) that Hamas began to use women. In comparison to the other Palestinian jihadist groups such as PIJ, Fatah, and al-Aqsa Martyrs' Brigade, Hamas has used women less in its organization, only 8 percent of the time according to Jessica Davis.[9] Hamas has truly struggled with the concept of women being more than wives and mothers in the struggle for Palestine. In Hamas, women cannot be members. However, many Hamas legislators and municipal councilors are women. Women also work in the charities to recruit for Hamas and to spread the goodwill of the organization. Women are also allowed to sit on the *Shura* Council and have set up a women's affairs committee. Women are not allowed to actually be in Hamas but are encouraged to get a college education and allowed supportive roles in the party, usually concerning family roles.[10] Recently in Hamas, women have become more important in logistical roles. In an article published in 2005, the following was stated:

Increased interest can be attributed to its confrontation with Israel—as female members helped Hamas militants in some resistance actions without appearing publicly—its competition with secular forces and its need for women take on active roles. Thus, it has completely integrated women in its organizational apparatuses—not in a separate section—and they participate in the implementation of Hamas activities, but [women] do not make decisions or create policies.[11]

Women in Hamas do have some leadership roles in the political party but the terrorist arm of Hamas, the one that does not control parliament, does not allow women in any leadership roles in the terrorist organization. Women are instrumental in getting people to vote for Hamas in the elections.

> Women played a crucial role in getting out the vote for Hamas, knocking on doors and often getting a sympathetic hearing. Hamas's strategy to build political support through its social programmes—the provision of health clinics, nurseries and food for the poor—sealed the loyalty of many Palestinian women.[12]

Hamas has become strategic in that it realizes that it must allow women to participate in the movement in order to get the majority of the Palestinians united behind it.[13] Part of this has to do with fulfilling what are traditionally viewed as government roles since the Palestinian Authority is incompetent. Women will serve at Hamas-run charity organizations or hospitals, etc.[14] Many Palestinians voted for Hamas and put the party in power because Fatah, the former ruling party, negotiated with Israel and was often incompetent from an administrative perspective. Many Palestinians could not support a political party that had tried to cooperate with Israel.[15]

For the Shiite terrorist organization Hezbollah in Lebanon, women continue to play a supportive role. In Hezbollah,

> Fighters (men) are rewarded for their efforts and sacrifices, while other employees (mostly women) are expected to stay on hold and wait until the battle is over and victory is achieved. Hezbollah's institutions constitute an alternative economic structure that hires and attracts Hezbollah's men and women. A girl in Hezbollah's community is brought up in Mahdi's or Al-Mustafa's schools (Hezbollah's schools). She is expected to work in Hezbollah institutions, marry a Hezbollah fighter, and promote Hezbollah's values both outside and inside her family.[16]

Approximately 65 percent of Hezbollah's employees are women. In Hezbollah, a woman's role is first as a mother and wife but she is also given the role of secretary. Women make up a large force of the workforce in Hezbollah, not as leaders or fighters, but primarily as support and the inner mechanism of Hezbollah. In fact, it is safe to say that Hezbollah could not function without its women.

Women run the charities and social organizations. "Many of Hezbollah's social services that are funded by the party are headed by women and Hezbollah has in the past nominated women to run for parliament."[17] Water tanks, health care services, agricultural services, education, martyr's organizations and philanthropy are part of the numerous services that Hezbollah has put in place to assist the community.[18] Hezbollah is not supportive of women running for political office. Rima Fakhri, a member of Hezbollah's political bureau, stated, "We have reservations about [women's] participation in parliamentary elections as it would be at the expense of their families."[19]

Women also raise money for Hezbollah by creating crafts and selling them. They also sponsor a fighter by providing everything that he needs by selling goods and crafts.[20] Women will engage in protesting when necessary. Rarely will women be responsible for the logistics of the group. In Hezbollah, "If women are allowed on the battlefield they are limited to tracking the enemy and transferring information and arms."[21]

In ISIS women are fulfilling the logistic and operator roles. BBC security correspondent Frank Gardner states, "Indeed, there is no question about it. They [women] are half of the society. They are playing an important role in many departments: the medical department, the educational department and even the tax collection department, so they are essential for the survival of Islamic State." Since ISIS adheres to the strictest version of Islam, women and men must be segregated. Therefore, there are jobs for women in the hospitals as a male doctor cannot be alone with a female patient unless there is another woman with her. However, the women of ISIS are not leaders, nor are they foot soldiers.[22]

The Muslim Brotherhood has probably been the most proactive in regards to their treatment of women. Women in the Muslim Brotherhood have probably progressed the most in terms of membership roles in the organization. In the early Muslim Brotherhood, women were teachers in the Muslim Brotherhood schools (1930s), making sure that "girls who really understood their religion would be truly Muslim and thus truly emancipated."[23] Damc Labiba Ahamd, the first head of the Muslim Sisters, stated, "The basis of reforming the [Muslim] nation is reforming the family, and the first step in reforming the family is reforming the female, since women are the world's educators, and the woman who rocks the cradle with her left hand, rocks the world with her right hand."[24] These women also fundraised for the Muslim Brotherhood and the distribution of finances to members of the Muslim Brotherhood network in the 1950s (after Qutb had been imprisoned, in addition to several members of the network).[25] In 2005 and later, the Muslim Brotherhood had women run for parliament as the Brotherhood needed the goodwill of the Egyptians and foreign supporters. "There were no elaborate discussions on democracy or feminism. We were just being practical."[26]

Since the Muslim Brotherhood and President Morsi had been thrown out of power by the Egyptian military in July 2013, women are now fulfilling more roles since the men are in prison. "They [Muslim Sisters] teach Muslim Brotherhood values to children, organize its protests, preserve its networks, and take an ever more prominent role in politics."[27] Pakinam Sharkaw served as an advisor to President Morsi during his presidency. She stated, "But women are not permitted into its highest office, the Guidance Bureau. They take part in internal elections at local level, but can neither run nor vote in elections for the shura council, the group's policy-making body."[28] However, "Divisions remain deep over whether a woman should lead men, or could occupy the role of General Guide itself. Even women who want reform say their role as wives and mothers is paramount."[29] Most likely these initial leadership roles for women will be reversed when the men get out of prison and the situation calms down.

In al-Qaeda, women are encouraged to play the support role for their husbands. An article in *al-Khansa*, an al-Qaeda's women's magazine, published by al-Qaeda's Arabian Peninsula Women's Information Bureau stated:

> We stand should to shoulder with our men, supporting them, helping them, and backing them up. We educate their sons and we prepare ourselves. May Allah know of the honesty of our intentions and of our good deeds, and [may he] choose us and make us *Shahids* [martyrs] for His sake, as we charge forward and do not retreat and as Allah is pleased with us. We will stand covered by our veils and wrapped in our robes, weapons in hand, our children in our laps, with the Koran and Sunna of the Prophet of Allah directing and guiding us. The blood of our husbands and the body parts of our children and the sacrifice by means of which we draw closer to Allah, so that through us, Allah will cause the *Shahada* for His sake to succeed.[30]

Academic Katharina Von Knop stated that in al-Qaeda "women are often strongly involved in the financial issues of a terrorist organization."[31] The wife of the operational chief of Jemaah Islamiah, Hambali (October 2002 Bali bombings) was the bookkeeper. The wife of Omar al-Faruk, another figure in the same group, was also Omar's bookkeeper. "In the aftermath of the 9/11 attacks the United States has closed several bank accounts of terrorist organizations or supporting institutions that were handled by women."[32] Sarah Olson, who married an Egyptian member of al-Qaeda, created a fake charity to help finance al-Qaeda operations throughout the world.[33]

Another woman, Aafia Siddiqui from Pakistan, was known as a "fixer," which is a person that is responsible for solving logistical problems and creating false documents for al-Qaeda operatives arriving in the United States.[34] She married a relative of Khalid Sheikh Mohammed. She was thrown in jail after creating a plan to assassinate American agents in Afghanistan. Angry at her capture, numerous jihadist groups have protested her imprisonment and capture.[35]

CONCLUSION AND CONSIDERATIONS

This chapter has provided an overview of the secretarial role that women play in jihadist terrorist organizations. As has been discussed in this chapter, this role is somewhat rare. There are a handful of women that will play a logistical or planning role but these women are few and far between in any of the groups. However, some important observations can be made in the chapter that shed some light on why this phenomenon occurs; why are not women allowed to have a greater role in a jihadist terrorist organization and why are the roles always so traditional and provincial for women?

As stated in the introduction and first chapter, women in Islamic societies have certain roles to play and these roles are elaborated upon and reinforced by the Quran and the Hadith. There is no reason for women to move outside of these roles, even when women commit their jihad. Although Muslim feminists will state that the interpretation of Islam appears to be the problem, they will still point to the primary roles for women in society as wife and mother as the ideal.

In an effort to get women involved in the struggle to a greater extent and perhaps because the women in their lives are asking to be a bigger part of the fight, jihadist groups that became or have political parties often give women minor leadership positions in the party. However, these positions are token positions that have little significance or power and they are positions that primarily affect the affairs of women. In Hamas, six women were elected to parliament in 2006. These women were concerned about things such as getting harsher sentences for men who commit honor killings of women or having some decision in whom they marry. While not in parliament, these women were training their children to be martyrs in the Palestinian struggle against Israel. Typically Hamas choses younger women to run that are still at the university; when these women marry, they are often sidelined by the organization.[36]

A member of parliament, Miriam Farhat, is known as the "Mother of Martyrs" as she has lost three sons in the fight against Israel. She has become a public figure for Hamas as the poster mother of the idolized Palestinian woman.[37] Mariam Salah became the minister for women's affairs in Hamas.[38] She consistently calls for women in Hamas to support and entreaty the martyrdom and sacrifice of their children for Islam.

In the Muslim Brotherhood, women are allowed to run for office. In the Freedom and Justice Party, which is the Muslim Brotherhood's political party in 2011, forty-six women were put on lists to run for the party. "The Freedom and Justice Party calls for equality between women and men, but says women must strike a balance between their family duties and public life. This means some constraints on women's role in society in general, and in politics in particular."[39] President Morsi appointed three women, two of which were Islamists, to his twenty-one-member team of advisers and aides. "Of the six women on the 100-member assembly writing the constitution, three are Brotherhood members."[40]

However, women in these leadership roles tote traditional Muslim rhetoric including traditional roles for women and follow the party line. "Azza el-Garf, one of the Brotherhood women on the constitution-writing panel, said the 'first' role of women in Egypt is 'inside the family, as a wife and mother,' while politics or work comes second. Women are responsible for raising the new generation—this means the future of Egypt is in our hands."[41] There were fewer than twelve women in the newly elected Egyptian parliament of five hundred members. Even when women were included in the party in leadership positions, they were placed on committees regarding women's issues or women's committees and nothing else. "As of 2012, the MB allowed women to be elected as heads of the regional women's committees. These committees communicated directly with the Guidance Bureau, the highest decision-making body within the movement. Previously, such positions were held only by men."[42]

One of the biggest fights in the Morsi-led administration was the "Islamist-backed clause that would call for equality between men and women but only if it does not contradict Islamic law, or Shariah."[43] This would continue to allow for men to have up to four wives, the practice of female genital mutilation, and for women to receive smaller inheritances as a result of their gender. Initially in the Muslim Brotherhood, women did social work types roles but were recruited into greater political roles when the men in the Muslim Brotherhood were killed or imprisoned. Obviously, after Morsi was thrown out of office in a military coup, women returned to their homes and families.

Hamas[44] and The Muslim Brotherhood[45] have argued that women are unfit to be commander-in-chief or presidents. They argue that the Prophet Muhammad and Islam are quite clear about women's inability to lead. The Quran states that men are in charge of women, because God has made some excel (faddala) some of the others.[46] The Quran also states, "And they (women) have rights similar to those (of men) over them in kindness, and men are a degree above them."[47] The Hadith state, "A people will not succeed who are commanded by a woman."[48]

By and large in recent decades, Islamic societies have become more traditional as time has progressed. Muslim women throughout the world have reverted back to the hijab when women who wore the hijab were becoming a minority in the 1980s. It does not help that jihadist groups such as Hamas and Hezbollah began campaigns to get women to wear the hijab and to modestly cover themselves, often harassing women who do not comply. Women who did not comply had acid thrown on them or were stoned by Hamas members. A few women were even gunned down for minor infractions. Men too are expected to grow long beards, wear long loose clothing, and to cover their heads for prayer. Early marriage and the halting of education for women are also necessities to keep women from polluting the family honor. With the rise of the Intifada, Palestinian society in particular went back to conservative Islam and the Palestinians helped to push the rest of the Islamic world towards conservatism. In addition, the onslaught of Western culture which is at odds with Islam in general is a defense mechanism to protect Muslim ideology and culture. For these reasons, it is highly suspect that the roles of women in jihadist terrorist organizations and in Muslim societies will progress. Women will continue to remain in traditional roles in the home and family.

One last point needs to be made: that there are random mentions and/or images of women in combat roles in these jihadist organizations and one can even find a couple pictures here and there for al-Aqsa Martyrs' Brigade or Hamas.[49] Although the author has seen these pictures, there are no documents, interviews, etc., to attest that women ever actually serve in combat roles. There are a few stories where a compound was attacked and women picked up guns to defend their homes and families. This is not the same as being a soldier in a jihadist terrorist organization. It is rather interesting that the camera is always poised to capture images of these women shooting guns, yet there is little to no information on whether these women are ever seen in the field of combat.

The author has two theories concerning these interesting images of jihadist women in combat. The first theory is that these women train with weapons and bombs only when the camera is there so it looks like the jihadist organizations are really ratcheting up their forces, including using women as a last line of defense. Most likely, this is just a media day show and is done to scare the Israelis from entering the Gaza Strip in the future. There are stories as part of the Gaza Strip military buildup where women are supposedly trained for combat by Hamas and PIJ when there is a lull in fighting.[50] If one looks closely at the feet, many of these women are wearing flip flops. It is also possible that these women are trained how to fight as a last resort doomsday scenario, at least nominally but are never actually allowed to do so.

The other theory is that women who are trained to be suicide bombers also undergo some type of military training while they are training to be suicide bombers. Interestingly enough the media seems to be there to capture these images also. This training is an excellent way to get these women fired up and make them feel committed to a cause while giving them a sense of empowerment while firing a weapon. What a great way to get these women jacked up about what they are doing. The author has not read any accounts in the media or in interview research where women in jihadist groups are actually trained like soldiers. These images appear to be a façade to scare the public and to induce women into participation in the jihadist organization, most likely to eventually become disposable weapons.

NOTES

1. Hilary Matfess, *Women and the War on Boko Haram: Wives, Weapons, Witnesses* (London: Zed Books, 2017), 138.

2. Anne Speckhard and Khapta Akhmedova, "Black Widows: The Chechen Female Suicide Terrorists" in *Female Suicide Bombers: Dying for Equality*, ed. Yoram Schweitzer (Tel Aviv: Jaffee Center for Strategic Studies, August 2006), 11.

3. Anne Nivat, *Chienne de Guerre*, trans. Susan Darnton (New York: Public Affairs, 2001), 201.

4. Yossef Bodansky, *Chechen Jihad: al-Qaeda's Training Ground and the Next Wave of Terror* (New York: Harper Collins, 2007), Chapter 21.

5. Yossef Bodansky, *Chechen Jihad: al-Qaeda's Training Ground and the Next Wave of Terror* (New York: Harper Collins, 2007), 242.

6. Paul J. Murphy, *The Wolves of Islam* (Washington, DC: Brassey's Inc., 2004), 182.

7. Viv Groskop, "Women at Heart of the Terror Cells," *The Guardian*, September 4, 2004, accessed July 25, 2018, https://www.theguardian.com/world/2004/sep/05/russia.chechnya1.

8. Yossef Bodansky, *Chechen Jihad: al-Qaeda's Training Ground and the Next Wave of Terror* (New York: Harper Collins, 2007), 280–90.

9. Jessica Davis, *Women in Modern Terrorism: From Liberation Wars to Global Jihad and the Islamic State* (Lanham: Rowman & Littlefield, 2017), 62.

10. Jeroen Gunning, *Hamas in Politics* (New York: Columbia University Press, 2009).

11. Adnan Abu Amer, "Women's Roles in Hamas Slowly Evolve," *al-Monitor*, March 2, 2015, accessed September 15, 2016, http://www.al-monitor.com/pulse/originals/2015/02/women--role-hamas-gaza-leadership-social-mobilization.html.

12. Chris McGreal, "Women MPs Vow to Change Face of Hamas," *The Guardian*, February 17, 2006, accessed August 27, 2018, https://www.theguardian.com/world/2006/feb/18/israel.islam.

13. Paola Caridi, *Hamas: From Resistance to Government* (New York: Seven Stories Press, 2012), 90–97.

14. Sara Roy, *Engaging the Islamist Social Sector* (Princeton: Princeton University Press, 2011).

15. Chris Hammer, "The Women of Hamas," *SBS News*, August 23, 2013, accessed August 27, 2018, https://www.sbs.com.au/news/the-women-of-hamas.

16. Hanin Ghaddar, "Hezbollah's Women Aren't Happy," *Tablet*, October 12, 2016, accessed June 26, 2017, http://www.tabletmag.com/jewish-news-and-poli tics/215483/hezbollah-women.

17. Victor Argo, "Hezbollah in the Words of Two South Lebanese Women," *Your Middle East*, December 13, 2013, accessed August 27, 2018, https://yourmiddleeast. com/2013/12/13/hezbollah-in-the-words-of-two-south-lebanese-women/.

18. Dalia Khalil, *Hizbullah, The Story from Within* (London: Saqi, 2005), 83–86.

19. Hanan Hamdan, "Lebanese Women Determined to Continue Fight for More Political Representation," *Al-Monitor*, May 31, 2018, accessed August 27, 2018, https://www.al-monitor.com/pulse/originals/2018/05/lebanon-2018-election-women -in-parliament-obstacles-quota.html.

20. Everywoman, "Women of Hezbollah," *Al Jazeera*, August 28, 2007, accessed August 27, 2018, https://www.youtube.com/watch?v=vFCOFt24LLE.

21. Mary Chastain, "List of Female Hezbollah Suicide Bombers Grows," *Breitbart*, August 18, 2013, accessed September 15, 2016, http://www.breitbart.com/national -security/2013/08/18/women-rise-in-hezbollah-still-not-equal-to-men/.

22. Frank Gardner, "The Crucial Role of Women within the Islamic State," *BBC News*, August 20, 2015, accessed September 15, 2016, http://www.bbc.com/news/ world-middle-east-33985441.

23. Richard P. Mitchell, *The Society of the Muslim Brothers* (New York: Oxford University Press, 1969), 289.

24. As cited in Hazem Kandil, *Inside the Brotherhood* (Malden, MA: Polity Press, 2015), 74.

25. Barbara H. E. Zollner, *The Muslim Brotherhood: Hasan al-Hudaybi and Ideol- ogy*, (London: Routledge, 2009), 42.

26. Hazem Kandil, *Inside the Brotherhood* (Malden, MA: Polity Press, 2015), 45.

27. Lin Noueihed, "Sisters in the Vanguard as Egypt's Muslim Brotherhood Bat- tles to Survive," *Reuters*, December 15, 2014, accessed August 7, 2018, https://www .reuters.com/article/us-egypt-brotherhood-women/sisters-in-the-vanguard-as-egypts -muslim-brotherhood-battles-to-survive-idUSKBN0JT1PD20141215.

28. Lin Noueihed, "Sisters in the Vanguard as Egypt's Muslim Brotherhood Bat- tles to Survive," *Reuters*, December 15, 2014, accessed August 7, 2018, https://www .reuters.com/article/us-egypt-brotherhood-women/sisters-in-the-vanguard-as-egypts -muslim-brotherhood-battles-to-survive-idUSKBN0JT1PD20141215.

29. Lin Noueihed, "Sisters in the Vanguard as Egypt's Muslim Brotherhood Bat- tles to Survive," *Reuters*, December 15, 2014, accessed August 7, 2018, https://www .reuters.com/article/us-egypt-brotherhood-women/sisters-in-the-vanguard-as-egypts -muslim-brotherhood-battles-to-survive-idUSKBN0JT1PD20141215.

30. As cited in Elena Mastors and Alyssa Deffenbaugh, *The Lesser Jihad* (Lanham: Rowman & Littlefield, 2007), 54.

31. Katharina Von Knop, "The Female Jihad: Al Qaeda's Women," *Studies in Conflict and Terrorism* 30 (5) (2007): 397–41, 410.

32. Katharina Von Knop, "The Female Jihad: Al Qaeda's Women," *Studies in Conflict and Terrorism* 30 (5) (2007): 397–414, 410–11.

33. Elena Mastors and Alyssa Deffenbaugh, *The Lesser Jihad* (Lanham: Rowman & Littlefield, 2007), 54.

34. Steven Emerson, *Jihad Incorporated* (Amherst, NY: Prometheus Books, 2006), 109.

35. Murad Batal al-Shishani, "Is the Role of Women in al-Qaeda Increasing?" *BBC News*, October 7, 2010, accessed September 26, 2018, https://www.bbc.com/news/world-middle-east-11484672.

36. Khaled Hroub, *Hamas: A Beginner's Guide,* 2nd ed. (New York: Pluto Press, 2010), 73–75.

37. Chris McGreal, "Women MPs Vow to Change Face of Hamas," *The Guardian*, February 17, 2006, accessed August 27, 2018, https://www.theguardian.com/world/2006/feb/18/israel.islam.

38. Beverley Milton-Edwards and Stephen Farrell, *Hamas: The Islamic Resistance Movement* (Malden, MA: Polity Press, 2010).

39. Said Shehata, "Profile: Egypt's Freedom and Justice Party," *BBC News*, November 25, 2011, accessed August 27, 2018, https://www.bbc.com/news/world-middle-east-15899548.

40. The Associated Press, "Egyptian Sisters of the Muslim Brotherhood Rise with Conservative Vision," *Hareetz*, November 10, 2012, accessed August 27, 2018, https://www.haaretz.com/egypt-muslim-sisters-rise-with-a-vision-1.5197442.

41. The Associated Press, "Egyptian Sisters of the Muslim Brotherhood Rise with Conservative Vision," *Hareetz*, November 10, 2012, accessed August 27, 2018, https://www.haaretz.com/egypt-muslim-sisters-rise-with-a-vision-1.5197442.

42. Anwar Mhajne, "How the Muslim Brotherhood's Women Activists Stepped Up in Egypt," *Middle East Eye*, January 15, 2018, accessed August 27, 2018, https://www.middleeasteye.net/essays/muslim-sisters-agents-resistance-2092726647.

43. The Associated Press, "Egyptian Sisters of the Muslim Brotherhood Rise with Conservative Vision," *Hareetz*, November 10, 2012, accessed August 27, 2018, https://www.haaretz.com/egypt-muslim-sisters-rise-with-a-vision-1.5197442.

44. Jeroen Gunning, *Hamas in Politics* (New York: Columbia University Press, 2009), 62.

45. Anwar Mhajne, "How the Muslim Brotherhood's Women Activists Stepped Up in Egypt," *Middle East Eye*, January 15, 2018, accessed August 27, 2018, https://www.middleeasteye.net/essays/muslim-sisters-agents-resistance-2092726647.

46. Shakir, Quran IV: 34.

47. Shakir, Quran II: 228.

48. Hadith, 3285.

49. Avax, "Female Martyrs Train with Al-Aqsa Martyrs Brigade," *Avax News*, May 22, 2011, accessed September 12, 2018, http://avax.news/sad/Female_Martyrs_Train_With_Al-Aqsa_Martyrs_Brigade.html.

50. Intelligence and Information Center, "As Part of the Gaza Strip Military Buildup, Women Are Trained for Combat and for Suicide Bombing Attacks," Israel Intelligence Heritage and Commemoration Center, September 7, 2008, accessed September 28, 2018, https://www.terrorism-info.org.il/en/18419/.

Chapter Five

The Disposables (Mujahidat)

V. G. Julie Rajan states in *Women Suicide Bombers*,[1] "What I have discovered is that women bombers, by and large, are represented in ways that highlight them first and foremost as women, in line with common sociologies about women. In some cases women bombers are noted marginally as political actors. Moreover, I have discovered that those representations are also marked by the political ideologies of the nations/regions that produce them."

In his 2002 Army of Roses Speech Yasser Arafat[2] published, "We are preparing for the new strike announced by our leaders and I declare that it will make America forget . . . the September 11 attacks. The idea came from the success of martyr operations carried out by young Palestinian women in the occupied territories. Our organization is open to all Muslim women wanting to serve the [Islamic] nation, particularly in this very critical phase."

In an early article from 2004, Debra Zedalis, former IMCOM-Pacific Region director, stated that "Research indicates that terrorist organizations will continue to use suicide bomber tactics and employ female suicide bombers. A comprehensive counterterrorism plan should recognize the increasing potential for use of suicide bombers, including females."[3] Today, as the use of female suicide continues to grow over a decade later, the creation of a comprehensive plan has not been created nor has the threat of female suicide bombers been taken seriously by governments or intelligence agencies in Western countries. To be fair, male suicide bombers have not received much scrutiny or evaluation either.

There are eight case studies that were chosen to illustrate the argument in this book and seven of these case studies use women as suicide bombers, some groups more frequently than others. Boko Haram and the Chechen separatists use more female suicide bombers than male as will be discussed later in this chapter. The Egyptian Muslim Brotherhood has never used a female suicide bomber. These eight case studies the author has chosen were selected because the groups are some of the most virulent terrorist groups in the world. In addition, the literature was available to be able to effectively explore the roles of women in these groups as the author was unable to conduct primary research on these groups.

However, almost any jihadist terrorist group could be used as an example to illustrate the disposable role of women in terrorist organizations as they have almost all begun to use women as suicide bombers. As illustrated in chapter 1, jihadist Muslims frequently use the Quran and Hadith as justification for martyrdom operations and the appeal for many jihadist women is alluring. Although critics may point to certain statements in the Quran or Hadith as not wholly representative of Islam, it is evident that jihadist groups use statements from these holy texts to legitimize their tactics.

As a side note, female suicide bombers do exist in groups that are not Muslim, although this is relatively rare. Marxist terrorist groups such as the Tamil Tigers (LTTE) use female suicide bombers. Other examples of this include Christian women in Palestine, who live next to the Lebanese border and are part of the Communist Party. These communist Christian women in Palestine are fighting against what they view as Israeli occupiers in a Muslim society. From a racial perspective, these women identify as Arab. However, it appears as though most of these women who blew themselves up like Loula Abboud did not target Israeli noncombatants. Instead Loula drew several Israeli soldiers in during a gunfight and then exploded herself. She was not part of any terrorist group.[4]

The title of this chapter refers to a disposable object that is used temporarily and then disposed of once it has achieved its purpose. This term refers to women who have chosen to become suicide bombers as they are often the socially undesirable. However, at times they are married women with children. Suicide bombers are often the lowly, the downtrodden, the deformed, or the socially ostracized. This categorization can also be applied to many male suicide bombers. Recruiters target the socially vulnerable and depressed. In Muslim society, women are already considered property, a disposable burden if they are unmarried, divorced, scandalized, cannot bear children, or simply want to achieve martyrdom. Therefore, they make the perfect bomb.

For the previous reasons, the journey of the female suicide bomber is often fraught with sadness and loneliness. The first female suicide bomber was Dalal al Maghribi, a Palestinian who blew up a bus going to Tel Aviv on March 11, 1978. There is not a tremendous amount known about her.[5] Wafa Idris, another example of an early female Palestinian suicide bomber, affiliated with the al-Aqsa Martyrs' Brigade, achieved martyrdom on January 27, 2002. By training and education, she was a nurse who had been responsible for caring for Palestinian people who had been wounded by Israeli soldiers. Although she had two brothers in Fatah, she was not part of the group, but was part of the al-Aqsa Martyrs' Brigade, who claimed responsibility for her attack. A divorcee who had been abandoned by her husband because she was infertile, Wafa had even participated in the party her ex-husband threw when he became a father for his new family. Ostracized as an infertile divorcee and a financial burden on her family in the Palestinian community, Wafa sacrificed herself, a disposable bent on the destruction of Israelis.[6] Before her death, she frequently repeated to her family that she was a financial and social burden to them.

Unfortunately, Wafa's story is all too common. The story of Shifa Adnan al-Qudsi, a twenty-six-year-old, is similar. Ostracized as a divorcee, Shifa sacrificed herself for al-Aqsa Martyrs' Brigade. Another young woman, Ayat al-Akhras, was plagued by rumors that her fiancée had impregnated her so she blew herself up outside a supermarket. Andalib Takatka, another female suicide bomber, was also rumored to be pregnant by a Fatah terrorist.[7] The story of jihadist female suicide bombers are similar and numerous examples can be recited. Recruiters are like predators in that they prey on the weak, the weary, and the unwanted. An editorial published in Egypt's *Al-Sha'ab* a few days after Wafa Idris's death stated,

> It is a woman who teaches you today a lesson in heroism, who teaches you the meaning of jihad, and the way to die a martyr's death . . . It is a woman who has shocked the enemy with her thin, meager and weak body. It is a woman who blew herself up, and with her exploded all the myths about woman's weakness, submissiveness, and enslavement.[8]

There are also several stories of jihadist women blowing up themselves with their husbands or alone. Many of these women were recently married. In these situations, some women chose to become suicide bombers next to their husbands although this appears to be more of a Western phenomenon. Some women run after their husbands have blown themselves up, neglecting to do the deed. Some married women commit suicide bombings alone, away from their husbands. These women are rarely forced into a suicide bombing; most of them have chosen it on their own although their circumstances in life are usually unideal.

In general jihadist female suicide bombers appear to have had little contact with men and society in general so there is a common romanticized notion of defeating the enemy and becoming one of the beautiful *houri* virgins in paradise. This is equivalent to the perception of the male terrorist "playing soldier." The possibilities are endless and magnificent directly before the bomb goes off. Throughout their lives these women are told where to go, who to talk to, and are not allowed to be in the company of a man who is not a direct family member.

For Palestinian women, even in prison, these female terrorists are not able to cope without being controlled by someone. "Many addressed the void in authority and missing guidance in their lives by submitting to the orders of a self-appointed fellow prisoner leader, who dictated what they can do, who they can talk to or with whom they could socialize with in the prison."[9] In this instance, women who refused to follow the authority of the prison leader met with boiling margarine and brown sugar thrown in their face. Women in ISIS are also subservient to the Al Khansaa Brigade who is responsible for monitoring the conduct of ISIS women.

Many women may choose the possibility of becoming a suicide bomber because there are so few options open to women in jihadist terrorist groups. Women are not able to volunteer for militant roles but they are also interested in helping their country and people. Many times, the women who do volunteer must repeatedly ask to become martyrs and must persuade the men in the group to let them do so, although sometimes women are actually asked by close males in their lives to martyr themselves. Speckhard makes the point that women in Palestinian groups were only used as suicide bombers when the "tactical advantages of using women also outweighed their sender's moral reservations that they gave in to using women as bombers."[10] In fact, it is possible that women become suicide bombers to shame the men in their culture to do more for the "cause."

In her article in *Studies in Conflict and Terrorism*, Karla Cunningham[11] looks at the utility of evolutionary theory for the phenomenon of female political violence including terrorism. Cunningham found that female terrorism is part of a survival strategy in that women who will not invest in the concepts of wife and motherhood are able to sacrifice themselves for the greater glory of their nation and its survival. By placing the bomb into her body as a surrogate womb, a woman is ensuring the survival of her nation through the destruction of her body, which ensures that others may live on. The next part of this chapter talks about the female suicide bombers in the eight case studies.

The Disposables

According to academic Ami Pedahzur,

> Similar to other acts of terrorism, suicide terrorism also aims at destroying or damaging a specific target. However, its real intention is to create an atmosphere of terror amidst a population not necessarily exposed directly to the incident but rather those who are informed about it from a secondary source. As the terrorists perceive it, public pressure in the wake of this collective anxiety should also

be translated into political gains . . . Or in other words, the terrorist's death by means of the detonation of an explosive charge is an integral part of the execution of the operation and constitutes an essential condition of its success.[12]

Pedahzur finds that suicide bombers can be classified into two groups, "1) members of an organization or social network and 2) individuals who were recruited—or volunteered—specifically for the suicide mission."[13] For the first group, commitment is a major incentive. Individuals have given time and energy for the success of organization and typically a crisis will help facilitate the martyrdom of a person who is predisposed to it. Typically, these people are not valuable members of the organization who have participated in it for several years—leaders are against sacrificing their best people.

Many jihadists groups have embraced women as suicide bombers over men for certain periods of time or in general. There are several reasons for this decision and they are mostly strategic in nature. The first is that in Islamic society, women are untouchable, meaning that it is difficult to frisk them. Since women are the honor bearers and honor securers in the family, they cannot be searched by men. Instead, they must be searched by female officers, which even then can be problematic as female police and security can be rare. The second reason is that women, particularly in Islamic societies, wear long flowing robes and dresses that allow them to hide weapons in their clothing or, more importantly, bombs. Their faces are even covered, which will hide any signs of nervousness or fear. Women can also appear pregnant while actually hiding a bomb. The third reason is that women are often the least suspected targets as many people still assume that women are not violent. Lastly, women are disposable in most Islamic societies. To summarize it efficiently, women are a quadruple threat.[14]

In Table 5.1: Case Studies and The First Female Suicide Bombers, the first female suicide bomber for each case study is listed. Hezbollah was the first jihadist group to use a female suicide bomber but the group only used a few during this time period and was at war with Israel. Since this is a Shiite group, it did not really catch on and women have not been used since the initial bombings. The next group to use female suicide bombers were the Chechens. The beginning of the Chechen use of female suicide bombers led to a revolution in suicide bombings for the Muslim Arabs. Shortly after, the Palestinian groups latched on to the idea of female suicide bombers and have never really stopped. When conflict flares up again with Israel, the Palestinian jihadist groups may revert back to the use of female suicide bombers.

One interesting fact is that the Egyptian Muslim Brotherhood has never used female suicide bombers. The Muslim Brotherhood is the origin of jihadist terrorism and several terrorist groups came from Muslim Broth-

Table 5.1:   Case Studies and The First Female Suicide Bombers

Terrorist Organization	Name	First Female Suicide Bombing	Were men included in the attack?	Type of Bomb
Al-Aqsa Martyrs' Brigade	Wafa Idris	January 27, 2002	Yes	Car bomb
Boko Haram	Unknown	June 8, 2014	No	Motorcycle Bomb
Chechen Separatists (Black Widows)	Khava Barayeva and Luisa Magomadova	June 7, 2000	No	Truck bomb
Hamas	Reem Raiyshi	January 14, 2004	No	Suicide Belt
Hezbollah	Sana Youssef Mheidleh-Bride of the South	April 9, 1985	No	Car Bomb
ISIS	Unknown-Hussienieh Ali Basha Shia Mosque	July 5, 2013	No	Suicide Belt
Muslim Brotherhood	NA	NA	NA	NA
Al-Qaeda	Nour Qaddour al-Shammari and Wadad Jamil Jassem	April 3, 2003	No	Car Bomb

erhood members as discussed in the Introduction. Many jihadist groups have also subscribed to the ideology and writings of the Egyptian Muslim Brotherhood. However, the Muslim Brotherhood has stayed away from female bombers although they have used male bombers many times. It is unclear why the Muslim Brotherhood have not used women in this capacity particularly since it has become quite popular among the other jihadist terrorist groups.

From a tactical perspective, the car bomb appears to be the favorite method of bombing for female suicide bombers as it is quite easy to drive a car into a target and requires little training. The suicide belt was invented by the LTTE in Sri Lanka in the early 1990s and it took the jihadist groups a while to catch on this method. What follows in this chapter is an examination of the use of women in suicide bombings from the case studies that are included in the book and the peculiarities concerning each organization beginning with al-Aqsa Martyrs' Brigade.

On January 27, 2002, Yasser Arafat, the leader of the PLO, called for women to step up their role in the Palestinian conflict, calling for "*Shahida* all the way to Jerusalem." "You are the hope of Palestine. You will liberate your husbands, fathers, and sons from oppression. You will sacrifice the way you, women, have always sacrificed for your family."[15] Later that afternoon Arafat received his wish in the form of Wafa Idris, the first female suicide bomber, later claimed by the al-Aqsa Martyrs' Brigade. After the death of Wafa Idris, al-Aqsa Martyrs' Brigade created a female suicide bombing sect in their organization called "Shawaq al-Aqsa.[16]

In the aftershock, Wafa's brother Khalil admitted that he was supposed to be the bomber but that his sister begged him to let her take his place. Yasser Arafat was afraid to claim Wafa at first. As usual, he waited for the response of the Palestinian public before claiming her death and martyrdom. If Wafa were a man, her family would have received 400 dollars per month instead of the usual 200 dollars for female suicide bombers.[17] Wafa literally became the martyr poster child for female suicide bombers, with poetry and songs written about her.

Boko Haram uses female suicide bombers more frequently than male suicide bombers and they are one of the few jihadist terrorist organizations to do this. Often these bombers are young girls who are kidnapped by the group and they will be pushed into committing a suicide bombing. Several of these young women have refused to become a sex slave, also known at times as forced marriage in Boko Haram, and the group will ask them to martyr themselves. Some of these women are cajoled into becoming suicide bombers and some make their own decisions.

Or in other cases, the man will get sick of his woman sexually and emotionally.[18] In one case, seventeen-year-old Nadia was kidnapped by Boko Haram and was chosen by the second in command to be a sex slave. Nadia fought him persistently and succeeded, although most likely she was repeatedly raped in her struggle. He then proposed marriage to her and she still refused. He then ordered her flogged by his troops. After he had grown tired of her refusal, she woke up one morning with a bomb strapped to her body as she had been drugged the previous night. She and two other girls were forced on a motorbike and dropped in Gamboro by Boko men. Luckily the three girls were not shot when they showed the Nigerian soldiers the bombs strapped to their bodies.[19]

In preparation for martyrdom in Boko Haram, women's hair will be braided and they will be painted with henna. "What they normally do is to dress you very beautifully, and put henna on your hands," said Aisha. Recruiting women for suicide bombings is as simple as asking a few questions. Fatima stated,

They gather all the women in one area and preach and preach. Then they ask: "Who wants to go to paradise?" Everyone raises her hand. Then they ask: "Who wants to go now?" Some raise their hands, so they take them and train them in suicide bombing. If nobody raises her hand, they say: "God created you, fed you, did everything for you, and this is how you reward him for all this?" They make sure they get at least one person.[20]

Children who are as young as five are recruited for suicide bombings, and receive similar treatment. "They say: 'Who wants to go and see their mother in paradise? If you want to see her, that's where she is.' The children accept it easily, because they don't know how dangerous it is. They tell them they won't feel any pain even if their body is destroyed. I heard them saying that to the children in my camp."[21] Or one social worker described, "They would tell the girls, 'In heaven there is a special house for you made of glass,' and that is how they got them to blow themselves up."[22] Boko Haram has also sent young women tied to vehicles to their deaths with remote control detonators. Many of these women will be shot first by Nigerian soldiers who are terrified of suicide bombings. In other cases, women will willingly go to their deaths as a martyr for Islam.

The first female Chechen suicide bombing occurred on June 7, 2000, when Khava Barayeva, the cousin of field commander Arbi Barayev, and Luisa Magomadova drove a truck full of explosives into temporary Russian Special Forces (OMON) headquarters in Alkhan Yurt in Chechnya.[23] Khava became so popular among the Chechen people as a *shakhidi* (female suicide bomber) that she was commemorated by Chechen songwriter Timur Mutsar-aeva.[24] In November 2001 Ayiza Gasouev exploded a bomb in the presence of a military commander (Gaidar Gadzhiyev) who had tortured and killed her husband. The Chechen female suicide bombers unit is known as the Riyadus-Salikhin Reconnaissance and Sabotage Battalion of Chechen Shahids or simply the Black Widows which was created in 2002.[25] Highlighted in the media as a terrifying phenomenon, Abu al-Walid stated, "These women, particularly the wives off the mujahedin who are martyred, are being threatened in their homes. Their honor and everything are being threatened."[26]

Many scholars such as Mia Bloom have stated that Chechen women are drugged or coerced into suicide bombings. For example, the Black Widow handler Black Fatima supposedly gives women psychopathic drugs and tranquilizers in orange juice to get them to commit their bombings. The raping of Chechen women by Chechen men is filmed and the women are then blackmailed into committing a suicide bombing. However, academic Yossef Bodansky states that this is not necessarily true. Bodansky finds that the treatment of Chechen civilians during the first rebellion from 1994–1996 was much worse than the second Chechen rebellion which began in 1999.

The first rebellion did not have any suicide bombers. The second Chechen rebellion was primarily Islamist in nature and the "Islamist-Jihadist recruiters and terrorist masters exploited religious devotion but also shame and despair to drive women to attempt martyrdom. In Chechnya, the oppressive circumstances of the war increased women's desperation—but it was the alien influence of enforced Islamicization that introduced and legitimized the idea of self-cleansing-through-revenge through martyrdom bombing."[27] Or as one female Chechen martyr stated in a letter to a friend before she crashed a plane:

> I know that many people will not understand us, and will make accusations. But I believe, that you will understand all. Do not trust anything that will be said about us. They will say that we bargained and demanded dollars and a plane in exchange for the hostages. It's not the truth. We go on jihad. We know that all of us will die. We are ready for it. We will not bargain and we will stand to the end.[28]

Bodansky also mentions that "Black Widows were gradually introduced into combat, first in tandem with male counterparts and in groups for self-reinforcement, and later alone—an approach that suggested caution on the part of the terrorists' masters.[29] "However, each example Bodansky gives ends with a woman blowing herself up, which appears to be the purpose for the entire mission. Chechen women are primarily used for operations that end in martyrdom.

Fulbright Scholar John Reuter found that the Chechens used female suicide bombers 70 percent of the time and women are used exclusively 50 percent of the time in a report published in 2004. Only 25 percent of the attacks are committed by males; the other 25 percent are unknown.[30] In a later piece, published in 2008, Anne Speckhard and Khapta Akhmedova[31] found that Chechen women committed a majority of suicide bombings when all female terrorist attacks were considered. 79 percent of attacks were committed by Chechen women, or to be more precise 22 out of the total 28 attacks at that time were perpetrated by women. 42 percent of all Chechen suicide bombings were committed by women. These attacks include: "wearing explosive bomb belts, carrying bomb-filled bags, driving cars or trucks filled with explosives, exploding themselves, exploding themselves on airplanes, in subways, and on trains."[32] The most infamous of these attacks included the Moscow Dubrovka Theater and the Beslan School mass hostage situation. However, some women such as Mareta Duduyeva, Zulikhan Elikhadzhiyeva, and Zarema Inarkaeva were forced to commit suicide bombings by the Chechen rebels and there is some indication of rape and drug abuse.[33]

Using the psychological autopsy method to interview the family members and friends of sixty-four Chechen female suicide bombers, Speckhard and Akhmedova[34] found that the bombers were on average twenty-five years of age and they ranged between fifteen to forty-five years of age. Many of these women were married with children. All of the women were volunteers who at least had minimal training and were equipped by the terrorist organization. Minimal training is apparent across the spectrum so why would the organization spend time and money on someone who only needed to perform the simple task of blowing oneself up? Many of these women had access to or had accumulated some higher education and several of them had professional jobs. However, traditional family structures and stereotypical gender roles were apparent. These women had adopted Middle Eastern dress to identify themselves as true believers of Islam although this apparel is not part of traditional Chechen culture. Over 65 percent of these women had finished high school; around 12 percent were in college, 4 percent had finished college, and over 19 percent had finished their university studies. Many of these women were experiencing financial hardships but this was due to a poor Chechen economy.

The next case study is Hamas, which has had a difficult time implementing female suicide bombers. Sheikh Ahmad Yassin, the founder of Hamas, when asked, "What makes Muslims want to commit suicide for the sake of a certain goal?" stated:

> Here your understanding is wrong. The person who kills himself in [one of] many ways, by shooting or taking drugs or to escape from life and its problems, because of personal distress, that is suicide, but the person who goes to fight an enemy who fights him who took his land, his country, or who took his property, fights him and is killed, such a person is considered a *shaheed* [martyr for the sake of Allah] and not someone who committed suicide.[35]

Although Hamas formally allowed women to participate in jihad in 2002, they still have not completely embraced nor felt entirely comfortable with female suicide bombers. Hamas was inspired by the Chechen Black Widows in 2000 to use female suicide bombers and began using their own female suicide bombers on January 14, 2004. They created the all-female suicide bombing unit called Martyr Izz ad-Din al-Qassam Brigades in summer 2005.[36] Hamas does not appear to have any particular persona that they chose for a suicide bomber. In 2004, they chose a young married woman with a child and in 2006, they chose a grandmother with many children and grandchildren to perform a suicide bombing.

However, Sheikh Yassin claimed that no woman "should be allowed to go out for jihad without a male chaperone."[37] This put a damper on actions that women could perform. Former Hamas chief Abdel Aziz Rantissi articulated that there was no reason that suicide bombings should be monopolized by men.[38] The rhetoric went back and forth, with Yassin stating that women could be used only when there was a shortage of men in Hamas. In reality, scholar Davis states that Hamas was recruiting many women for suicide bombings in 2004 despite the rhetoric from leadership. Before 2004 women were only used as recruiters and logisticians.[39] As Hamas tended to incorporate more women into the Hamas movement, more woman joined Hamas. There was even one report of a female bomb maker for Hamas who was captured by Israel in October 2005. She had taught her husband how to make bombs in case she was captured. However, the gender progression in the organization ends there.[40]

Sheik Yassin claimed that in paradise, female suicide bombers become "even more beautiful than the seventy-two virgins. If they are not married, they are guaranteed a pure husband in paradise, and of course they are entitled to bring seventy of their relatives to join them there without suffering the anguish of the grave."[41] Martyred women will also have wedding celebrations given in their honor to a local man who symbolically marries them. Nicknames like "Bride of the South" or "Bride of Haifa" are also given to Hamas female bombers after their martyrdom.

Hezbollah executed approximately thirty-six suicide attacks against Israel and UN Coalition forces (including France and the United States) from 1983–1986. Of those forty-one attackers, six were women. Although some of these groups involved were under the Syrian Socialist Nationalist Party, they were still under the umbrella organization of Hezbollah.[42] Between 1988 and 1990, Hezbollah conducted few suicide attacks using men and suicide attacks were again orchestrated in 1995, 1996, and 1999. Since then Hezbollah has quit suicide bombings.[43] Hezbollah has rarely used women for suicide bombers since the 1980s but recent statements may signify a change in this practice. For Hezbollah, "The list of women willing to commit suicide attacks is as long as the men's."[44]

However, journalists Keck and Sparks make the argument that Hezbollah has now abandoned suicide bombing altogether even though they refuse to acknowledge this change in tactics publicly. Hezbollah, a Shiite organization, frequently supports bombings by Sunni organizations. This change in Hezbollah is interesting considering that Shiites have a strong tradition of martyrdom. Keck and Sparks believe that Hezbollah has not used suicide bombings because it has become more powerful and is not facing such a vastly superior enemy any longer like Israel. Hezbollah now has more financial resources at its disposal.[45]

ISIS used its first female suicide bomber in Iraq on July 5, 2013. Currently, the list of female martyrs for ISIS is not very long as women typically have a traditional role in the organization. Female terrorist expert Mia Bloom stated in a *CNN* interview that "Up until now ISIS has been very clear. The role for women is cooking, cleaning, and childcare. They do not have women on the front lines."[46] The first female European suicide bomber for ISIS, Hasna Ait

Boulahcen, detonated herself on November 18, 2015, in a Saint-Denis raid in France. Even then, Boulahcen's act was in self-defense to get away from the police, not an act she perpetrated in public to kill noncombatants. In late February 2016, ISIS used female suicide bombers in Libya so it is likely that this trend will continue.[47]

The ISIS ideology has spread throughout the world and many national terrorist organizations have declared their allegiance to ISIS, including adopting the use of ISIS tactics. Several of these attacks have been perpetrated by female suicide bombers and even entire families have begun to martyr themselves together. The group Jama'ah Ansharud Daulah (JAD), who is affiliated with ISIS, sponsored an attack by Dian Yulia Novi who tried to commit a suicide bombing with her husband in 2016 in Indonesia. Their attack failed. On May 13, 2018, in Indonesia, Dita Oepriarto and his wife Puji Kuswati, along with their four children, carried out suicide attacks against three Christian Churches. The next day a family of five drove two motorcycle bombs, which were detonated in front of the Surabaya police headquarters. The family of five consisted of Tri Murtiono and his wife Tri Ernawati, who were accompanied by their sons aged eighteen and fourteen and their seven-year-old daughter.[48]

Considering that the founding of al-Qaeda occurred in 1988, al-Qaeda only recently came into using female suicide bombers considering the organization's extensive history. This change occurred with the creation of al-Qaeda in Iraq under the leadership of Abu Musab al-Zarqawi in October 2004. It is speculated that Osama bin Laden was not a fan of using female suicide bombers although as Pape[49] points out, male suicide bombers were used frequently in al-Qaeda from 1995–2003 throughout the world. As discussed in the Introduction, there was a falling out between Osama bin Laden and Ayman al-Zawahiri (bin Laden's successor) and al-Zarqawi over the brutality of terrorist attacks. Bin Laden and al-Zawahiri were not happy with the brutality that al-Zarqawi was using against the local population, many of them Sunni. Al-Zarqawi also purposefully targeted Shiites. Although bin Laden and al-Zawahiri presented a united front to the public, al-Qaeda officially disowned ISI (later became ISIS) in 2013. Al-Zarqawi was using female suicide bombers for ISI in Iraq or Al-Qaeda in Iraq in 2003. Most likely, had the leadership of bin Laden not been hijacked in Iraq, bin Laden would not have used female suicide bombers. In a book published in 2010, academic Ariel Merari supports this argument when he finds that less 3 percent of al-Qaeda bombers were women until the end of 2008. Merari also mentions that most of these attacks were in Iraq after the American invasion. Until the end of 2008, female suicide bombings did not occur at all in Afghanistan and Pakistan had women bombers about 1 percent of the time.[50]

However, Osama's successor Ayman al-Zawahiri was likely converted to using female suicide bombers albeit reluctantly. His wife Umayma al-Zawahiri wrote a letter in 2009, before Osama bin Laden's death in May 2011. In that letter she stated:

> Incidentally, a question has arisen about the role of women in the current jihad. So I say, and Allah will grant success: Jihad is an individual obligation on every Muslim man and woman, but the path of combat is not easy for a woman. It requires a Mahram [a male Muslim relative], because the woman must have a Mahram in her comings and goings. However, we must support our religion in many ways, so we put ourselves in the service of the mujahideen and do what they ask, whether it is helping with money or service, or giving them information or opinion, or participation in battle or even with martyrdom-seeking acts. There are many women who did martyrdom-seeking acts in Palestine, Iraq and Chechnya, and hurt the enemy and defeated them. So we ask Allah to accept them and make us follow them in goodness.[51]

Umayma al-Zawahiri reminds women of their duties as Muslim women in her letter and she emphasizes the need for women to be mothers of jihadists and wives of jihadists. Although jihad is not the main purpose for women, it is one that she supports and she encourages other Muslim women to support female jihad.

Since the death of Osama bin Laden in May 2011, al Qaeda has claimed female suicide bombings all over the world including Iraq, Morocco, Uzbekistan, Egypt, Belgium, France, Germany, Denmark, and the Netherlands in addition to other countries. Some of these attacks were committed by terrorist organizations who have declared their loyalty to al-Qaeda and others were committed by al-Qaeda members. Western women who marry jihadist Muslim men are the newest sources of female suicide bombers.[52] However, unlike Boko Haram and the Chechens, it is unlikely that al-Qaeda will plan a majority of female suicide bombings in comparison to male. Al-Qaeda is old school and more fundamentalist by nature. Malika al-Aroud, the Belgian widow of one of the suicide bombers who killed the Afghan leader Ahmad Shah Massoud (September 2001), stated (under the pseudonym Oum Obeyda)[53]: "It's not my role to set off bombs—that's ridiculous. I have a weapon. It's to write. It's to speak out. That's my jihad. You can do many things with words. Writing is also a bomb."

CONCLUSION

In conclusion, seven of the eight case studies in this book use female suicide bombers and have somewhat varying views of women as the disposable role. However, it is evident that women throughout these groups have a lesser value than men in the organization. The value of women in these organizations is based on traditional Islamic views of women in the household and family. Although the Shiite organization Hezbollah has not used female suicide bombers for decades, it is evident that female bombers may become an option in the future. The Egyptian Muslim Brotherhood also has never used female suicide bombers, and the reasons for this are unknown although it is speculated that the Egyptian Muslim Brotherhood has stuck to tradition and has refused to innovate their tactics.

In Western terrorist organizations, women are not used as suicide bombers or disposable ammunition. For the most part, Western terrorist organization have never used suicide bombers, let alone female suicide bombers. Women may die in combat but they do not use their bodies as bombs in Western terrorist organizations. The tactic/concept of female suicide bombing is only associated with Marxist organizations like the Tamil Tigers and jihadist terrorist organizations like the case studies in this book.

It must also be reiterated that the concept of martyrdom in Islam is not similar to suicide in Western nations. As the scholar Frances S. Hasso states, "Muslim and Christian Palestinians often use the term 'martyrdom' rather than 'suicide operations' to describe these attacks because the former indicate 'respect and honor for the bomber' and the family left behind, while suicide is forbidden by Islam."[54] To put it more succinctly, the Ramallah religious leader Sheikh Bassam Jarrar stated, "Suicide is running away, it is weakness and fear facing life and its troubles. But martyrdom operations . . . [are] known throughout history and . . . respected by all nations. People who carry out such attacks are those who are very brave, braver than others."[55] However, many of the female suicide bombings in this chapter appear to be running away from problems and have looked to martyrdom as a heroic and rewarding solution to their problems. This indicates a problem in Islam in the interpretation and translation of the Islamic religious texts.

Critics of this book may point to the fact that if Islam justifies or invites martyrdom through Islamic texts and scriptures, then why is not every Muslim martyring themselves? This question can be answered quite simply. Most people do not want to die. Therefore, for the reasons of self-preservation and natural selection, most people will not commit suicide or martyr themselves. The examples used in this chapter make the point that it is often the desperate and socially ostracized women who become suicide bombers, although the author argues that these women still have agency. Western culture and even Christianity place a higher value on life and the concept of Christian martyrdom is something that has been confined to early Christianity. If Christians are martyred for their faith in modern times, it often at the hands of Muslim extremists in the Middle East or Africa.

Throughout this chapter, there are several generalizations that can be made. The first is that female suicide bombers do not play a lead role in the planning of their attacks. They do, however, play a lead role in actually carrying out their suicide attacks. There are several instances where women have lost their nerve and turned back or have allowed themselves to be arrested in the process. Barbara Victor attests to this in the book *Army of Roses*,[56] where she interviews several women who have changed their minds. After all, one cannot interview a successful female suicide bomber so researchers must rely on women who have failed. It is possible that there are differences between the failures and the successful suicide bombers. But the data simply does not exist to make that argument.

Another item that can be learned from this chapter is that the decision to sacrifice women over men varies by Islamic country culture and perhaps is slowly changing throughout the Islamic world. One reason for this may be that there of plenty of men in certain cultures to use as suicide bombers so women are not necessary. Another reason (as stated earlier) might be that female suicide bombers guilt men into joining an organization or volunteering for martyrdom missions. Ayat Akhras, a successful Palestinian female suicide bomber (al Aqsa Martyrs Brigade), stated the following in her final video. "I say to the Arab leaders. Stop sleeping. Stop failing to fulfill your duty. Shame on the Arab armies who are sitting and watching the girls of Palestine fighting while they are asleep. It is intifada until victory."[57]

Thirdly, for the Palestinians, unmarried women living at home should be sacrificed over men when it comes to suicide bombings. As one mother states when her brother-in-law cajoled her daughter into committing a suicide bombing, "He had no right to involve my daughter. He has children of his own. The only reason he picked on Shireen was because she is the only one who is not married. I have sixteen children. Shireen is the youngest."[58] A family who has a daughter living at home is worried about the family honor falling victim for their unmarried daughter's actions. If she is of marrying age and still living at home for too long, she becomes a financial and reputation burden. Conversely in Palestinian society, Dr. Mira Tzoreff states from Ben Gurion University that "There are still constraints among religious Muslims about keeping a daughter at home. To sacrifice a son brings enormous honor."[59]

Another observation can be made in that women for the most part listen to or are controlled by the men in their prospective terrorist organizations as to what women should do in the organization. In the case of the disposable role, there are a few examples where women have chosen to become suicide bombers before the religious leaders in their organizations allowed it. For example, Dareen Abu 'Aisheh (2002) challenged Hamas Sheikh Yassin's statement that jihad is a man's duty. Dareen stated in her final recorded speech that she was following in the footsteps of Wafa Idris and that "women's roles will not be confined to weeping over a son, brother, or husband."[60] Itaf Ilayan, from Palestinian Islamic Jihad, also questioned the need to take a male chaperone while participating in jihad as commanded by Sheikh Yassin. She stated "From a practical angle, how can a female seeking martyrdom take a *mahram* [proper escort], a brother or son, with her? The operation and the task of jihad will fail. Therefore necessities permit what is not allowed."[61] So perhaps there is a feminist angle here to women creating their own destinies although this is feminist in a non-Western sense.

In addition, it is evident even in committing a suicide bombing, the woman's traditional role is pronounced and reiterated by jihadist groups and sympathizers. She is using her body to care and fight for her nation or people. Unlike a male suicide bomber who kills the enemy as it is in his nature to fight and defend, she is making a sacrifice. She is never a soldier but a strange and heroic anomaly. The day she dies is her wedding day as she is a bride of Allah. She shames the men as they should be the ones to martyr themselves. Her femininity can never be separated from her act.

Lastly, it is puzzling why the Egyptian Muslim Brotherhood have not used female suicide bombers. The author would surmise that it is because the Muslim Brotherhood is one of the first jihadist terrorist organizations and therefore they are one of the most fundamentalist jihadist groups. The Quran is somewhat restrictive towards female jihad as the Prophet Muhammad states (although there are contradictory verses as discussed in the first chapter) so it is likely that the Egyptian Muslim Brotherhood takes the hard line towards female martyrdom.

NOTES

1. V. G. Rajan, *Women Suicide Bombers, Narratives of Violence* (New York: Routledge, 2011), 2.

2. Al Jazeerah News, "Bin Laden Has Set Up Female Suicide Squads: Report," *Arab News*, March 13, 2003, accessed May 23, 2018, www.aljazeerah.info/News%20 archives/2003%20News%20archives/March%202003%20News/13%20News/ Bin%20Laden%20has%20set20%20up%20female%20suicide%20squads%20%al jazeerah.info.htm.

3. Debra D. Zedalis, "Female Suicide Bombers," *Strategic Studies Institute*, June 2004, accessed September 18, 2018, https://www.globalsecurity.org/jhtml/ jframe.html#https://www.globalsecurity.org/security/library/report/2004/ssi_zedalis. pdf|||Female%20Suicide%20Bombers.

4. Joyce M. Davis, *Martyrs: Innocence, Vengeance, and Despair in the Middle East* (New York: Palgrave Macmillan, 2003), Chapter 4.

5. Mia Bloom, *Bombshell* (Philadelphia: Penn State University Press, 2011), 23.

6. Ami Pedazhur, *Suicide Terrorism* (Cambridge: Polity Press, 2005), 138+.

7. Ami Pedazhur, *Suicide Terrorism* (Cambridge: Polity Press, 2005), 138+.

8. Paige Whaley Eager, From Freedom Fighters to Terrorists: Women and Political Violence (Burlington, Vermont: Ashgate, 2008), 188–89.

9. Anat Berko and Edna Erez, "Gender, Palestinian Women, and Terrorism: Women's Liberation or Oppression? *Studies in Conflict and Terrorism*, 30 (6) (2007): 493–519, 509.

10. Anne Speckhard, "Female Terrorists in ISIS, al Qaeda and 21rst Century Terrorism," *Trends Research: Inside the Mind of a Jihadist*, May 4, 2015, accessed September 9, 2016, http://trendsinstitution.org/wp-content/uploads/2015/05/Female-Ter rorists-in-ISIS-al-Qaeda-and-21rst-Century-Terrorism-Dr.-Anne-Speckhard11.pdf.

11. Karla J. Cunningham, "Female Survival Calculations in Politically Violent Settings: How Political Violence and Terrorism are Viewed as Pathways to Life," *Studies in Conflict and Terrorism* 32:7, (2009), 561–75.

12. Ami Pedahzur, *Suicide Terrorism* (Malden, MA: Polity Press, 2005), 11.

13. Ami Pedahzur, *Suicide Terrorism* (Malden, MA: Polity Press, 2005), 125.

14. Also see Anne Speckhard for early literature on female suicide bombers. Anne Speckhard, "The Emergence of Female Suicide Terrorists," *Studies in Conflict and Terrorism* 31 (11) (2008): 995–1023.

15. Barbara Victor, *Army of Roses* (Emmaus, PA: Rodale, 2003), 20.

16. V. G. Rajan, *Women Suicide Bombers, Narratives of Violence* (New York: Routledge, 2011), 247–48.

17. Barbara Victor, *Army of Roses* (Emmaus, PA: Rodale, 2003), 20.

18. Diane Searcey, "Boko Haram Strapped Suicide Bombs to Them. Somehow These Teenage Girls Survived," *The New Times*, October 25, 2017, accessed August 8, 2018, https://www.nytimes.com/interactive/2017/10/25/world/africa/nigeria-boko -haram-suicide-bomb.html.

19. Ruth Maclean, "Dressed for Death: the Women Boko Haram Sent to Blow Themselves Up," *The Guardian*, May 5, 2017, accessed August 8, 2018, https://www. theguardian.com/world/2017/may/05/dressed-for-death-the-women-boko-haram -sent-to-blow-themselves-up.

20. Ruth Maclean, "Dressed for Death: the Women Boko Haram Sent to Blow Themselves Up," *The Guardian*, May 5, 2017, accessed August 8, 2018, https://www. theguardian.com/world/2017/may/05/dressed-for-death-the-women-boko-haram sent-to-blow-themselves-up.

21. Ruth Maclean, "Dressed for Death: the Women Boko Haram Sent to Blow Themselves Up," *The Guardian*, May 5, 2017, accessed August 8, 2018, https://www.

theguardian.com/world/2017/may/05/dressed-for-death-the-women-boko-haram
-sent-to-blow-themselves-up.

22. Hilary Matfess, *Women and the War on Boko Haram: Wives, Weapons, Witnesses* (London: Zed Books), 1.

23. Anne Speckhard and Khapta Akhmedova, "Black Widows and Beyond: Under-standing the Motivations and Life Trajectories of Chechen Female Terrorists," in *Female Terrorism and Militancy: Agency, Utility, and Organization* ed. Cindy D. Ness (New York: Routledge, 2008).

24. John Reuter, "Chechnya's Suicide Bombers: Desperate, Devout, or Deceived?" *The Jamestown Foundation*, August 23, 2004, accessed July 25, 2018, https://james town.org/report/chechnyas-suicide-bombers-desperate-devout-or-deceived/.

25. Gordon M. Hahn, *Russia's Islamic Threat* (New Haven: Yale University Press, 2007), 38.

26. As cited in Yossef Bodansky, *Chechen Jihad: al-Qaeda's Training Ground and the Next Wave of Terror* (New York: Harper Collins, 2007), 258.

27. Yossef Bodansky, *Chechen Jihad: al-Qaeda's Training Ground and the Next Wave of Terror* (New York: Harper Collins, 2007), 259.

28. Elena Pokalova, *Chechnya's Terrorist Network: The Evolution of Terrorism in Russia's Northern Caucus* (Santa Barbara, CA: Praeger 2015), 216.

29. Yossef Bodansky, *Chechen Jihad: al-Qaeda's Training Ground and the Next Wave of Terror* (New York: Harper Collins, 2007), 262.

30. John Reuter, "Chechnya's Suicide Bombers: Desperate, Devout, or Deceived?" *The Jamestown Foundation*, August 23, 2004, accessed July 25, 2018, https://jame stown.org/report/chechnyas-suicide-bombers-desperate-devout-or-deceived/.

31. Anne Speckhard and Khapta Akhmedova, "Black Widows and Beyond: Under-standing the Motivations and Life Trajectories of Chechen Female Terrorists," in *Female Terrorism and Militancy: Agency, Utility, and Organization* ed. Cindy D. Ness (New York: Routledge, 2008).

32. Anne Speckhard and Khapta Akhmedova, "Black Widows and Beyond: Under-standing the Motivations and Life Trajectories of Chechen Female Terrorists," in *Female Terrorism and Militancy: Agency, Utility, and Organization* ed. Cindy D. Ness (New York: Routledge, 2008), 100.

33. John Reuter, "Chechnya's Suicide Bombers: Desperate, Devout, or Deceived?" *The Jamestown Foundation*, August 23, 2004, accessed July 25, 2018, https://james town.org/report/chechnyas-suicide-bombers-desperate-devout-or-deceived/.

34. Anne Speckhard and Khapta Akhmedova, "Black Widows: The Chechen Female Suicide Terrorists," in *Female Suicide Bombers: Dying for Equality*, ed. Yoram Schweitzer (Tel Aviv: Jaffee Center for Strategic Studies, August 2006).

35. Anat Berko, *The Path to Paradise, The Inner World of Suicide Bombers and Their Dispatchers* (Westport, CT: Praeger Security International, 2007), 53.

36. Yossef Bodansky, *Chechen Jihad: al-Qaeda's Training Ground and the Next Wave of Terror* (New York: Harper Collins, 2007), 308.

37. Jessica Davis, *Women in Modern Terrorism: From Liberation Wars to Global Jihad and the Islamic State* (Lanham, MD: Rowman & Littlefield, 2017), 55.

38. Jessica Davis, *Women in Modern Terrorism: From Liberation Wars to Global Jihad and the Islamic State* (Lanham, MD: Rowman & Littlefield, 2017), 55.

39. Jessica Davis, *Women in Modern Terrorism: From Liberation Wars to Global Jihad and the Islamic State* (Lanham, MD: Rowman & Littlefield, 2017), 56.

40. Amos Harel, "First Known Female Hamas Bomb Maker Among Many Detainees," *Haaretz*, October 11, 2005, accessed August 22, 2018, https://www.haaretz.com/1.4877573.

41. Barbara Victor, *Army of Roses* (Emmaus, PA: Rodale, 2003), 112.

42. Robert A. Pape, *Dying to Win* (New York: Random House, 2005), Appendix 1.

43. Zachary Keck and Matthew Sparks, "The Shia Shift: Why Iran and Hezbollah Abandoned Martyrdom," *The National Interest*, May 28, 2018, accessed August 14, 2018, https://nationalinterest.org/feature/the-shia-shift-why-iran-hezbollah-aban doned-martyrdom-25992.

44. Mary Chastain, "List of Female Hezbollah Suicide Bombers Grows," *Breitbart*, August 18, 2013, accessed September 15, 2016, http://www.breitbart.com/national -security/2013/08/18/women-rise-in-hezbollah-still-not-equal-to-men/.

45. Zachary Keck and Matthew Sparks, "The Shia Shift: Why Iran and Hezbollah Abandoned Martyrdom," *The National Interest*, May 28, 2018, accessed August 14, 2018, https://nationalinterest.org/feature/the-shia-shift-why-iran-hezbollah-aban doned-martyrdom-25992.

46. Tiffany Ap, "What ISIS Wants from Women," *CNN*, November 20, 2105, accessed September 8, 2016, http://www.cnn.com/2015/11/20/europe/isis-role-of -women/.

47. Samuel Osbourne, "Isis Starts Using Female Fighters and Suicide Bombers for the First Time," *Independent*, February 29, 2016, accessed September 8, 2016, http:// www.independent.co.uk/news/world/africa/isis-starts-using-female-fighters-and-sui cide-bombers-for-the-first-time-a6903166.html.

48. Devianti Faridz, Euan McKirdy, and Eliza Mackintosh, "Three Families Were Behind the ISIS-Inspired Bombings in Indonesia's Surabaya, Police Said," CNN, May 15, 2018, accessed September 19, 2018, https://edition.cnn.com/2018/05/13/ asia/indonesia-attacks-surabaya-intl/index.html.

49. Robert A. Pape, *Dying to Win* (New York: Random House, 2005), 109–111.

50. Ariel Merari, *Driven to Death* (Oxford: Oxford University Press, 2010), 64–65.

51. Insite Blog on Terrorism and Extremism, "Translated Message From Zawahiri's Wife To Muslim Women," *Insite Blog on Terrorism and Extremism*, 2008, accessed September 19, 2018, http://news.siteintelgroup.com/blog/index.php/about us/21-jihad/227-translated-message-from-zawahiris-wife-to-muslim-women.

52. Katharina Von Knop, "The Female Jihad: Al Qaeda's Women," *Studies in Conflict and Terrorism* 30 (5) (2007): 397–414, 410.

53. Christopher Dickey, "The Role of Women in al-Qaeda," *Newsweek*, January 2, 2010, accessed August 9, 2018, https://www.newsweek.com/role-women-al -qaeda-70757.

54. Frances S. Hasso, "Discursive and Political Deployments by/of the 2002 Palestinian Women Suicide Bombers/Martyrs," *Feminist Review* 81 (2005): 23–51, 27.

55. Lori Allen, "There Are Many Reasons Why: Suicide Bombers and Martyrs in Palestine," *Middle East Report* 223 (Summer 2002): 34–37, 36.

56. Barbara Victor, *Army of Roses* (Emmaus, PA: Rodale, 2003).

57. Frances S. Hasso, "Discursive and Political Deployments by/of the 2002 Palestinian Women Suicide Bombers/Martyrs," *Feminist Review* 81 (2005): 23–51, 29.

58. Barbara Victor, *Army of Roses* (Emmaus, PA: Rodale, 2003), 262.

59. Barbara Victor, *Army of Roses* (Emmaus, PA: Rodale, 2003), 263.

60. Frances S. Hasso, "Discursive and Political Deployments by/of the 2002 Palestinian Women Suicide Bombers/Martyrs," *Feminist Review* 81 (2005): 23–51, 31.

61. Frances S. Hasso, "Discursive and Political Deployments by/of the 2002 Palestinian Women Suicide Bombers/Martyrs," *Feminist Review* 81 (2005): 23–51, 32.

Chapter Six

The Women of Cohar

Convicted Jihadist Terrorists in an Israeli Prison

In September 2017, I interviewed four women in a maximum-security prison in Israel; three women were part of a terrorist group and one woman was not affiliated with any group. These women had been sentenced for committing some act of terrorism by the Israeli government. It took over a year to gain access to these women including asking several academics for help at Israeli universities and asking several American political representatives, both in the United States' Congress and in the South Carolina Congress. In the end, a family member was able to get me access to these women through his connections in Israel. Gaining access entailed permission from the minister of public security in Israel, which is a cabinet level position for the prime minister in the Israeli government. The stipulations for access to these women were as follows: I was allowed twenty minutes with each woman and I could only speak with five women. When the interviews occurred, I was actually allotted over one hour with each woman. What follows in this chapter is an account of the raw interviews and research that I conducted with each of these women. The research question that I sought to answer in this chapter is, "What is the role of Islam in female terrorism?" The reader will find that my research uncovered much more than this question.

LITERATURE REVIEW

Since this research is the reporting of raw data (i.e., the results of interviews), there is not much that can be cited in reference to academic literature pertaining to this topic. Only a few journalists come to mind, concerning interview research with female terrorists. The first of the scholars is Eileen MacDonald.[1] An older book, *Shoot the Women First* was published in 1992 and is a collection of essays, containing the results of a few interviews with female terrorists such as Leila Khaled, the infamous Black September hijacker and leader, and Kim Hyon Yui, the North Korean airplane bomber. MacDonald's interviews are editorial in style as she is a British journalist by occupation. In her basic quest to explain and understand these women, MacDonald did not publish academic research but did add tremendously to data that had previously not existed. MacDonald was the first to start talking to female terrorists.

The next book concerning interview research was published by another journalist, Barbara Victor,[2] who was interested in publishing the stories of Palestinian women. Victor's book titled *Army of Roses* focuses on the individual stories of female terrorists in Palestinian groups but it is not comprehensive or analytical in nature, as Victor is also a journalist and author. Victor's contribution was also highly significant.

As time progressed, academics finally got involved in understanding and researching female terrorists. However, interviewing female terrorists and hearing their stories were part of the following academic research: Debra Zedalis,[3] Rosemarie Skaine,[4] Margaret Gonzalez-Perez,[5] Cindy Ness,[6] Julie Rajar,[7] and Mia Bloom[8] have all published important works on female suicide bombers and terrorists. Zedalis was literally the first to begin researching female terrorists, publishing a short article, which was later published into a mini-book. Zedalis is actually a military analyst by trade and not an academic, although her work "got the ball rolling" so to say in academia. Zedalis produced a short descriptive work on female suicide bombers.

Skaine, a sociologist, published a book on the profiles of female suicide bombers and researched why traditional female roles from Western societies affect consideration of women and violence throughout the world. Gonzalez-Perez looked at the participation of women in terrorist groups all over the world and the motivations for women to join these groups. Ness also published an edited book on the involvement of women in terrorist organizations concerning several topics with authors who had already published on female terrorism. Mia Bloom, in her book *Bombshell*, uses in-depth case studies to understand female motivation for committing suicide bombings. Bloom finds that women are motivated to commit suicide bombings as a result of revenge, redemption, relationship, and respect.[9] Rajan also published a book on female suicide bombers throughout the world titled *Women Suicide Bombers: Narratives of Violence*. Rajan's work focused on female suicide bombers through the lens of feminist research methodology.

In 2009, the research on female terrorism began to branch out more to focus on details rather than sweeping accounts of female terrorism. The data has come a long way allowing more academics to conduct comprehensive research on female terrorists. In their book *Women as Terrorists: Mothers, Recruiters, and Martyrs*, Cragin and Daly[10] look at female terrorism through the lens of three roles that women play in terrorist organizations. This book looks at terrorist organizations throughout the world.

Since MacDonald's first book was published in 1992, there have also been some journal articles and smaller publications that have been published on female terrorism, although none of these have used interview methodology. However, as can be seen from the literature encompassed in this literature review, very few works have used interviews and the personal stories of these female terrorists to understand the phenomenon of female terrorism. In addition, no one has written scholarship that has focused primarily on women in jihadist terrorist organizations. In fact, most jihadist terrorist organizations have been lumped together with the rest of the international terrorist organizations and research has failed to look at the religion of Islam as the primary variable. In today's society where jihadist terrorist attacks occur in Western cities on a weekly basis, academics can no longer afford to ignore Islam and jihadist organizations as a possible variable in international terrorism research. The next part of this chapter will focus on the methodology and research parameters used to conduct these interviews.

METHODOLOGY

To complete this research, I was required to go through the Institutional Review Board process at the University of South Carolina where I was given an exemption status to conduct my research. I was also instructed by the Institutional Research Board at the University of South Carolina to address the corresponding Institutional Research Board at an Israeli University. I chose to work with Ariel University. Ariel University then directed me to the Israeli Prison Services who were responsible for supervising the research that I conducted.

In order to do this research, I had to submit my interview questions ahead of time to the Israeli Prison Service (IPS). I also had to have consent forms for each of the women. The consent form was originally in Hebrew. I was fortunate that IPS has their own consent forms and I was not required to give information that might pose a security problem in the future. In addition, like the IPS form states, I am not allowed to give any identifying information such as the names of these women so that they can be identified. Therefore, all names used in conjunction with this research are pseudonyms.

The women chose whether they wanted to speak with me. These women were told by IPS that an American scholar was coming to Israel to speak with them about Palestinian women and the plight of these women. The women who were interested in speaking to me at the prison filled out consent forms. From a language perspective, these women all spoke very little English, so I had a young female Saudi Arabian translator with Israeli citizenship who could speak Hebrew, Arabic, and English. These women could leave the interview at any time and were not required to answer any questions they did not feel comfortable answering.

I was originally only supposed to receive twenty minutes with each of these women. When I did the interviews I was given over an hour with my translator to speak to these women and have them answer all the questions. Therefore, there will be some information concerning these women that will be included in this chapter that the interview questions do not address.

Originally I was allowed to speak with five women, but the women became hesitant after the first day when we began asking them what crime they committed. One woman backed out, which is why I was only able to interview four women. In compensation, IPS tried to get one more woman for me to speak with but no one else volunteered. According to IPS, the women feared that my publication may affect their legal trial or that I was with al-Mossad or Shin Bet. One of the women that I spoke with was the spokesperson for the Women's Prison. I implored her to assuage the fears of the fifth inmate so that we could speak with her, but the spokeswoman was not able to convince her to come speak with us.

The room that we were given to speak with these women in was approximately ten by ten feet. Three of the women were handcuffed and one of the women was not handcuffed. The differences for the reasons behind the handcuffs is unknown. A guard was located outside but was not in the room, and was not within hearing distance. The inmates were free to speak to us without fear of retaliation from a guard. My translator was seated facing the woman and I was seated behind my translator. We were not allowed to have any recording or filming devices. My translator and each woman would conduct the interview in Arabic without interruption. I would then proceed to ask questions in English, which would be translated by my translator between us after all of the official questions were asked. My translator took notes and we would spend at least one hour communicating what each prisoner stated immediately after each interview was over. I also took notes the whole time, writing down what I was able to understand and observe.

Results

The answers to the interview questions will be mostly provided in order of the questions, although there are times when the questions will get a little out of order or information will be added, according to context. As a side note, two of the women chose not to answer every question.

Case Study 1: Haajar

The first woman I spoke with (Haajar) was a member of the Popular Front for the Liberation of Palestine. As a note, Haajar would not answer every question she was given; she picked which questions she wanted to answer and would dodge the questions she did not want to answer. She was not feeling well when we met with her so perhaps this explains her lack of cooperation. Haajar was approximately fifty-four years and wore short sleeves and capri pants. She was a secular Sunni Muslim, which explains her involvement with the PFLP. Haajar had a bachelor's degree in mathematics and was originally a teacher. Originally from the Palestinian territories, she was serving an administrative detention sentence of six months for unknown reasons. She stated that she did not know why she was in administrative detention and IPS could not divulge her information to me. Most likely her involvement with the PFLP and her proselytizing of Palestinian girls had something to do with her sentence, as she stated that she mostly gave speeches and talked to young women.

Haajar admitted that she was a feminist and that her husband knew that when he married her. When I asked her if she thought she was equal to her husband, she responded that "I am equal to him, but he does not think I am equal to him." She stated that she wants an equal world with men and she wants an equal society where women have freedom. She stated that "Men use religion to control and in history, women are less than men." Haajar was very curious about my research and asked me several questions about whether I was solely looking at the Palestinian girls. She stated that "The Palestinian situation is different than the rest of the world. You cannot look at the situation of girls here as similar to other places."

From a familial standpoint, Haajar stated that her husband was not proud or embarrassed of her crime but that he just wanted her back home. He came to visit her with her children. She stated that her "Community is retarded. They will look at women as something to use, like an object." This might imply that her community was not in favor or proud of her actions as there seemed to be some friction there.

In response to terrorism, Haajar was against female terrorism and stated that "Palestinian women have only respect for their selves and life." She had never heard of Leila Khaled or Wafa Idris, which was very surprising considering her age and sentence. Haajar was also against male and female suicide bombings. She also mentioned that she did not support ISIS or the situation in Syria. "I do not like terrorist people committing suicide bombings in the name of Islam." Haajar defined terrorism as "killing people without the right to kill." Haajar stated that she did not think that politics and religion should be mixed together.

Case Study 2: Zaheen

Zaheen is a thirty-year-old mother of three with kind light brown eyes. She comes in wearing a niqab and is dressed completely in black. After the door is mostly closed, she will lower the cover over her mouth to speak with both of us women but when someone passes or makes a noise, she will recover her mouth. Zaheen is a Sunni Muslim with a high school education with a few years of college. She has three children and is originally from the West Bank in the Palestinian territories. She speaks with her hands and is pleasant to talk to.

Zaheen was convicted of belonging to ISIS. Both her and her husband who was an ISIS fighter migrated to Iraq where he fought for ISIS for fourteen months (was also in Turkey two to three months) and she worked as a nurse in the ISIS hospital (for two months). Both left of their own free will to join ISIS so that they could live under an Islamic caliphate. Zaheen joined ISIS and was recruited from YouTube videos. She stated that she saw many people joining ISIS from the United States, Great Britain, and Switzerland. She is obviously a very religious person and believes that all Muslims should live in an Islamic State under Sharia Law. ISIS paid her 200 dollars per month as a salary but this was not always consistent.

Besides being a nurse for two months in an ISIS hospital, which Zaheen did to take care of her pregnant friend, she did little else in ISIS. Since ISIS is a very patriarchal organization, women were primarily in the home taking care of the children and the household. Zaheen took her three children with her to Iraq. Zaheen did state that she would rarely see any women. In ISIS, Zaheen stated that she was not treated well generally. She was not allowed to move freely and was often criticized if she went out by herself, although she stated that she ignored the criticism and went about her business. Zaheen stated that most men were respectful towards her. She rarely met other women as most women stayed in the house. Zaheen and her husband were not happy in ISIS and eventually borrowed the money to return home from Zaheen's parents.

She stated that she was actually surprised as to how bad it was in Iraq and Mosul. Every time her and her husband tried to leave, ISIS accused him of being a spy, which would mean certain death. Eventually they escaped.

Zaheen saw many Yazidi Christian slaves including the slave market where these slaves were bought and sold. She believed that these Yazidi people were not people of the book as they "were praying for fire." However, she was against slavery. She said that she could see "sadness in everyone's eyes, in slaves [Yazidi Christians] and in citizens. Most men use slaves for their sex lives." They would get these sex slaves pregnant and then marry them. She mentioned that many Arab men came for the sex slaves although Saudi Arabians were predominately there for the sex slaves. However, Zaheen's husband would not have a slave in their household nor did he want a second wife. The two are still married and appear to be very much in love from her perspective. She stated that she is the only woman whose husband had stayed with her while she is in prison. Her husband is also currently in prison.

In regards to her family, Zaheen's parents would not speak to her for a long time after she returned and would not visit her in prison although they are caring for her three children. Her community also rejected her and would not visit her. Her mother is not religious and both parents were against her joining ISIS. Her children come to visit her. The girls in prison sometimes treat her well but define her as a traitor because she went to Iraq instead of staying home to fight for Palestine. Zaheen believes Palestine should have freedom but they are going about it in the wrong way. There appeared to be some friction in the prison community regarding her relationship with ISIS.

In regards to terrorism, Zaheen stated that she was against it and everything having to do with it. She stated that "Killing innocent people is wrong and is not written in the Quran. To do it in the name of Islam is wrong." She did not think it was right to kill people in anger or for one's country.

As a side note concerning the Yazidi Christians, Zaheen told a story about how she heard a Yazidi slaves screaming one night so she asked her husband to help the girl. Her husband took the slave girl and gave her to a friend and last they heard, the girl was "well taken care of." Many of the girls that Zaheen saw were very young that were used as sex slaves.

Case Study 3: Rameen

Rameen was a twenty-three-year-old single woman, who appeared shy and nervous. Single and without any children, Rameen was once engaged to a man who jilted her after she went to prison. She did not belong to any group and was extremely difficult to talk with. She only had a high school education and is a Sunni Muslim. She wore an al-Amira that consisted of flowers in turquoise, black, and purple. She would refuse to answer interview questions but then would refuse to leave. She would go back and forth about answering the questions and it was almost like she was a child playing a game with us.

Rameen was accused of stabbing an IDF man. He in turn shot her several times where she was forced to undergo numerous surgeries. Rameen did not entirely admit to her crime. In reference to her family, Rameen did not want to talk about them and even got angry when we asked why her fiancé left her. We were left with the impression that her fiancé put her up to the stabbing and then left after she was put into prison. We also thought that her family was very hard on her, perhaps even physically abusive. She was naïve concerning social media and the world and was extremely sheltered. Her community viewed her as a hero for the stabbing and she loves her community. Rameen also stated that she was happy in prison.

In reference to the questions concerning terrorism, Rameen stated that "All Jews should leave Palestine." She stated that "Palestinians need to do everything to make Palestine theirs again." She believed that "Arabs should kill Jews." Rameen supported suicide bombings "if it is to kill Jews."

In regards to feminism, Rameen was not a feminist. She does not fight for nor does she believe in the rights of women. She believes that women should stay with their families. She believed that the Quran was "our book" and it describes what women can do and what men can do. It also states what women should do.

In the end, Rameen gave us enough information to understand her. I cannot define her as a terrorist as she did not belong to any group nor did she attack any noncombatants. Although she stabbed an Israeli soldier, this was an act of war that young Palestinian children have been doing for about the past decade. The stabbing of Israeli soldier has become a fad in the Palestinian territories. Rameen is most likely a product of her environment. Raised in a conservative Muslim family with a dominating, perhaps abusive father, she follows the roles prescribed for her in the Quran and believes in the same things as her radical Islamic family. Although her ideology is quite possibly in line with terrorism, her actions are not.

Case Study 4: Yelda

The last lady we spoke with (Yelda) was actually the spokeswoman for the prison. Had we spoke with her first, we might have been able to speak with the fifth inmate. However, this information was not given to us until later. Yelda wore an al-Amira with hot pink and light pink flowers all over it. She was the only prisoner that did not wear any handcuffs. We had to give her all of the questions ahead of time before she would answer anything. Once this was done, she became quite loquacious. She then proceeded to question me about my research and what I thought about the Israelis bulldozing the homes of Palestinian terrorists. She is thirty-three years old and is married with four kids. She is a Sunni Muslim with only a high school education from the West Bank Palestinian territories.

Yelda was put in prison for trying to carry out a suicide bombing attack for Hamas, although she is not a member of Hamas. Yelda is a member of the Palestinian Islamic Jihad. She was caught with a bomb strapped on her while posing as a pregnant Jewish women with four men from Hamas escorting her. When asked, Yelda stated that she was never going to commit suicide and bomb Israelis but that her goal was to place her bomb under a bus of IDF soldiers and walk away. However, she also stated that Palestinians are blowing themselves up because they are so miserable in Palestine as they have no jobs, no education, and no future. "Martyrdom is a way to get to heaven and have one's sins forgiven," she stated. It is doubtful that she was not trying to commit suicide considering this last statement.

Yelda stated that the Quran agreed with what she did. "We have to fight against all that take land that is not their land (crusaders)." "We need to fight Israel until we get our land back." Yelda stated that she respected the Jewish quest for a homeland. She believes that Palestine should be composed of the old Palestine, before the British arrived. She would meet women in the group every two weeks to socialize and talk about religion. These women were friends of hers.

Yelda stated that the men in PIJ treated her well and the men from Hamas who tried to make her a suicide bomber were always respectful towards her. They are now full of remorse for their actions towards her. Yelda joined the PIJ because they had the same ideas as she did and same goals.

In reference to her religious community, Yelda stated they did not care about what she did and were not accepting of her. She stated that she "hates her community in West Bank as it does not give women a chance to live their lives." Her father supported her, whatever she did, but did not say whether he accepted her actions. Yelda's mother is afraid for her and still denies that her daughter could be a suicide bomber. In reference to Yelda's husband, he was aware that Yelda belonged to PIJ but was not supportive of it. He also was not aware of her suicide bombing attempt nor does he even want to talk to her about it. He views it as something that is in the past and just wants her to come home. He has stayed with her this entire time.

Yelda stated that a female terrorist is something that is created by the community. "Women are kind creatures and good, and will never do something terrible like terrorism. Men make women terrorists. They are the creators of female terrorists." Yelda is against both male and female suicide bombings and now regrets her actions. Her definition of terrorism is "going and killing innocent people without really fighting for something."

As a side note, Yelda views herself as a feminist. She believed that women should be foot soldiers and leaders in politics or organizations if they wanted to. "Women can be raised to be leaders." She stated that women have no rights in the world and that women deserve rights. She stated that there should be companies or organizations to help women achieve rights. "Women think with their heart but can think with their brain. Women are more diplomatic than men and can decide and do better with the world than men." In her definition of feminism, Yelda stated that "Islam respects women and gives her all her rights."

DISCUSSION

In Table 6.1: The Women of Cohar, the results from the interviews are displayed and I will discuss the highlights of the interviews in the following section. I have found that three of these women were treated well by the women in their group. The fourth, Rameen, was not part of any group. The women were also treated well by the men in their group. Although Yelda was recruited by members of Hamas to be a suicide bomber, they apparently treated her well although one would think that recruiting her for a suicide bombing is not great treatment. However, Yelda did not have any opinion regarding this except to state that the men were "very sorry for their actions."

I have looked at whether community and family have accepted the actions of the daughter or friend. In previous research, I have found that unsuccessful suicide bombers such as Yelda were rejected by their communities while unsuccessful male suicide bombers were accepted and even portrayed as a hero despite their inability to get the job done. The only woman who was accepted by her community for her actions was Rameen as she was successful in stabbing the Israeli soldier. In the past decade, there has been a tremendous increase in young Palestinian women stabbing male IDF soldiers. A lot of these girls are too young, mostly in the early teens, to make any intelligent decisions. Most likely family or friends put them up to the stabbing. This is probably what happened in Rameen's situation. Most of the women were not accepted by their family or community for their actions. This may be due to the strong stigma of female honor bearing for the family in Muslim society. Haajar was accepted by her family but she is a lot older, most likely a grandmother at this point, so she has some power in the family. Most of them except for Rameen were also feminists and strong women; perhaps the patriarchal society of Palestine is also the reason for their rejections or ostracism from society.

Table 6.1: The Women of Cohar

Name	Group	Age	Married?	Kids?	Sect	Feminist	College	Family	Community	Repentant	Role
Haajar	PFLP	54	Yes	Yes	Sunni	Yes (Islam)	BA Math	Accept	Reject	No	Secretary
Zaheen	ISIS	30	Yes	Yes	Sunni	Yes (Islam)	1-2 Years	Reject	Reject	No	Domestic
Rameen	NA	23	No-Fiancée	No	Sunni	No	High School	Reject	Accept	Yes?	Disposable
Yelda	HAMAS/PIJ	33	Yes	Yes	Sunni	Yes (Islam)	High School	Reject	Reject	Yes	Disposable

Ironically every woman said they were against terrorism and suicide bombers, whether male or female, yet when I probed deeper, the answers got a lot
more complicated. Haajar said that "terrorism was killing people without a
reason." People could only kill if they had a right to. Zaheen stated that "Killing innocent people is wrong and is not written in the Quran. To do it in the
name of Islam is wrong." Rameen did not believe that what the Palestinian
people did on any level could be called terrorism. Yelda proceeded to ask if
I thought Israel committed state terrorism against the Palestinians during our
interview. She stated that "Terrorism is going and killing innocent people
without fighting for something." She believed that ISIS should help Palestine
and should be there fighting for the Palestinians. Obviously, these women's
definitions of terrorism are not the same as a Western definition of terrorism. These women view the Palestinians as revolutionaries who are working
towards the independence of Palestine, regardless of the morality of their
methods. The radical views of people who join terrorist organizations are
definitely present in their responses although they were trying to make their
answers as politically correct as possible for me.

   Another thing that is interesting about these women is that they are not
highly educated, except for Hajaar. The rest of these women only had a few
years of college or a high school education. Lack of education can lead to a
lot of prejudice. Most of these Palestinian women had never met a Jew or an
Israeli before prison, so they had these preconceived prejudices about Israelis
before they committed their attacks. In Israel, the Israelis and Jews are kept
apart for security reasons so prejudice and hate is allowed to flourish. Israel
also has a much higher standard of living and is a wealthier country while
Palestine is extremely poor in many parts. The author thinks that a lot of these
women were racist/prejudiced against Jews before prison and formed a different view after prison as their guards were usually Jewish Israeli men and
women. All of these women, except for Haajar, were sorry for their actions.
Perhaps one way to solve problems in Israel is to expose Israelis and Palestinians to one another at an early age so as to alleviate prejudice and hatred that
is perpetrated in the community.

   In another interesting twist, many of these women showed regret for their
actions. Zaheen, Rameen, and Yelda all made sure to express regret for their
actions. Haajar refused to admit to anything and pretended that she was clue-
less as to why she was in prison. These admissions of guilt resonate with the
work of Yoram Schweitzer who found in interviews with female Palestinian
terrorists that:

   Most prominent was the women's contradictory versions of their stories, and
   the general effect that collective time with fellow prisoners had on their auto-

biographies. This aspect emerged especially in the personal interviews but in some of the media interviews as well, conducted in the earlier stages of their imprisonment, before they were briefed by their domineering cellmates. In these personal interviews, the women expressed a strong feeling that their difficult personal situation had been exploited to lead them to volunteer for their mission, without their having fully thought through the deed they planned to commit. In contrast, personal remarks were generally absent from the media interviews conducted with them after they had already spent time in prison. The latter interviews were primarily products of an indoctrination process, formal or informal, in prison. They bore a dominant nationalistic character, and reflected the uniform dogmatic messages that the organizations wish to deliver.[11]

Schweitzer makes the important point that the stories concerning the motivations of female terrorists change once the women have spent some time in prison. The culture in prison forces the women to change their stories or outlooks. The last woman that the author spoke with was the spokeswoman for the woman's prison. It was evident that she was a leader and that the other women did as she said. One does have to wonder whether the prison culture had forced these women to change their outlooks and stories concerning their imprisonment.

In this book, I theorize that jihadist terrorist organizations stereotypically use women in at least three capacities. I use the terms the disposable, the domestic, and the secretary to describe these roles. The disposable refers to the use of women as suicide bombers, a throwaway weapon, with little cost. The domestic refers to the use of women in Islamic terrorist organizations as the sex slaves, supporters, child care providers, or wives of men who go off to battle. Women may be forced into these positions like in ISIS or al-Qaeda where women are used as brides for new recruits. These are traditional Muslim female love and support roles. Lastly, the secretary role refers to women performing clerical duties such as reproducing propaganda, taking notes, or transporting weapons for male terrorists in the organizations. Another word for this role could be the logistician or even recruiter.

In my interviews at the prison, each woman neatly fits into these roles. Both Rameen and Yelda fulfilled the disposable role as they both were sent on a mission to martyr themselves for Islam. Zaheen fulfills the domestic role as she is the wife of an ISIS fighter and mother to ISIS children who will be raised to live in an Islamic State. Haajar, the most educated and distinguished of the four women, fulfills the propagandizing recruiting component.

CONCLUSION

In conclusion, this research demonstrates that there is a lot to be learned from speaking to convicted female terrorists in person. As social scientists, we spend a lot of time trying to understand the motivations of others and, at times, we may put words in other people's mouths or falsely attribute something to them. Even the word "terrorist" applies a label to a person regardless of aims or motivations. The author can say that she was not surprised by anything that she learned as the research she has read and completed was in line with the interviews. However, these women deserved to be heard in their own words.

Several things were learned from completing this research such as the differences between Israeli and Palestinian reporting of a crime. Most of the time what the Israelis publish regarding a person and what Palestinians in the prison watches publish are two very different stories. The prisoner would not always admit to either story so things can get confusing. However, since these women were imprisoned for their crimes, it is highly likely that the Israelis had evidence in their convictions.

In addition, the women were scared when the author asked them what crime they had committed. A few of the women thought that the author would contribute to their guilt at their trials when this research was published or their statements would be a published admission of guilt. A few others thought that the author was doing undercover work for Shin Bet or al-Mossad. For future reference for any researcher, an investigator should not ask prisoners about their crimes in these situations unless necessary and what is published about the women should be used to answer that question.

NOTES

1. Eileen MacDonald, *Shoot the Women First* (New York: Random House, 1992).

2. Barbara Victor, *Army of Roses* (Emmaus, PA: Rodale, 2003).

3. Debra D. Zedalis, *Female Suicide Bombers* (Honolulu, Hawaii: University of the Pacific, 2004).

4. Rosemarie Skaine, *Female Suicide Bombers* (Jefferson, NC: McFarland & Company, 2006), 143.

5. Margaret Gonzalez-Perez, *Women and Terrorism: Female Activity in Domestic and International Terror Groups* (New York: Routledge, 2008).

6. Cindy D. Ness, ed., *Female Terrorism and Militancy: Agency, Utility, and Organization* (New York: Routledge, 2008).

7. V. G. Julie Rajan, *Women Suicide Bombers: Narratives of Violence* (New York: Routledge 2011).

8. Mia Bloom, *Bombshell* (Philadelphia: Penn State University Press, 2011).

9. Mia Bloom, *Bombshell* (Philadelphia: Penn State University Press, 2011), 235.

10. R Kim Cragin and Sara A. Daly, *Women as Terrorists: Mothers, Recruiters, and Martyrs* (Santa Barbara, CA: Praeger Security International, 2009).

11. Yoram Schweitzer, "Palestinian Female Suicide Bombers: Reality vs. Myth" in *Female Suicide Terrorism*, ed. Yoram Schweitzer (Tel Aviv: Jaffe Center Publications, 2006), 25–41, 31.

Chapter Seven

Female Home-Grown and Emigrant Terrorism in the United States

When women give in to the desire to trash convention by the sensational rejection of a role they never chose for themselves, but was assigned to them by those who wrote their history, they are destined to suffer a tremendous loss of identity. They find themselves in a place that does not recognize their differences and problems, and they discover that they no longer understand themselves or other women ("women in armed struggle do not understand women they are estranged from being women, through militancy . . . they can become perfectly autonomous, but they do it by radically negating themselves"—Franceschini, 1988).[1] Here, in armed subversion, we find that the risk of an extreme search for supplementarity between men and women is laid out in an extreme manner. When the qualitative difference, which is essential because it renders the two sexes complementary, reaches extreme levels, it ends up erasing every difference and, thus, all tension towards the other. Women in armed struggle become totally interchangeable with their comrades in arms, physically and psychologically.[2]

Since 2001, only 7 percent of terrorist attacks have been committed by women in the United States. The other 93 percent were committed by men. That being said, every terrorist attack that has been committed by women in the United States has been committed by women in jihadist terrorist organizations. According to *New America*,[3] the following women were involved in terrorist attacks or were charged with some type of terroristic activity. This information is listed by year in Table 7.1: Female Home-grown and Emigrant Terrorism in the United States, 2001–2018.

Table 7.1: Female Home-grown and Emigrant Terrorism in the United States, 2001–2018.

Year	Name	Conversion to Islam?	Tactic/Charge
2001	-		-
2002	1. October Martinique Lewis (Portland Seven)	1. Afghan born Muslim	1. Joining and financing al-Qaeda
2003	-	-	-
2004	-	-	-
2005	-	-	-
2006	-	-	-
2007	-	-	-
2008	1. Aafia Siddiqui	1. Pakistani born Muslim	1. Attempted murder/ assault US personnel (Courier and financier for al-Qaeda)
2009	1. Jihad Jane (Colleen Renee LaRose or Fatima LaRose)	1. American born convert	1. Conspiracy to commit murder and providing support to terrorists
2010	1. Jamie Paulin-Ramirez (Jihad Jane II)	1. American born convert	1. Conspiracy to commit murder and providing support to terrorists
	2. Nima Ali Yusuf (Minnesota Shabaab)	2. Somalian born Muslim	2, 3, and 4. Financing and recruiting for al-Shabaab
	3. Hawo Hassan (Minnesota Shabaab)	3. Somalian born Muslim	
	4. Amina Ali (Minnesota Shabaab)	4. Somalian born Muslim	
	5. Nadia Rockwood (King Salmon Alaska Plot)	5. British born Muslim Convert	5. Lying to the FBI
	6. Prosovia Kampire Nzabanita (South Park Threat)	6. Ugandan born Muslim	6. Plea bargain, had to leave US
2011	1. Oytun Ayse Mihalik	1. Turkish born Muslim	1. Provided aid to terrorists and sent back to Turkey
2012	-	-	-
2013	1. Saynab Abdirashid Hussein	1. Somalian born Muslim	1. Lying under oath

Table 7.1: Female Home-grown and Emigrant Terrorism in the United States, 2001–2018. (con't.)

Year	Name	Conversion to Islam?	Tactic/Charge
2014	1. Amina Mohamud Esse (Shabaab Funding)	1. Somalian born Muslim	1. Funding a terrorist organization
	2. Muna Osman Jama (Shabaab Funding)	2. Somalian born Muslim	2. Funding a terrorist organization
	3. Hinda Osman Dhirane (Shabaab Funding)	3. Somalian born Muslim	3. Funding a terrorist organization
	4. Daniela Greene	4. American born convert	4. FBI agent married ISIS fighter
	5. Shannon Maureen Conley	5. American born convert	5. Tried to marry an ISIS fighter and provide money
	6. Yusra Ismail	6. Kenyan born with Somalia ties	6. Went to Syria to marry ISIS fighter
	7. Heather Elizabeth Coffman	7. American born covert	7. Tried to go to Turkey to marry an ISIS fighter
2015	1. Keona Thomas	1. American born convert	1. Tried to marry an ISIS fighter
	2. Sedina Unkic Hodkic	2. Bosnian born Muslim	2, 3, and 4. Sending money and supplies to ISIS
	3. Mediha Medy Salkicevic	3. Bosnian born Muslim	
	4. Jasminka Ramic	4. Bosnian born Muslim	
	5. Tashfeen Malik	**5. Pakistani born Muslim**	**5. San Bernardino Shooting, killed 14 people, wounded 22**
	6. Asia Siddiqui	6. Saudi Arabian Muslim	6. Conspiracy to commit and attack a police funeral
	7. Noelle Valentzas	7. American born convert	7. Conspiracy to commit and attack a police funeral
	8. Jaelyn Deishaun Young	8. American born convert	8. Tried to join ISIS with husband

(continued)

Table 7.1: Female Home-grown and Emigrant Terrorism in the United States, 2001–2018. (con't.)

Year	Name	Conversion to Islam?	Tactic/Charge
2016	1. Safya Roe Yassin	1. American born convert	1. Threatening communication across state lines
	2. Michelle Marie Bastian	2. American born (conversion unknown), husband is American born convert	2. Gave imprisoned husband bomb-making and ISIS materials
	3. Marie Castelli	3. American born convert	3. ISIS propagandist
2017	1. Zoobia Shahnaz	1. Pakistani born Muslim	1. Funding ISIS, money laundering
2018	1. Tnuza J. Hassan	1. American born Muslim	1. Arson, trying to join al-Qaeda, the Taliban, or al Shabab
	2. Waheba Issa Dais	2. Palestinian Muslim	1. ISIS propagandist
	3. Samantha El-Hassani	3. American born convert	3. Joined ISIS

As can be seen in the Table 7.1, there is some variation among jihadist female terrorists in the United States. This chapter looks at the similarities and differences between American home-grown female jihadists and American emigrant jihadists. Home-grown jihadists are women who are American citizens that were either born in the United States or received American citizenship. These women may be Muslim from birth or they may have converted to Islam shortly before they committed their crime. They are committing terrorist attacks or performing terroristic actions in the United States.

The American emigrant jihadists are women who have left the United States and are American citizens who join terrorist organizations. These women are often called foreign fighters, although they never fight but are important components in recruitment and support. We are primarily referring to ISIS members concerning these women. These women may also be born in the United States and have converted to Islam or may be women who have earned American citizenship and were born Muslim in another country. The next section will analyze similarities and differences among home-grown female jihadists.

Home-grown Female Jihadists

As the reader will remember, in chapter 1, the author quoted Wafa Sultan, Syrian Muslim critic and former Muslim, who stated,

> No one can be a true Muslim and a true American simultaneously. Islam is both a religion and a state. A true Muslim does not acknowledge the U.S. Constitution, and his willingness to live under that constitution is, as far as he is concerned, nothing more than an unavoidable step on the way to that constitution's replacement by Islamic Sharia Law.[4]

Sultan is referring to the United States' democracy in the previous quote. However, the author advocates that this quote is getting at something larger in that jihadists are unable to live peacefully in any country that is not under Sharia Law. That includes dictatorships, democracies, monarchies, oligarchies, etc. In fact, many jihadists will advocate that leaders who are anti-Islam or are not practicing Muslims (in their opinion) deserve death. Like one ISIS member in Indonesia, Dian Yulia Novi, said, "A Muslim is not a true adherent of Islam if they follow a political leader such as a president."[5] The reason for this is that Muslims are compelled in Islam to live under Sharia Law. According to jihadists, any Muslim who does not live under Sharia Law is not a true practicing Muslim.

Therefore, American Muslims are in some sense apostates according to jihadist interpretation. To solve this problem, they must either convert the political system they live under into a theocracy controlled by Sharia Law (or die trying) or they must emigrate to a Muslim country that is controlled by Sharia Law. Umm Layth, an ISIS propagandist, argued, if they cannot make it to the battlefield, "to bring the battlefield to yourself."[6] The establishment of the caliphate by ISIS is the best option for every jihadist and this explains the massive number of Muslims emigrating from all over the world to the caliphate located in Iraq and Syria under ISIS control.

In the last decade, Western countries in particular have received an onslaught of terrorist attacks from home-grown jihadists who are trying to change Western countries like the United States and advocate a legal system of Sharia Law. In his book *Islamist Terrorism in Europe*,[7] senior research fellow at the Norwegian Defense Research Establishment Peter Nesser documented terrorist attacks in Europe from groups such as al-Qaeda, the GIA, Af-Pak, and other terrorist organizations. In all, Nesser looked at attacks from thirty-nine different terrorist organizations. He argues that Europe has not received a lot of attention in Jihadi ideology as Europeans are not the main target of jihadists. Although he did not particularly specify which country is the main target, it is probable that the United States is the primary target.

Nesser also found that Europe is a sanctuary for jihadists who travel to war zones to fight in the Middle East and North African region (MENA) due to European proximity. Lastly, he states that jihadists who live in non-Muslim countries cannot harm those who provide protection according to Islamic religious texts, although this stipulation has been violated several times.

In his research, Nesser also provides a typology of four terrorist cell members. First there is the entrepreneur, who is crucial for the cell to take action. They are religious-political activists who have a strong sense of justice. They are the planners and leaders of the cell and are always foreign fighters. The second type is the protégé who is subordinate to the entrepreneur. The protégé is concerned with injustice against Muslims and is inclined to act for that reason in addition to their admiration for the entrepreneur. The misfit is the next category and these people are usually victims of personal misfortune. They are not as ideologically informed and may have a criminal record. They radicalize out of loyalty to friends or family or to deal with personal problems. The drifter is the final typology as they are people who join a terrorist cell to fulfill social commitments or get societal rewards. They end up in the cell because of some type of social tie. Cells must always contain the entrepreneurs but the other characters are optional.[8] This book predominately contains research based on terrorist organizations and Nesser's research is completely based on terrorist cells. Since jihadist terrorist organizations do not exist in the United States, at least with any membership numbers that are significant, the terrorist cells who are the extension of terrorist organizations can be analyzed. Therefore, Nesser's research is helpful to a certain point although Nesser does not specifically apply his research to women.

However, two of Nesser's personality types may pertain to women. As discussed throughout the book, the entrepreneur type cannot be applied to women as women in jihadist groups are not leaders or planners. The protégé role cannot be applied to women as women are not second in command nor could a male entrepreneur develop a good relationship with a Muslim woman who is not his wife or close family member like what occurs in the protégé type. The misfit might be a possible typology for a woman in a jihadist terrorist cell although it is highly unlikely that any jihadist woman would have a criminal record, which Nesser states is typical for this personality type. The misfit type does tend to have a weaker and more hesitant personality, which fits many jihadist women. Misfits also radicalize due to loyalty to family and friends or to deal with a personal problem, which again applies to jihadist women. The last type, the drifter, can also possibly be tied to female jihadists as these people lack a strong agenda and they are fulfilling social commitments or obtaining social rewards by joining a jihadist group. Drifters can be at the wrong place at the wrong time and can get caught up in the moment, thus they are suddenly part of a terrorist organization.

Going back to Table 7.1 and looking at the women described in it, it is important to notice that many of these women are playing supportive roles or the domestic roles in these organizations and they are similar to the women that have been explained throughout this book. The domestic role includes providing funding or support for men in jihadist organizations and include women like Amina Mohamud Esse, Muna Osman Jama, and Hinda Osman Dhirane who were convicted of sending money to al-Shabaab throughout Internet chat rooms in Minneapolis.[9] Or Zoobia Shahnaz who laundered and gave over 150,000 dollars to ISIS and was caught trying to catch a flight to Pakistan. It is likely that a brief stint in Jordan as a volunteer for the Syrian American Medical Society in January 2016 helped to further radicalize Shahnaz.[10]

The most controversial female jihadist is Tashfeen Malik (in bold in Table 7.1), who was one of the San Bernardino shooters, along with her husband Rizwan Farook. The terrorist attack occurred on December 2, 2015, in San Bernardino, California. The couple shot and killed fourteen people and wounded twenty-two others. Tashfeen was born in Pakistan and was also radicalized in Pakistan. Online chat rooms helped to complete her transformation into a jihadist terrorist. She was raised in Saudi Arabia by a conservative Sunni family and would read al-Qaeda writings online. During the shooting spree, the couple pledged their loyalty to ISIS and Abu Bakr al-Baghdadi, the caliph of ISIS on Facebook. The pair were found by the police a few hours after the shootings and opened fire; they were subsequently killed in the shootout.[11] The pair did not worry about the young daughter they had orphaned as a result of their shooting spree.

Although she does fit into the domestic role as both a wife and mother, the foot soldier actions of Tashfeen do not fit into any role. She is the only foot soldier that the author has been able to find although she is technically part of a terrorist cell, not a terrorist organization. Perhaps there are more roles for women in terrorist cells living in Western countries. Muslims living in Western countries are subjected to stricter laws regarding the treatment of women and the West is much more progressive concerning the treatment of women. It is logical since Tashfeen was part of a terrorist cell in a Western nation that she was able to transcend the defined roles that women have in jihadist terrorist organizations. In addition, it is highly unlikely that she had any contact or affirmation with ISIS to commit her terrorist attack. Her husband most likely had a lot of influence over her actions. Although the couple publicly declared their loyalty to ISIS, that does not mean that ISIS accepted and confirmed their membership. Technically the pair acted as lone wolves.

In Figure 7.1: Female Jihadist Attacks by Place of Birth (US), 2001–2018, American born female jihadists versus foreign born female jihadists are presented. From 2001 to 2018 there are approximately fourteen American born female jihadists and eighteen foreign born female jihadists. It is evident that there have been more terrorist actions/attacks from jihadist women born in other countries who immigrated to the United States and earned their citizenship. It is also evident that American born female jihadists who convert to Islam are on the rise. With the creation of ISIS, is it apparent that American converts to Islam were inspired by ISIS, mostly through Internet radicalization, and many decided to make their jihad. In the next section, American emigrant jihadists will be discussed.

The American Emigrant Jihadists

In his book *Words Are Weapons*, philosopher Philippe-Joseph Salazar makes an enlightening argument about Muslim women who have journeyed to Iraq or Syria to seek the establishment of the caliphate under ISIS. He states that this decision is at odds with Islam for three reasons. 1) Like Muhammad when he left Mecca for Medina, these women are typically journeying from Western nations to live under the caliphate. They are leaving their homes to live with a community of believers where the universality of Islam has been established. They are throwing off the immorality of the Western nation.

The woman that decides to return, modeling herself on the earliest emigrant women who undertook their *hegira* at the time of the foundation of Mohammedanism, is defying or shattering her family ties; there is no need for the consent or the accompaniment of her husband, her father, or her

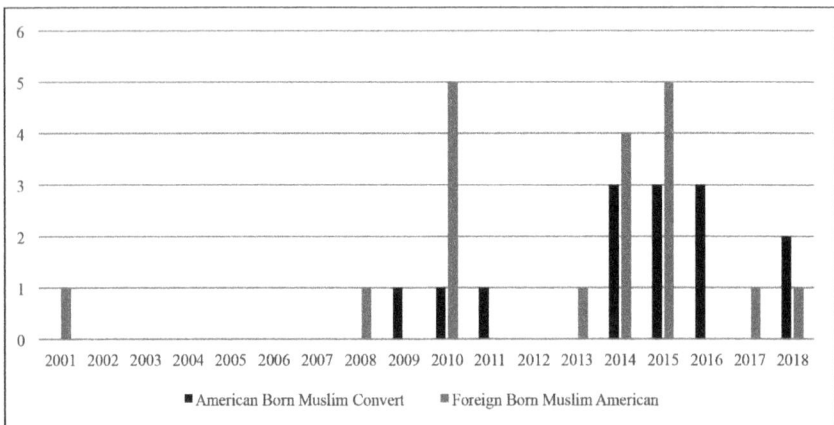

Figure 7.1.   Female Jihadist Attacks by Place of Birth. *Source*: Author

brother-or any male relative.[12] 2) By leaving on her own, the Muslim woman is asserting rights over her body, even if she is leaving while pregnant. She can rest assured that if she loses her baby on her journey it will be buried in the land of Allah. 3) The Muslim woman who leaves also declares herself to be a slave of Allah, which gives her the right to admonish the men who have not yet left to live under the caliphate. These men are only half men if they choose to criticize or block women who emigrate to live under the caliphate.[13]

The need for Muslim women to leave and live under the Islamic caliphate literally pokes Islam in the eye and defies the restrictions placed on women. However, the women's reasons are difficult for Muslims to question. Besides the motivation to live under the Islamic caliphate, the romance of jihad also calls many Muslims home. Ahlam al-Nasr is literally known as "The Poetess of the Islamic State." Al-Nasr was most likely born in Damascus and married Abu Usama al-Gharib, who is a major propagandist for ISIS. Al-Nasr writes jihadist poetry that has inspired many Muslims to make their jihad or to marry a jihadist. Al-Nasr's first book *Blaze of Truth* was published online and is often sung in propagandist videos. Since it is illegal to use musical instruments, Muslims will sing poetry. Al-Nasr has praised Abu Bakr al-Baghdadi, the caliph of ISIS, and she has also described the romantic life of living and cooking for a jihadist. Although al-Nasr's poetry is popular among jihadists, there are many Muslim poets who praise jihad and the lifestyle. Osama bin Laden would quote jihadist poetry in his talks and would also look for poets among his men.[14]

Besides the romantic poetry, which is enticing, there is also the medieval sexual atmosphere of jihad, which appeals to young jihadists, including women. The handsome young Arab men are often portrayed training like soldiers without shirts in recruiting videos. The poetry with drums is being chanted in the background. The adventure of war and death is in the air and when they are not fighting, jihadists are reciting poetry or swimming. Paradise is talked about ad nauseam and imagined. Every women can find a husband.[15] Women are promised a life of ease where they are treated like sultanas by their husbands. The family is first and Muslim men are responsible for providing for their families. Children are gifts that are to be cared for. Women will speak of the respect they earned from their Muslim brothers and the ease of their lifestyles. The entire atmosphere of jihad is meant to recruit and sustain young men and women to the movement.

In the United States, (referring to Table 7.1: Female Home-grown and Emigrant Terrorism in the United States, 2001–2018) women have tried to marry ISIS fighters and were caught before or soon after they left, such as

Shannon Maureen Conley or the FBI agent Daniela Greene. These stories also fall under the domestic role of wife and sexual jihad where women go to provide sexual comfort and domestic chores for jihad men. Conley, at age nineteen, is an American born Muslim convert who tried to travel to Turkey to marry her fiancé Yousr Mouelhi whom she met in an Internet chat room. After taking first-aid and firearms training, she planned to join ISIS and work as a nurse.[16] She was recruited by a housewife on the Internet who was married to an ISIS fighter.[17]

The FBI agent Daniela Greene was a tremendous embarrassment to the FBI after she traveled to Syria in 2014 to marry a German rapper turned ISIS fighter. Greene earned her master's from Clemson University and was hired by the FBI as a translator. She was supposed to monitor the rapper turned ISIS fighter known as Dennis Cuspert, Deso Dogg, or Abu Talha al-Almani, each name depending on his environment. Within weeks after she made it to Syria, Greene escaped and returned to the United States where she was arrested upon her arrival. She was sentenced to two years for her crimes, although the sentence should have been around thirteen years in comparison to other women who had committed similar crimes.[18]

Yusra Ismail stole a passport from her friend to travel to Syria to join ISIS and marry an ISIS fighter.[19] She has not been heard from since. Samantha Elhassani and her husband went to Syria to join ISIS and lived under the caliphate for two years. She was found living in a Kurdish detention camp with her four children who are also American citizens. She is an American born Muslim convert who stated that her husband tricked her into going to join ISIS. Samantha was extradited back to Indiana where she awaited trial. She stated that she had left ISIS after her husband had been killed fighting for ISIS although her crime also concerns lying to the FBI.[20]

In another strange story, Muhummad Dakhlalla (Mo) was a young Muslim college student at Mississippi State University who was born in the United States. His father was an imam and his mother was also Muslim. Mo met Jaelyn Young, who converted to Islam and married Mo shortly thereafter. According to the story, Jaelyn was radicalized by watching ISIS videos and convinced Mo to join the terrorist organization. On August 8, 2015, the couple tried to board a plan near Columbus, Mississippi to fly to Turkey to join ISIS. To their surprise, they were arrested by FBI. Jaelyn was sentenced to twelve years in prison while Mo received eight years in prison.[21]

A few women on the chart bear closer scrutiny as they appear to defy the typology of the domestic, the secretary, or the disposable. The first of these is Aafia Siddiqui who is a Pakistani born American citizen. Dr. Siddiqui, who completed her PhD in neuroscience, fled to Pakistan after the FBI began investigating her for her ties to al-Qaeda in 2002. She is called Lady al-Qaeda as terrorist groups including ISIS have tried to exchange hostages for her. Siddiqui had wanted to commit a massive terrorist attack on several New York landmarks. She was captured in Afghanistan and shot at officers after she was left unsecured in a questioning room. She was shot twice in the abdomen. After her recovery she was sentenced to eighty-six years in prison and is currently serving her time in Fort Worth, Texas.[22]

The stories about Siddiqui are almost stranger than fiction and there are numerous conspiracy theories concerning her life. However, what is clear is that at most, Siddiqui is a recruiter and financier for al-Qaeda, thus fulfilling the domestic and secretary roles. Although she appears to have married the uncle of Khalid Sheikh Mohammed, Ammar al-Baluchi, in her third marriage, she is not a founder, leader, foot soldier, planner, or any other leader position for al-Qaeda. It is likely that her scientific expertise may be of use to the organization, which is why ISIS has tried to get her. However, Siddiqui has been diagnosed as suffering from mental disease.[23]

Another interesting character is Jihad Jane and her co-defendant Jihad Jane II. Colleen LaRose or Jihad Jane plotted to kill a cartoonist who satirized the Prophet Muhammad after she had a one night stand with a Muslim in 2007. Born in the United States, LaRose converted to Islam. In a letter to a journalist LaRose stated why she committed the crime. "There's many reasons but the simplest reason is I did it for love. Love for my Prophet, love for my Ummah [community] and love for the brother that gave me the assignment."[24] She also stated:

> Also I think I did it for pride. Sisters are never given assignments like the one I was given. I felt my brother had enough confidence and trust in me that he honored me by giving me the assignment. I felt if he loved me that much then I had to do what he told me needed to be done.[25]

It is evident that LaRose has feminist aspirations in her actions; jihadist women are not usually asked to assassinate unless it is in the form of a suicide mission. Larose was radicalized in an online chat room. It was also reported that LaRose was sexually abused by her father, had worked as a prostitute, and had abused drugs.[26] She had no idea how and where to get a gun when she flew to Europe with the goal of killing the cartoonist Lars Vilks.[27] It is unlikely she would have been successful had she not gotten caught. It is probable that Jane was fulfilling the disposable role for ISIS.

Jihad Jane II or Jamie Paulin Ramirez (also born in the United States) flew to Ireland to marry her ISIS fiancé with her small son. She was also part of the plot with Jihad Jane to kill Lars Vilks. She was caught in Ireland after the wedding and has since returned to the United States for eight years of prison. Ramirez was teased as a child for a hearing disability and had a string of failed marriages. She converted to Islam and was also radicalized online with Jihad Jane I.[28]

There are numerous examples of Western women outside of the United States, whether born Muslim or newly converted to Islam, who have left Western nations in particular to live under the ISIS Caliphate. Wasserstein states that as many as 10 percent of the Western recruits to ISIS are women[29] or Perešin[30] puts that number at around 550 women. Khadiza Sultana, Amira Abase, and Shamima Begum all left London together and went to Syria to join ISIS. These were Western Muslim girls raised in strong to moderate Muslim families in England. Austrians Samra Kesinovic and Sabina Selimovic, two women of Bosnian descent, left Austria to join the Islamic State in Syria.[31]

When they reached the Islamic State, these women were expected to follow the following on women's dress and decorum:

> Proper covering includes: (1) having the entire body and hands concealed, (2) being thick, not thin, (3) being unadorned, (4) being loose-fitting, not tight-fitting, (5) being unperfumed, (6) not resembling men's clothing, and (7) not resembling infidel women's clothing. Improper showing includes: (1) showing anything of the body before unfamiliar men, (2) showing any part of the clothing beneath the veil, (3) suggestive ambling in front of men, (4) leg slapping, which is highly arousing, (5) coy and flirtatious talking, and (6) mixing with men, touching their bodies, shaking their hands, and crowding together with them in cramped vehicles.[32]

Obviously these young women were introduced to an ISIS that they had never read about or heard of. A lot of women who travel to ISIS to join the caliphate are shocked at the conditions when they arrive. Some women like the American Nadia Rockwood from the FBI escape and find a way home but others remain in the Caliphate where they are killed as bystanders like the British girl Kadiza Sultana[33] who was killed in an airstrike in Syria. The worst possibility is that these girls are murdered by ISIS fighters when they are caught trying to escape such as the Austrian teenager Samra Kesinovic who was beaten to death with a hammer in one of her many attempts to escape. Samra was kept with her friend Sabina Selimovic and both were sex slaves, passed from fighter to fighter as presents. Sabina has since disappeared and was most likely killed in the fighting.[34]

What is interesting is the radicalization process that occurs on the Internet for future female jihadists who emigrate from Western countries. Malika El-Aroud is an infamous Belgium holy warrior for al-Qaeda online. "The holy warrior of al-Qaeda" stated in 2008, "I have a weapon. It's to write. It's to speak. That my jihad. You can do many things with words. Writing is also a bomb."[35] Her job is to inspire both men and women in particular to martyr themselves in the name of Islam and al-Qaeda. El-Aroud stays at home collecting welfare and unemployment while she uses her rights of free speech to inspire jihadist Muslims to attack Belgium.

Concerning online recruiting, typically women will meet someone on a social networking site and start speaking with them in a chat room. This recruiter may be a woman who becomes a female friend or a man who is a potential spouse. Through numerous conversations, the recruiter will get the woman to trust him or her and to buy in to the idea that they should join the caliphate of ISIS. At the time of this book, ISIS has been severely beaten by the United States and has retreated into Africa. However, it is unlikely that they will dissipate and is highly possible that ISIS will regroup in Africa with a willing foundation such as Boko Haram in Nigeria who has already declared their allegiance to ISIS. The Internet will continue to be used as a tool to recruit women and men to join ISIS throughout the world.

In her master's thesis, Hillary Peladeau[36] from the University of Western Ontario analyzed more than fourteen thousand individual tweets of women from al-Qaeda affiliated networks. Peladeau found that there were emotionally supportive tweets, ideologically supportive tweets (propaganda and education), logistically supportive tweets (fundraising and recruitment), and lastly active participation on the battlefield tweets. The most interesting of these, the active participation on the battlefield tweets, either refer to defense, training, or martyrdom although none of these tweets support women being in combat. Peladeau also found that women in al-Qaeda use Twitter to extend supportive roles for recruiting, fundraising, etc. in the organization. Al-Qaeda women are not empowered through Twitter to become more active in the organization but it does allow women a greater voice and access to people through propagandizing.

In a later article published with coauthors Huey and Inch, Peladeau[37] investigated ISIS women who had Twitter accounts. The coauthors found after analyzing one hundred thousand tweets from ninety-three Twitter accounts that ISIS women had eight roles online and in real-time social networks including: fan-girls, baqiya (family members), propagandists, recruiters, the muhajirah (women who have migrated to ISIS territory), widows, terrorists, and leavers (women who leave Twitter). Women in ISIS still primarily stick to the gendered roles that have been prescribed for them even in the online realm. However, the authors did find two women that were later convicted of terrorism over the yearly course of the study. One fifteen-year-old British girl left to join ISIS but was caught and another sixteen-year-old British girl had information on her person likely to be used to commit an act of terrorism. Lastly, a third individual, the "ISIS Superstar" as is her nickname, was arrested after she threatened the FBI over Twitter.

In an article in *Perspectives on Terrorism*, scholar Anita Perešin[38] finds that many women emigrate from the West to join ISIS for religious reasons. However, these religious reasons vary from woman to woman. Some women want to join the caliphate as Abu Bakr al-Baghdadi reminds Muslims that it is their religious duty to do so. Other women want to take part in the state-building process and leave a corrupt Western society that has no respect for women. Yet others believe that Muslims or the *ummah* are under attack and need to be defended or they are wanting to protect their religion from the onslaught of the West. Lastly, other women believing they are taking part in a humanitarian cause, helping Muslims in a war zone.

When it comes to young adolescent girls who leave Western countries and join ISIS, they are troubled by an identity crisis provoked "by liberalism and modernity in multicultural Western societies."[39] Conservative Islam does not seem to fit and ISIS offers a third way, outside of conservative Islam or Western modernity. Or young people are simply bored and want to be part of a movement that will change history. Still other teenage girls are attracted to the danger in joining ISIS. The previous reasons are the most typical reasons for Western women to join ISIS although other motivations can also be found. In the end, women typically want to participate in combat although ISIS and/or al-Qaeda does not allow them. Several women who cannot leave and are held captive by ISIS will most likely be able to integrate peacefully into society. Other militant jihadist women who are true believers and return are likely to be a large security threat to Western nations that allow these women to return home.

Scholars Perešin and Cervone[40] argue that female lone wolves are a great threat to Western governments whether they are already in the West or they return from ISIS in Syria and Iraq. Although women in ISIS are strictly relegated to traditional female roles such as the domestic and secretary roles described in this book, it is evident that there is somewhat of a gender crisis between male and female jihadists. There are instances where female jihadists want to be involved in combat but are not allowed by both their male and female comrades. Perešin and Cervone believe that ISIS women who return to Western countries will be inclined to commit lone wolf attacks to fulfill their violent aspirations. The authors suggest intelligence collection, surveillance, judicial actions, disruption of money flows, counterterrorism actions, counter-ideology efforts, and rehabilitation, de-radicalization, and reconciliation programs to assist these women in their transition back or into Western society.

CONCLUSION

Terrorism expert Anne Speckhard and her coauthors Grace Wakim and Ardian Shajkovci[41] add that there should rehabilitation and reintegration programs in society for former ISIS members and for society. In Iraq, approximately five hundred thousand people lived under ISIS dominated territory. There is a social stigma in Iraq that mental illness should be dealt with privately and shows personal weakness. In 2006, the United States instituted the Detainee Rehabilitation Program for the US Department of Defense for over twenty-three thousand Iraqi detainees. However, the Department of Defense had serious problems finding qualified Iraqi psychologists and social workers to administer the program. Nonetheless, the Iraqi government is instituting programs to deal with these people, however small of a start it may be. ISIS members and supporters will likely bear the cost of revenge and social ostracism for their actions and support of ISIS from Iraq society. Many women have been raped and many family members have been killed by ISIS. In particular, the Shite-dominated Iraq was attacked and killed by ISIS and minority Sunni in the country, causing even more sectarian violence.

However, particular attention should be paid to female jihadists in that there should be programs to directly address their needs. In his article, Associate Research Fellow at the International Center for Political Violence and Terrorism Research in Singapore Nur Irfani Binte Saripi states that "the rehabilitation of female jihadists, focusing on countering the sources of their violent ideologies and special narratives used for their recruitment and radicalization and reintegrating them back into society is important."[42] In this rehabilitation, Saripi believe that three aspects are important: the extent of their indoctrination, an understanding of their motives for traveling to Iraq and Syria, and lastly, there needs to be an understanding of why these women returned and left the caliphate. There should be a specific program to rehabilitate these women as they cannot be lumped in with women from other terrorist organizations or women in general. These jihadist women should get education and there should be prominent religious figures involved in counter-ideological teachings.

In an effort to counteract ISIS recruitment in Iraq before the person actually joined the organization, Speckhard, Ardian, Wooster,[43] and Izadi developed a Facebook Brand Awareness and Safety Ad campaign that was broadcast for twenty-four days. The purpose was to show off the real ISIS instead of the caliphate dreamland that is often advertised by ISIS. The authors' efforts reached 1,287,557 people in their ad with 2,339,453 impressions and close to 1.7 million video views. The campaign worked to address violent ISIS narratives and to create a discussion that would channel anger into conversation and participation. Although President Trump and other state leaders have tried to eradicate ISIS, it is evident that the group is still alive and well on the Internet. In December 2017, the group put out three hundred online items and those numbers increased to seven hundred in January 2018. ISIS is still around and should be always be considered a threat.[44]

NOTES

1. Luisella de Cataldo Neuberger and Tiziana Valentini, *Women and Terrorism* (New York: St. Martin's Press, 1996), 93.

2. Luisella de Cataldo Neuberger and Tiziana Valentini, *Women and Terrorism* (New York: St. Martin's Press, 1996), 94.

3. Peter Bergen, Albert Ford, Alyssa Sims, and David Sterman, "Part II. Who are the Terrorists?" *New America*, 2018, accessed October 25, 2018, https://www.newamerica.org/in-depth/terrorism-in-america/who-are-terrorists/.

4. Wafa Sultan, *A God Who Hates* (New York: St. Martin's Press, 2009), 243.

5. Febriana Firdaus, "The Making of a Female ISIS Bomber," *New Naratif*, June 4, 2018, accessed September 16, 2018, https://newnaratif.com/journalism/making -female-isis-bomber.

6. H. Khaleeli, "The British Women Married to Jihad," *The Guardian*, September 6, 2014, accessed November 5, 2018, https://www.theguardian.com/world/2014/sep/06/british-women-married-to-jihad-isis-syria.

7. Petter Nesser, *Islamist Terrorism in Europe: A History* (Oxford: Oxford University Press, 2015).

8. Petter Nesser, *Islamist Terrorism in Europe: A History* (Oxford: Oxford University Press, 2015), Introduction.

9. Amy Forlitti, "Minneapolis Woman Gets Probation in Terrorism Case—At Prosecution's Urging," *Twin Cities Pioneer Press*, April 27, 2017, accessed October 30, 2018, https://www.twincities.com/2017/04/27/minneapolis-woman-gets-proba tion-in-terrorism-case-at-prosecutions-urging/.

10. Nicole Fuller, "Feds: Brentwood Woman Laundered Money to Support ISIS," *Newsday*, December 14, 2017, accessed November 2, 2018, https://www.newsday.com/long-island/crime/brentwood-money-laundering-islamic-state-1.15455156.

11. Counter Extremism Project, "Tashfeen Malik," *Counter Extremism Project*, 2018, accessed October 31, 2018, https://www.counterextremism.com/extremists/tashfeen-malik.

12. Philippe-Joseph Salazar, *Words are Weapons* (New Haven: Yale University Press, 2017), 105.

13. Philippe-Joseph Salazar, *Words are Weapons* (New Haven: Yale University Press, 2017), Chapter 7.

14. Robyn Creswell and Bernard Haykel, "Battle Lines: Want to Understand the Jihadis? Read their Poetry," *The New Yorker*, June 8 & 15, 2015, accessed August 20, 2018, https://www.newyorker.com/magazine/2015/06/08/battle-lines-jihad-creswell-and-haykel.

15. Thomas Hegghammer, "The Soft Power of Militant Jihad," *The New York Times*, December 18, 2015, accessed August 20, 2018, https://www.nytimes.com/2015/12/20/opinion/sunday/militant-jihads-softer-side.html.

16. Ben Markus, "Arvada Teen Sentenced to 4 Years in Prison For ISIS Terror Plot," *Colorado Public Radio*, January 23, 2015, accessed October 30, 2018, https://www.cpr.org/news/story/arvada-teen-faces-sentencing-over-terror-plot.

17. Michael Martinez, Ana Cabrera, and Sara Weisfeldt, "Colorado Woman Gets 4 Years for Wanting to Join ISIS," *CNN*, January 24, 2015, accessed October 30, 2018, https://www.cnn.com/2015/01/23/us/colorado-woman-isis-sentencing/index.html.

18. Scott Glover, "The FBI Translator Who Went Rogue and Married an ISIS Terrorist," *CNN*, May 1, 2017, accessed November 1, 2018, https://www.cnn.com/2017/05/01/politics/investigates-fbi-syria-greene/index.html.

19. Department of Justice U.S Attorney's Office, District of Minnesota, "Minnesota Woman Charged with Stealing Passport to Travel to Syria," *United States Department of Defense*, December 2, 2014, accessed October 30, 2018, https://www.justice.gov/usao-mn/pr/minnesota-woman-charged-stealing-passport-travel-syria.

20. Sarah Childress and Joshua Baker, "American Mom Who Lived Under ISIS Charged with Lying to the FBI," *Frontline*, July 24, 2018, accessed November 2, 2018, https://www.pbs.org/wgbh/frontline/article/american-woman-who-lived-under-isis-charged-with-lying-to-fbi/.

21. Scott Bronstein and Drew Griffin, "Young ISIS Recruit: I was Blinded by Love," *CNN,* December 6, 2016, accessed November 2, 2018, https://www.cnn.com/2016/12/02/us/mississippi-isis-muhammad-dakhlalla-interview/index.html.

22. Terrence McCoy, "'Lady al-Qaeda': The American-educated PHD the Islamic State Desperately Wants Freed," August 28, 2014, accessed October 30, 2018, https://www.washingtonpost.com/news/morning-mix/wp/2014/08/28/lady-al-qaeda-the-american-educated-doctor-the-islamic-state-desperately-wants-freed/?utm_term=.b8b7ea4db9c4.

23. Benjamin Webster, "Court to Hear New Reports on Pakistani Scientist's Fitness for Trial," *The New York Times*, July 5, 2009, accessed October 30, 2018, https://www.nytimes.com/2009/07/06/nyregion/06competency.html.

24. Tracy Connor and Stephanie Seigel, "'Jihad Jane' Colleen LaRose Became a Terrorist for Love," *NBC News*, January 14, 2015, accessed October 30, 2018, https://www.nbcnews.com/news/investigations/jihad-jane-colleen-larose-became-terrorist-love-n284636.

25. Tracy Connor and Stephanie Seigel, "'Jihad Jane' Colleen LaRose Became a Terrorist for Love," *NBC News*, January 14, 2015, accessed October 30, 2018, https://www.nbcnews.com/news/investigations/jihad-jane-colleen-larose-became-terrorist-love-n284636.

26. Anne Speckhard, "Female Terrorists in ISIS, al-Qaeda and 2rst Century Terrorism," *Trends Research: Inside the Mind of a Jihadist,* May 4, 2015, accessed

November 5, 2018, http://trendsinstitution.org/wp-content/uploads/2015/05/Female-Terrorists-in-ISIS-al-Qaeda-and-21rst-Century-Terrorism-Dr.-Anne-Speckhard.pdf, 7

27. John Hurdle, "10 Years for Plot to Murder Cartoonist," *New York Times*, January 6, 2014, accessed October 31, 2018, https://www.nytimes.com/2014/01/07/us/jihad-jane-given-10-year-prison-sentence.html.

28. John Hendren and Clayton Sandell, "American Held in Ireland, No 'Jihad Jamie,' Is Released," *ABC News*, March 13, 2010, accessed October 31, 2018, https://abcnews.go.com/WN/woman-released-arrest-terror-plot/story?id=10094548.

29. David J. Wasserstein, *Black Banners of ISIS* (New Haven, CT: Yale University Press, 2017), 124.

30. Anita Perešin, "Fatal Attraction: Western Muslims and ISIS," *Perspectives on Terrorism* 9(3) (June 2015): 21–38, 22.

31. David J. Wasserstein, *Black Banners of ISIS* (New Haven, CT: Yale University Press, 2017).

32. Fatwa no. 44 December 14, 2014 from IS Department of Fatwas and Research. As cited in David J. Wasserstein, *Black Banners of ISIS* (New Haven, CT: Yale University Press, 2017), 127.

33. Rohit Kachroo, "Bethnal Green Schoolgirl Kadiza Sultana Who Joined Islamic State 'Killed in Airstrike in Syria,'" ITV News Reveals, *ITV News*, August 11, 2016, accessed November 5, 2018, https://www.itv.com/news/2016-08-11/bethnal-green-schoolgirl-kadiza-sultana-who-joined-islamic-state-killed-in-airstrike-in-syria/.

34. Lizzie Dearden, "SISI Austrian Poster Girl Samra Kesinovic 'Used as Sex Slave' before Being Murdered for Trying to Escape," *The Independent*, December 31, 2015, accessed November 5, 2018, https://www.independent.co.uk/news/world/middle-east/isis-austrian-poster-girl-samra-kesinovic-used-as-sex-slave-before-being-murdered-for-trying-to-a6791736.html.

35. Elaine Sciolino and Souad Mekhennet, "Al Qaeda Warrior Uses Internet to Rally Women," *The New York Times*, May 28, 2008, accessed November 5, 2018, https://www.nytimes.com/2008/05/28/world/europe/28terror.html.

36. Hillary Peladeau, "Support for Sisters Please"; Comparing the Online Roles of al-Qaeda Women and the Islamic State Counterparts," (Master's Thesis, University of Western Ontario, 2016).

37. Laura Huey, Rachel Inch, and Hillary Peladeau, "'@ me if you need shoutout': Exploring Women's Roles in Islamic State Twitter Networks," *Studies in Conflict & Terrorism* (2017), accessed November 5, 2018, https://www.tandfonline.com/doi/abs/10.1080/1057610X.2017.1393897.

38. Anita Perešin, "Fatal Attraction: Western Muslimas and ISIS," *Perspectives on Terrorism* 9(3) (June 2015): 21–38.

39. Anita Perešin, "Fatal Attraction: Western Muslimas and ISIS," *Perspectives on Terrorism* 9(3) (June 2015): 21–38, 24.

40. Anita Perešin and Alberto Cervone, "The Western Muhajirat of ISIS," *Studies in Conflict and Terrorism* 38(7) (2015): 495–509.

41. Anne Speckhard, Grace Wakim, and Ardian Shajkovci, "Ensuring a Long-term Win Against ISIS in Mosul: The Need for Rehabilitation and Reintegration Programs

& Restoring Security and Justice," *International Center for the Study of Violent Extremism*, July 27, 2017, accessed November 6, 2018, https://www.academia.edu/34049265/Ensuring_a_Long-term_Win_Against_ISIS_In_Mosul_The_Need_for_Rehabilitation_and_Reintegration_Programs_and_Restoring_Security_and_Justice.

42. Nur Irfani Binte Saripi, "Female Members of ISIS A Greater Need for Rehabilitation," *Counter Terrorist Trends and Analyses* 7(3) (April 2015): 26–31, 28.

43. Anne Speckhard, Ardian Shajkovci, Claire Wooster, and Neima Izadi, "Mounting a Facebook Brand Awareness and Safety Ad Campaign to Break the ISIS Brand in Iraq," *Perspectives on Terrorism* 12 (3) (June 2018): 50–66.

44. Anne Speckhard and Adrian Shajkovci, "Is ISIS Still Alive and Well on the Internet?" *International Center for the Study of Violent Extremism* (January 14, 2019).

Conclusion

Wrapping It All Up:
The Roles of Women in Jihadist
Terrorist Organizations and Islam

Work from my first article[1] on female terrorism in *Women, Politics, and Policy* where the impetus for this book began can be reconciled with the idea the jihadist women are doing terrorist acts to bring respect and notoriety for their gender. Jihadist women want to be involved in the struggle to reestablish the caliphate and create a society governed by Sharia Law. They are not feminists in the Western sense as gender equality is not a priority nor is it necessary for them, as least from the Western perspective. Like one ISIS member stated in response to Western feminism, "Islam has given all my rights to me as a woman and I feel liberated, I feel content and equal in society . . . if you knew your place as a woman, if there was Shar'iah implementation, you would not be complaining like you are now."[2] Instead, women in jihadist terrorist organizations are fulfilling roles they are expected to embody by their society and religion, which are closely intertwined. One women who left Scotland to join ISIS stated, "The main role of the *muhajirah* [female migrant] here is to support her husband and his jihad and [God willing] to increase this *ummah* [Islamic community]."[3] Some female jihadists are also seeking to slightly enlarge those roles. One female terrorist described it perfectly when she stated, "We are smarter than women who did not do acts related to security."[4]

In Table C.1: The Roles of Women in Jihadist Terrorist Organizations, the roles of women in the eight case studies addressed in this book are presented. Jihadist female terrorists will not become the foot soldiers in ISIS nor are they looking to lead terrorist organizations. Speckhard and Akhmedova state that "In Chechen society, males play lead roles and women follow . . . Neither had a Chechen female played a significant leadership role within a terrorist organization."[5] A leadership role for women is not in line with Islam. For the most part, jihadist women are content to participate as the disposable, seeking

179

Table C.1:   The Roles of Women in Jihadist Terrorist Organizations

Terrorist Group	Sect of Islam	Domestic	Secretary	Disposable
Al-Aqsa Martyrs' Brigade	Sunni	✓	?	✓
Boko Haram	Sunni (Salafi)	✓	✓	✓
Chechen Separatists	(Sunni) Wahhabi	✓	✓	✓
Hamas	Sunni	✓	✓	✓
Hezbollah	Shiite	✓	✓	✓
Isis	Sunni	✓	✓	✓
Egyptian Muslim Brotherhood	Sunni	✓	✓	NA
Al-Qaeda	Sunni (Wahhabi)	✓	✓	✓

martyrdom, the domestic, fulfilling women's roles within a terrorist organization, or as the secretary, ensuring that the logistics are taken care of.

Jihadist terrorist organizations that base their identity on the history and religious texts of Islam cannot accept female fighters. The concept of women fighting is contrary to their nature for jihadist Muslims. As feminist scholar Dorit Naaman states,

> When women opt to fight alongside men, they challenge the dichotomy of woman as victim/man as defender. Women fighters are physically strong, are active (therefore agents), and, most important, are willing to kill (hence, they are violent). They challenge not only the images of women as victims of war but also the traditional patriarchal binary opposition that postulates women as physically and emotionally weak and incapable of determining and defending the course of their own lives. As a result, women fighters have often been represented—especially in mass media—as deviant from prescribed forms of femininity, forms that emphasize a woman's delicacy and fragility but also her generosity, caring nature, motherliness, and sensitivity to others' needs.[6]

In the case of Boko Haram, PhD candidate Matfess has written about there being rumors about female fighters in Boko Haram. However, she was never able to find any person who saw any female fighters and found that women in the group were genuinely confused by the question as to whether they had seen women fighters.[7]

Even the concept of gender equality in jihadist terrorist organizations is an anathema. If the groups are to be compared across the board and we are looking at female terrorists who have the most equality within their group, the Chechen Separatists or Black Widows appear to be the most progressive. In a study completed by Speckhard and Akhmedova, published in 2008, 65.3 of the 110 female terrorists they studied had a high school education; 11.5 percent were in college; 4 percent had finished college; and 19.2 percent had finished their university studies with one woman who had wanted to be a lawyer until the Chechen Wars derailed her plans.[8] In reference to the other case studies in this book, the number for the Chechens are high concerning education for women.

As academics Berko and Erez[9] find, the concept of membership in a jihadist terrorist organization in Muslim or particularly Palestinian societies is a liability for women. The experience of being a female terrorist and returning from jail does not enhance her reputation. Instead, she is sullied and unclean for marriage and motherhood as she has been a terrorist. Jihadist men can only enhance their masculinity or virility by being part of terrorist organization as a soldier. She (the jihadist female terrorist) is relegated to the dreary drudges of society after she retires. One interesting and possible contradictory example to this theory is Leila Khaled, who will be discussed in the next section. In addition, the role of suicide bomber or the disposable is regarded highly in society but only for the successful martyrs. If she fails, she is an embarrassment to her faith and her family for being unable to martyr herself. If he fails, he does not face the same fate as she does. Failure is not a societal option for the designated and trained female martyr.

Interestingly enough, in a study of 7,849 adults in fourteen Muslim countries, academics Fair and Shepard[10] found that females (may vary by country), young people, and those who believe Islam is under threat are more likely to support terrorism. This falls in line with one reason for jihad which is to protect the religion of Islam. Perhaps terrorism is a vehicle for women to assert a stronger role in society, although in the end, the participation of Muslim women in terrorist organizations leads to their later decline in societal relationships as previously discussed. The obvious exception to this theory is the idea of female martyrdom or *shahida*. For it is with martyrdom that female terrorists finally achieve equality with men in Muslim society.

The Women in Western Terrorist Organizations and How They Differ from Women in Jihadist Terrorist Organizations

Throughout this book it has been substantiated that jihadist female terrorists are different from and have different roles than Western female terrorists. In their work on the roles of women in terrorist organizations titled *Women as Terrorists*, published in 2009, academics Cragin and Daly[11] find that women tend to have a logistician role or what the author calls the secretarial role in most terrorist organizations, except for the Japanese Red Army. The authors also find that women recruit primarily in jihadist organizations and in the LTTE, PIRA, FARC, and Shining Path. Women are martyrs or disposables primarily in the jihadist terrorist organizations and the LTTE. Finally, Cragin and Daly find that women are political leaders and guerillas only in the non-jihadist groups. This book is an updated extension of the book *Women as Terrorists*, in addition to paying particular attention to women in jihadist groups.

In Western terrorist organizations, women have played substantial founder, leadership, planning, and foot soldier roles. They have commanded men and fought alongside men. They have planted bombs and carried weapons. For example, the Italian Red Brigades, a Marxist terrorist organization in Italy, was partly formed by a woman, Margherita Cagol. Cagol was killed during a shootout with the police when a kidnapping attempt went awry. She actually broke her husband Renato Curcio out of prison.[12]

Or the Red Army Faction in Germany which formed in 1970 had two female founders, Ulrike Meinhof, a journalist and Gudrun Ensslin, a university drop out student. Andreas Baader, Ulrike Meinhof, and Gundrun Ensslin banded together to form the Baader-Meinhof group that later became the Red Army Faction. Both Ulrike and Gudrun underwent military training in Jordan, planted bombs, and robbed banks. The RAF included several other women such as Imgard Möller, Brigitte Margret Ida Mohnhaup, Susanne Albrecht, and Adelheid Schul, to name a few.[13]

In the United States, Black women such as Kathleen Cleaver, Fredricka Newton, Charlotte Hill O'Neal, Elaine Brown, Rosemari Mealy, Assata Shakur, Erika Huggins, Barbara Easley Cox, Afeni Shakur, and Chaka Khan were part of the Black Panther Party.[14] These women also participated in violence as foot soldiers and leaders in the Black Panther Party. The Weather Men or Weather Underground also had several prominent women such as Bernadine Dohrn who helped to found the organization and Naomi Jaffe who wrote for many of the organization's essays.

Although women in Western terrorist organizations participated in founder, leadership, planning, and foot soldier roles, they faced many obstacles during their tenure in the organizations including misogyny, sexism, and racism during the mid-twentieth century. Many of these terrorist organizations were composed of the radical fringes of prominent social movements such as the Civil Rights movement, the anti-Vietnam War movement, and the Second Wave of Feminism. It is logical that they would face some of the "isms" that they were fighting against as societal change needed to occur, thus the very purposes for their terrorist organizations. This is not to say that terrorism is excusable but that repeated frustration over time can lead to violence in the form of terrorism. Most terrorist organizations start out peacefully as social movements and radicalize over time.[15]

It is obvious that female jihadists also face gender inequality of different magnitudes in their terrorist organizations. There are a few women that would like to play foot soldier, planning, and leadership roles in jihadist organizations. They are not allowed by the men and even women in jihadist organizations to fulfill these aspirations. The words are available regarding the support of women from other jihadists who take up their jihad but women performing any violent acts are still extremely taboo in Islam and in jihadist terrorist organizations. Martyrdom appears to be tolerated but death through the destruction of others is the only higher role that a woman can play besides the domestic or secretarial roles.

Other important differences are evident when comparing female jihadists with Western female terrorists. In their book on *Women and Terrorism*, Neuberger and Valentini[16] interview several female terrorists from 1970s terrorist organizations including the Prima Linea (Italy), the Communist Combat Formations (Italy, Germany, and England), and the Red Brigades (Italy). They find that most of these women did not show repentance for their actions or regret for joining a terrorist organization. The reason for this is that women as the sacrificial mother give everything to the cause and in the end, the lack of success of the revolutionary organizations leads to the questioning of their utility. The view that "we did it all for nothing" prevails.

In the interviews the author completed for this book in chapter 6 with the four women in the Israeli prison, three of these jihadist women were repentant for their crimes. The women were subjected to a prison hierarchy system and the author believes that they were towing the lines of their prospective terrorist organizations. This does not necessarily mean that these jihadist women did not feel some personal regret for the actions they committed but it does mean that they are most likely counseled concerning what they could say during their interviews.

In his book *Female Suicide Terrorism*, Yoram Schweitzer makes the point that Palestinian female suicide bombers tend to change their mind about their motivations for suicide bombing after spending time in prison.[17] For the female Palestinian suicide bombers, religious and Palestinian nationalistic motives become the official story after these women are indoctrinated in prison. Schweitzer states,

> In the many interviews granted by female suicide terrorist to the various media, some of which were conducted after they underwent indoctrination by their cellmates, they indicated that they regarded themselves as fulfilling the function of publicizing nationalistic messages. This theme often comes in stark contradiction to the personal interviews that they granted soon after their arrest. They explained their volunteering for missions in terms of equal protection in the national struggle their people. Particularly in the Arab media, they are thus

marketed as independent and determined women with strongly held opinions, who decided to take their fate into their hands with a feeling of completeness and destiny—rather like a modern version of Joan of Arc.[18]

Another difference between jihadist women and Western terrorist women is the masculinization of women that occurs in the Western terrorist organizations that does not occur in jihadist terrorist organizations. It appears that in order for women to have any status in Western terrorist organizations they must become masculine in many ways. Neuberger and Valentini state,

> In the context of subversion, women instead seem forced to depolarize their femininity, to transform themselves into androgynous beings . . . In the revolutionary world, women replicate men exactly, in all their functions, the point of losing or renouncing even their own function as mothers. This equality empties the relationship of all tension.[19]

This is similar to what happens when women join the military in Western countries. Their hair is usually cut short for maintenance purposes, they are given relatively masculine attire or uniforms, and their bodies become more muscular due to physical training and a lower body fat percentage. Terrorist organizations, in most cases, develop an army that can be compared to state militaries.

In jihadist terrorist organizations, the women remain women and their femininity is not lost. Perhaps this is because the women do not engage in combat operations or leadership roles of any kind. In fact, the loss of the femininity of women in jihadist terrorist organizations would be entirely distasteful to everyone in both Muslim society and jihadist organizations.

Regarding the women that I interviewed in chapter 6, it is evident that these women had no physical training at all nor were they in excellent physical shape. It is doubtful even that they have ever exercised. The concept of physical fitness for women in Muslim culture does not appear to be a priority like physical fitness is for both genders in Western culture. Whether women are in the military or not, Western culture places a lot more emphasis on exercise, health, and physical fitness. The female body is also always on display in Western culture unlike the veiled women in Islam so it is susceptible to more criticism.

In addition, the persona of women in jihadist terrorist organizations is much softer than women in Western terrorist organizations. Jihadist women have a more traditional feminine persona. They are quiet, polite, and respectful. They are not as self-assertive as Western women in that they do not argue or show much confidence in themselves. This is most likely a cultural difference but it is interesting that the gender roles and gender personalities are quite traditional in Muslim society in comparison with Western societies. The next section will talk about the similarities between Western female terrorists and jihadist female terrorists.

THE WOMEN IN WESTERN TERRORIST ORGANIZATIONS AND HOW THEY ARE SIMILAR TO WOMEN IN JIHADIST TERRORIST ORGANIZATIONS

Although there are few similarities between Western female terrorists and female jihadists, there are a few things that need to be mentioned. Foremost, it is apparent that both jihadist and Western female terrorists are women. They love, marry, and have children like other women throughout the world. They marry and divorce and live relatively similar lives. Their passion for their political objectives is apparent and strong. These women have goals that they want to accomplish and they have all sacrificed much in the obtainment of these goals. The reasons for their radicalization and the process for the radicalization is most likely very different but the passion they have for their causes is similar. The next part of the chapter will focus on the possible counterexamples to the theories presented in this book including Leila Khaled and female members of the Mojahedin Khalq in Iran.

COUNTEREXAMPLES? LEILA KHALED AND THE MOJAHEDIN KHALQ IN IRAN

The one possible counterexample to the entire argument present in this chapter is the Black September organization leader, Leila Khaled. Not only was Leila Khaled a leader in the group Black September but she is also one of few female leaders in an Islamic terrorist organization to have ever existed. Leila Khaled was responsible for planning and executing two plane hijackings, one in 1969 and the other in 1970. Khaled, a Palestinian, also trained with men and joined the Popular Front for the Liberation of Palestine (PFLP).[20]

The one major difference between Leila Khaled and all the other jihadist female terrorists presented in this book is primarily her religion. Leila Khaled is an atheist who was born in Israel—therefore, she is not a jihadist. Khaled, although she fought with Muslim men, did not believe in nor did she subscribe to Islam. Instead, Khaled's loyalty lies where it always has, even today. Leila Khaled is loyal only to Palestine, not Islam. It is rumored that Khaled once stated, "I represent Palestinians, not women." In a 2001 interview, Khaled stated, "I no longer think it's necessary to prove ourselves as women by imitating men," she says. "I have learned that a woman can be a fighter, a freedom fighter, a political activist, and that she can fall in love, and be loved, she can be married, have children, be a mother."[21] Khaled also stated, "When the religious leaders say that women who make those actions are finally equal to men, I have a problem. Everyone is equal in death—rich, poor, Arab, Jew, Christian, we are all equal. I would rather see women equal to men in life."[22]

In addition, the Popular Front for Liberation of Palestine that Khaled belonged to is a secular Palestinian Marxist–Leninist and revolutionary socialist organization founded in 1967 by George Habash. As was stated in the Introduction of this book, the only other type of terrorist organizations that have female leaders and suicide bombers are the Marxist groups such as the LTTE and the PFLP. These groups allow gender equality under Marxism as was championed by Karl Marx and Friedrich Engels in *The Communist Manifesto*, written in 1848.

Another oddity that needs to be explored in the context of this book is the Mojahedin Khalq (MEK) terrorist organization in Iran. The MEK was founded by a husband and wife team, Massoud and Maryam Rajavi, in 1965 to overthrow Shah Mohammad Reza Pahlavi and was deeply against American imperialism. The organization is founded on principles of Islamism, feminism, and Marxism and consists of mostly of female soldiers. Supposedly, older women were required to divorce their husbands in the late 1980s, and younger women are not allowed to marry or have children.[23] In some circles, this terrorist organization is also considered a cult.

The group even has a female founder and female foot soldiers and it holds true to Marxist ideology which argues for the equality of women. Therefore, since it is Marxist and not jihadist, the group does not present an exception to the theory presented in this book. Women play leadership roles, foot soldiers, logisticians, and planning roles in this organization. The MEK was a target of the Ayatollah Khomeini even though it participated in the Iranian Revolution that brought the Ayatollah to power. Saddam Hussein sponsored the group until his death and the United States tried to vanquish the group in their 2003 invasion of Iraq. Currently the United States has removed the group from the State Department's list of Foreign Terrorist Organizations. The members are now "protected persons" under the Geneva Convention.[24] The next section will focus on Indonesia, the largest Muslim country in the world, and the rising jihadist segments in Indonesian society.

INDONESIA

If Islam or its religious texts can truly be a cause of jihadist terrorism, then the largest Muslim country in the world must be taken into account. Indonesia is the largest Muslim country in the world and receives few terrorist attacks in comparison to countries such as Afghanistan and Pakistan. However, recent attacks, primarily from ISIS sympathizers, have increased terrorist attacks tremendously in Indonesia.

Dian Yulia Novi was supposed to be the first female suicide bomber for the Islamic State (ISIS) in Indonesia. Dian had planned to blow up a pressure cooker bomb in the Indonesian presidential palace. She was radicalized online by ISIS and Indonesian ISIS sympathizers. However, her plans were discovered by the police and her house was raided in Bekasi. She was sentenced to 7.5 years in prison for her actions.[25]

The terrorist group responsible for Novi's attack is Jamaah Ansharud Daulah, who has pledged their allegiance to ISIS. Amam Abdurrahman is the founder of the group. Shortly before the 2016 attacks he was responsible for, Aman issued a fatwa that was widely circulated among extremist groups. He stated:

Emigrate to the Islamic State and if you cannot emigrate, then wage jihad with spirit wherever you are, and if you cannot wage war or you lack the courage to do so, then contribute your wealth to those who are willing to do so. And if you cannot contribute, then urge others to undertake jihad. And if you cannot do that, then what is the meaning of your loyalty oath [bai'at]?[26]

Jamaah Ansharud Daulah takes issue with the Pancaslia, which is the foundation of the Indonesian state. It was created by the Indonesian nationalist leader Sukarno on June 1, 1945. Sukarno argued that the Indonesian state should be based on the Five Principles: Indonesian nationalism; internationalism, or humanism; consent, or democracy; social prosperity; and belief in one God.[27] These concepts expressed in the Pancaslia are not in line with jihadist Islam and will continue to create conflict and terrorist attacks for jihadist terrorist organizations.

Jamaah Ansharud Daulah was responsible for three separate suicide bombings involving women and their families on May 13 and 14, 2018. All of these families had recently returned from Syria. On May 13, 2018, one family of five attacked three churches. The two teenage sons blew up the Santa Maria Catholic Church in Surabaya. The father drove a car bomb into the Surabaya Centre Pentecostal Church. The mother, with her twelve- and eight-year old daughters, attacked the Diponegoro Indonesian Christian Church. All of these attacks occurred within a few minutes of one another. That night, another family died outside of Surabaya when their bomb exploded prematurely. Only three children survived. On May 14, a third family attacked a police station in Surabaya. Using two motorcycles, the family created two motorcycle bombs. An eight-year-old girl survived the attacks because she was sandwiched between her mother and father.[28]

Unfortunately, Indonesia appears to be subjected to the wrath of jihadist Islam that is clearly affecting most of the world. Al-Qaeda sympathizers who found that al-Qaeda was too benevolent have latched on to ISIS. ISIS has taken terrorist attacks and violence to an entirely different level than al-Qaeda. Indonesia is obviously in the path of ISIS and attacks will continue to increase unless the government finds a solid way to deal with jihadists who have recently returned from Syria and Iraq under the ISIS caliphate or who are ISIS sympathizers. Online radicalization for female jihadists such as Novi are also a large problem for the country.

SOME THINGS TO THINK ABOUT

One question that must be on the reader's mind is whether the modernization of Muslim societies will ever lead to modern roles for women in Islamic society; modern meaning that women will be allowed to participate as full citizens in society. Modern roles include women having the choice not to get married or have children without social ostracism, or to even have a career or education. Granted not all Muslim societies deny women education but it is not common to see Muslim female professionals in Islamic countries unless they are obstetricians.[29] If Islamic society modernizes, will women then play greater or more substantial roles in jihadist terrorist organizations? The answer to that question in my mind is no. Foremost, the author would hope that no one would want women to play more progressive roles in jihadist terrorist organizations. Moving past that point, Islam cannot by its very nature allow women to be equal to men. The concept of feminine subordination to men is too deeply ingrained in the Quran and the Hadith. Many people have stated that Muslims are several hundred years behind the West in their thinking and that modernization will eventually lead to gender equality among other things. This gender inequality is part of Islam and was incorporated into the Quran by Muhammad. Although Muslim women will state they are feminists, they will also state that Islam gives them all the rights they need in the same sentence. In Islam, these rights are the right to motherhood and marriage, and nothing else. Most Muslim women do not entirely understand nor do they want the Western concept of gender equality. The concept of Western gender equality is grotesque or unnatural to many Muslim women living in Islamic countries. In the last few decades Muslim societies such as Egypt have reverted back to conservative Islam, with women returning to the veil. Many Muslim societies have socially regressed when it comes to human rights instead of progressing.

Putting It All Together: Policy Implications and Prescriptions

One resounding question throughout this book is, why does jihadist Islam offer an individual an outlet to join in terrorism? Besides Quranic scripture and the Hadith that justifies martyrdom, there is the culture of Islam. Muslims have a family-first mentality. After a loss of any kind, Muslims will equip a person with a new family and the need to belong to a group. Whether motivations are sincere or not is irrelevant. Loyalty to family, friends, and Islam is also a highly sought after characteristic for people contemplating joining a terrorist organization. There is a solidarity among the *ummah* that cannot be underestimated. Muslims are bound to help and protect other Muslims in the Quran and Hadith. The Muslim community surpasses borders and boundaries and they will help and protect their own people. One need only look to Afghanistan and Chechnya where jihadists flocked from all over the world to help Muslims who were being attacked.

In addition, for some women like the Chechen women who have lost family to the Russians, the empowerment of sacrifice helps one overcome survivor guilt. The promise of paradise, where one will reunite with lost loved ones, provides a brighter future. Trauma survivors are often short-sighted in their need to heal.[30] Islam justifies martyrdom and provides the martyr with highly coveted rewards in paradise.

Many scholars have surmised that if women in Muslim countries were given more rights overall, then women would fare better and misogyny would be defeated. However, changes in the home environment often lead to increased tension and higher rates of domestic violence when the superiority of the male sex is questioned. Expert on Boko Haram Hilary Matfess[31] ponders ideas such as female legislative quotas, gender representation in the legislature, women's rights legislation, and proportional representation (which tends to have more egalitarian representation for minority groups) as possible ideas for improving the status of women in Nigeria. These ideas are helpful and may improve the plight of women in Muslim countries. However, the problem lies with the male gatekeepers of society who are hesitant or dead set against giving up some of their power to women. Government changes will help but there must be an entire attitude change in the Muslim culture, both among men and women to bring equality to women. Women are both the victims and the aggressors to some extent in their own tragedy. Equality is something that takes centuries to ascertain and cannot be done overnight. Many Muslim women in light of Western influence have returned to the veil and *purdah* to maintain their honor and chastity. This is not progression but instead is regression for women's rights.

Another problem that must be addressed is Western ignorance and denial of Muslim abuse and misogyny of women. The West has stayed silent regarding this problem for far too long. The Quran justifies the abuse of women by allowing husbands to beat their wives so long as it is not debilitating or too frequently. In the Quran, women are toys or playthings for men to use at will. This is not justifiable under any human rights documents. Female genital mutilation, forced marriages, child marriages, child rape, sexual slavery, and the full gamut of Islamic abuse are intolerable and cannot be accepted any longer. Turning a blind eye to these atrocities does not work and when it comes to human rights abuses, there is no such thing as cultural relativism. Muslim women must also take a stand when it comes to their treatment as they bear some of the responsibility for the misogyny of their gender as they are perpetuating the stereotypes.

The research presented in this book is most important to counterterrorism and security and was primarily written for that audience. It is still evident that counterterrorism operations do not necessarily consider women a risk. This is obviously a dangerous fallacy as many of the organizations presented in this paper have as many willing female suicide bombers as they do male suicide bombers. Part of this fallacy comes from the media who spins stories according to their entertainment value and refuses to only report the facts. The media cannot take the phenomenon of female terrorism seriously. Female terrorists are evaluated by their appearance and the shape of their nails. They are sensationalized over and over again by the international news. As the phenomenon of the husband and wife terrorist team grows, women must be taken seriously. Scholar Brigitte Nacos puts it perfectly when she states, "the lesson is that gender reality must inform the measures designed to prevent and respond to terrorism and, perhaps more important, the implementation of anti-and counterterrorist policies."[32]

However, women instead of participating in jihadist terrorism can also be used as a way to counteract and stop jihadist terrorism. Speckhard and Shajikovci suggest several ways that women can be used to counteract terrorism in the Sandjak region of Serbia and Montenegro. The first way is for women to receive the same training as male imams so they are able to provide religious education to women and girls, an environment that male imams are rarely allowed to access. The sexism that is evident in religious arenas should cease and allow women to attend anti-radicalization meetings; women should be allowed to have similar training at mosques. A third way is to use the highly influential role of women in their own families to counteract jihadist ideas and to teach their children moderate ways of political participation. Children are impressionable and can be taught that violence is not acceptable from an early age.[33]

In their book *Understanding and Addressing Suicide Attacks*, Cook and Allison argue that policy makers have embraced an attitude of defeatism regarding Islamist suicide attacks, which are the main tactic for Islamist groups. Policy makers in general believe that jihadist attacks cannot be stopped and that they are in fact, inevitable. Cook and Allison provide four ideas in order to understand and defend against jihadist suicide attacks. They are as follows:

1. Focus on the religious aspects of the problem of suicide attacks. Many scholars and policy makers shy away from considering the role of religion as a key determining factor in creating suicide attackers, a factor that yet may be cardinal, if not *the* cardinal factor in the contemporary creation of radical Muslim suicide attackers.
2. Confront the problem of perceived humiliation among Muslims that has such a prominent role in the continual recruitment of suicide attackers.
3. Make political and religious leaders accountable for their continued support of suicide attacks. While many Muslim leaders insist that certain suicide attacks (mainly those that target Muslims) are illegitimate, they refuse to systematically condemn the genre as a whole. Doublespeak needs to cease, or the tactic will continue to be used and supported.
4. Engage the Muslim world in a discussion about suicide attacks, using its own communication means (such as existing and popular satellite television channels, websites, and other media).[34]

Many scholars advocate that religion is an insignificant determinant of actions and that culture is irrelevant. Hopefully, this book has made an attempt to bring back the legitimacy of religion and culture in determining the actions of people. On the opposite side of the coin, scholars will often state that jihadist terrorist organizations such as ISIS misinterpret Islam. The same scholars that state that religion and culture are not important in why people act are often the same scholars that state jihadists misinterpret Islam. Unfortunately, this is a contradiction. One cannot state that religion and culture are irrelevant in political actions and then state that the same religions are being misinterpreted. For example, Associate Research Fellow at the International Center for Political Violence and Terrorism Research in Singapore Nur Irfani Binte Saripi states that "female propagandists and recruiters lace their discourse with misinterpreted religious narratives, hashtags, and youngster slang."[35] Interpretation is not the problem but the content of religious texts, in this case Islam, is the problem. The religion of Islam bears responsibility for instigating suicide attacks. Besides the Quran and Hadith which support, justify, and reward martyrs as can be seen in chapter 1 of this book, Muslims in general are highly supportive of martyrdom operations. According to public opinion polls, Muslims support suicide attacks throughout the world.[36]

In addition, Muslim clerics and religious authorities support martyrdom through fatwas. Western and Turkish apologists are the few that disagree with martyrdom operations. In a study performed by Cook and Allison of sixty-one fatwas: thirty-two mention the Israeli-Palestinian conflict, two mention Palestine and the entire world, two mention Chechnya, two mention the entire world, and one mentions India. The fatwas are issued by clerics from over twenty countries.[37]

In this book, the author is picking on Islam. However, the larger problem is religion in general. Religion throughout history has been one of the largest killing forces ever created. The crusades or the Spanish Inquisition were responsible for millions of deaths. Religious texts and their passages can be used to justify any great number of evil deeds. Culture then reinforces these actions by making it socially acceptable to use religion to suppress, torture, or kill individuals who are unbelievers or undedicated followers. The culture must change and then religion will follow.

For example in Christianity, there are passages in the Bible that state women should veil and that woman exists for men. In 1 Corinthians 11, the Bible states:

> So a man who prays or proclaims God's message in public worship with his head covered disgraces Christ. And any woman who prays or proclaims God's message in public worship with nothing on her head disgraces her husband; there is no difference between her and a woman whose head has been shaved. If the woman does not over her head, she might as well cut her hair. And since it is a shameful thing for a woman to shave her head or cut her hair, she should cover her head. A man has no need to cover his head, because he reflects the glory of God. But woman reflects the glory of man; for man was not created from woman, but woman from man. Nor was man created for woman's sake but woman was created for man's sake. On account of the angels, then, a woman should have a covering over her head to show that she is under her husband's authority.[38]

Passages in the Bible that justify human rights abuses or misogyny are plentiful. However, predominately Christian countries such as the United States do not force women to veil and indeed veiling is somewhat socially taboo in Western societies. While Christian women used to veil throughout history, they rarely do so in modern times. Women used to be property of their husbands. Women now have equal rights although progress is still needed in that area. The concepts of liberalism and gender equality in addition to the political system of democracy are part of Western culture. Therefore, the West for the most part has moved beyond fundamentalist interpretation of religious texts and their enforced application to society. This refers to the separation of church and state.

The Middle East and North Africa regions, where Muslims predominately reside, have not moved past a fundamentalist interpretation of Islam where jihadists interpret every word literally. The Islamic texts support jihadism as do many MENA cultures in general whether or not mass society participates in that support. There are enough fundamentalists to support jihad so that it is allowed to exist and thrive in society. However, time will tell as to whether Islam as an international movement, particularly in the MENA region, will embrace progressivism, gender equality, women's rights, human rights, tolerance, and other important values. Until that time occurs, jihadism will remain a danger to any culture or religion that threatens its existence.

NOTES

1. Christine Sixta, "The Illusive Third Wave: Are Female Terrorists the New "New Women" in Developing Societies?" *Journal of Women, Politics, and Policy* 29 (2) (2008): 261–88.

2. Simon Cottee, "What ISIS Women Want," *Foreign Policy*, May 17, 2016, accessed September 9, 2016, http://foreignpolicy.com/2016/05/17/what-isis-women-want-gendered-jihad/.

3. Aryn Baker, "How ISIS Is Recruiting Women from Around the World," *TIME*, September 6, 2014, accessed September 8, 2016, http://time.com/3276567/how-isis-is-recruiting-women-from-around-the-world/.

4. Anat Berko and Edna Erez, "Gender, Palestinian Women, and Terrorism: Women's Liberation or Oppression? *Studies in Conflict and Terrorism* 30 (6) (2007): 493–519, 506.

5. Anne Speckhard and Khapta Akhmedova, "Black Widows and Beyond: Understanding the Motivations and Life Trajectories of Chechen Female Terrorists," in *Female Terrorism and Militancy: Agency, Utility, and Organization* ed. Cindy D. Ness (New York: Routledge, 2008), 106.

6. Dorit Naaman, "Brides of Palestine/Angels of Death: Media, Gender, Performance in the Case of the Palestinian Female Suicide Bombers," *Signs* 32 (Summer 2007): 933–55, 935.

7. Hilary Matfess, *Women and the War on Boko Haram* (London: Zed Books, 2017), 130–34.

8. Anne Speckhard and Khapta Akhmedova, "Black Widows and Beyond: Understanding the Motivations and Life Trajectories of Chechen Female Terrorists," in *Female Terrorism and Militancy: Agency, Utility, and Organization* ed. Cindy D. Ness (New York: Routledge, 2008), 108.

9. Anat Berko and Edna Erez, "Gender, Palestinian Women, and Terrorism: Women's Liberation or Oppression? *Studies in Conflict and Terrorism* 30 (6) (2007): 493–519.

10. C. Christine Fair and Bryan Shepard, "Who Supports Terrorism? Evidence from Fourteen Muslim Countries," *Studies in Conflict and Terrorism* 29 (2006), 51–74.

11. R. Kim Cragin and Sara A. Daly, *Women as Terrorists* (Santa Barbara, CA: ABC CLIO, 2009), 106.

12. Leonard Weinberg and William Lee Eubank, *The Rise and Fall of Italian Terrorism* (Boulder, CO: Westview Press, 1987).

13. Leith Passmore, *Ulrike Meinhof and the Red Army Faction* (New York: Palgrave Macmillan, 2011) and Charity Scribner, *After the Red Army Faction: Gender, Culture, and Militancy* (New York: Columbia University Press, 2015).

14. Christina Coleman and Veronica Hilbring, "Black Panther 50—Here Are The Women Of The Black Panther Party," *Essence*, October 21, 2016, accessed November 7, 2018, https://www.essence.com/holidays/black-history-month/women-black-panther-party/.

15. See for example Christine Sixta Rinehart, *Volatile Social Movements and the Origins of Terrorism, The Radicalization of Change* (Lanham, MD: Lexington Books, 2014).

16. Luisella de Cataldo Neuberger and Tiziana Valentini, *Women and Terrorism* (New York: St. Martin's Press, 1996), Chapter 3.

17. Yoram Schweitzer, *Female Suicide Terrorism*, ed. Yoram Schweitzer (Tel Aviv: Jaffe Center Publications, 2006).

18. Yoram Schweitzer, "Palestinian Female Suicide Bombers: Reality vs. Myth" in *Female Suicide Terrorism*, ed. Yoram Schweitzer (Tel Aviv: Jaffe Center Publications, 2006), 25-41, 39–40.

19. Luisella de Cataldo Neuberger and Tiziana Valentini, *Women and Terrorism* (New York: St. Martin's Press, 1996), 95.

20. Leila Khaled, *My People Shall Live* (Raleigh, NC: NC Press, 1975).

21. Katharine Viner, "I Made the Ring from a Bullet and the Pin of a Hand Grenade," *The Guardian*, January 25, 2001, accessed September 15, 2016, https://www.theguardian.com/world/2001/jan/26/israel.

22. Barbara Victor, *Army of Roses* (Emmaus, PA: Rodale, 2003), 63–64.

23. Ronen A. Cohen, *The Rise and Fall of the Mojahedin Khalq 1987–1997,* (Brighton, England: Sussex Academic Press, 2009).

24. Jonathan Masters, "Mujahadeen-e-Khalq (MEK)," *Council on Foreign Relations*, July 28, 2014, accessed November 7, 2018, https://www.cfr.org/backgrounder/mujahadeen-e-khalq-mek.

25. Febriana Firdaus, "The Making of a Female ISIS Bomber," *New Naratif*, June 4, 2018, accessed November 7, 2018, https://newnaratif.com/journalism/making-female-isis-bomber/.

26. Karina M. Tehusijarana and Moses Ompusunggu, "What is JAD? Terror Group behind Mako Brimob Riot," *The Jakarta Post*, May 14, 2018, accessed November 7, 2018, http://www.thejakartapost.com/news/2018/05/14/what-is-jad-terror-group-behind-mako-brimob-riot-surabaya-bombings.html.

27. Encyclopedia Britannica, "Pancasila: Indonesian Political Philosophy," 2018, accessed November 7, 2018, https://www.britannica.com/topic/Pancasila.

28. Febriana Firdaus, "The Making of a Female ISIS Bomber," *New Naratif*, June 4, 2018, accessed November 7, 2018, https://newnaratif.com/journalism/making -female-isis-bomber/.

29. It is not permitted for male doctors to look at a woman naked as it destroys her virtue and modesty. Therefore, most Muslim women have female gynecologists in Islamic countries.

30. Anne Speckhard and Khapta Akhmedova, "Black Widows and Beyond: Under-standing the Motivations and Life Trajectories of Chechen Female Terrorists," in *Female Terrorism and Militancy: Agency, Utility, and Organization* ed. Cindy D. Ness (New York: Routledge, 2008), 116–17.

31. Hilary Matfess, *Women and the War on Boko Haram: Wives, Weapons, Witnesses* (London: Zed Books, 2017).

32. Brigitte L. Nacos, "The Portrayal of Female Terrorists in the Media: Similar Framing Patterns in the News Coverage of Women in Politics and Terrorism," *Studies in Conflict and Terrorism* 28 (5) (2005): 435–51.

33. Anne Speckhard and Ardian Shajikovci, "The Roles of Women in Supporting, Joining, Intervening In, and Preventing Violent Extremism, in Sandjak," *International Center for the Study of Violent Extremism*, December 21, 2016, accessed November 7, 2018, https://www.researchgate.net/publication/324900640_THE_ROLES_OF _WOMEN_IN_SUPPORTING_JOINING_INTERVENING_IN_AND_PREVENT ING_VIOLENT_EXTREMISM_IN_SANDJAK.

34. David Cook and Olivia Allison, *Understanding and Addressing Attacks: The Faith and Politics of Martyrdom Operations* (Westport, CT: Praeger Security Inter-national), 2007, xiv.

35. Nur Irfani Binte Saripi, "Female Members of ISIS A Greater Need for Reha-bilitation, *Counter Terrorist Trends and Analyses* 7(3) (April 2015): 26–31, 27.

36. Alex P. Schmid, "Public Opinion Survey Data to Measure Sympathy and Support for Islamist Terrorism," *International Centre For Counter-Terrorism—The Hague*, February 2017, accessed November 8, 2018, https://icct.nl/wp-content/up loads/2017/02/ICCT-Schmid-Muslim-Opinion-Polls-Jan2017-1.pdf.

37. David Cook and Olivia Allison, *Understanding and Addressing Attacks: The Faith and Politics of Martyrdom Operations* (Westport, CT: Praeger Security Inter-national), 2007, 12–13.

38. 1 Corinthians 11: 4–10 (New Revised Standard Version).

Bibliography

Abirafeh, Lina. "Gendered Aid Interventions and Afghan Women, Images Versus Realities." In *Muslim Women in War and Crisis*, edited by Faegheh Shirazi, 77–91. Austin: University of Texas Press, 2010.

Africa. "Boko Haram Crisis: Nigeria Arrests 'Female Recruiters.'" *BBC News.* July 4, 2014. Accessed August 8, 2018. https://www.bbc.com/news/world-africa -28168003.

Alcott, Amanda. "Gendered Narratives of "Black Widow" Terrorism in Russia's Northern Caucasus Region." Master's Thesis, Central European University, 2012.

Al Jazeerah News. "Bin Laden Has Set Up Female Suicide Squads: Report." *Arab News.* March 13 2003. Accessed May 23, 2018. www.aljazeerah.info/News%20 archives/2003%20News%20archives/March%202003%20News/13%20News/ Bin%20Laden%20has%20set20%20up%20female%20suicide%20squads%20 %aljazeerah.info.htm.

Al-Shishani, Murad Batal. "Is the Role of Women in al-Qaeda Increasing?" *BBC News.* October 7, 2010. Accessed September 26, 2018. https://www.bbc.com/ news/world-middle-east-11484672.

Alexander, Yonah. *Middle East Terrorism, Selected Group Profiles.* Washington, DC: Edward and Esther Reiner Philanthropic Foundation, 1994.

———. *Palestinian Religious Terrorism: Hamas and Islamic Jihad.* Ardsley, New York: Transnational Publishers, Inc., 2002.

Ali, Ayaan Hirsi. *The Caged Virgin: An Emancipation Proclamation for Women and Islam.* New York: Free Press, 2006.

Ali, Kecia. *Sexual Ethics and Islam: Feminist Reflections on Qur'an, Hadith, and Jurisprudence.* Oxford: One World, 2006.

Alison, Miranda. "Cogs in the Wheel? Women in the Liberation Tigers of Tamil Eelam." *Civil Wars* 6 (4) (Winter 2003), 37–54.

Allen, Lori. "There Are Many Reasons Why: Suicide Bombers and Martyrs in Palestine." *Middle East Report* 223 (Summer 2002), 34–37.

Amer, Adnan Abu. "Women's Roles in HAMAS Slowly Evolve." *Al-Monitor*. March 2, 2015. Accessed September 15, 2016. http://www.al-monitor.com/pulse/originals/2015/02/women--role-hamas-gaza-leadership-social-mobilization.html.

Ap, Tiffany. "What ISIS Wants from Women." *CNN*. November 20, 2015. Accessed September 8, 2016. http://www.cnn.com/2015/11/20/europe/isis-role-of-women/.

Argo, Victor. "Hezbollah in the Words of Two South Lebanese Women." *Your Middle East*. December 13, 2013. Accessed August 27, 2018. https://yourmiddleeast.com/2013/12/13/hezbollah-in-the-words-of-two-south-lebanese-women/.

Arraf, Jane. "ISIS Wives, With Children In Tow, Are Handed Long Jail Sentences Or Death Penalty." *National Public Radio*. June 9, 2018. Accessed August 1, 2018. https://www.npr.org/2018/06/09/613067263/isis-wives-with-children-in-tow-are-handed-long-jail-sentences-or-death-penalty.

The Associated Press. "Egyptian Sisters of the Muslim Brotherhood Rise with Conservative Vision." *Hareetz*. November 10, 2012. Accessed August 27, 2018. https://www.haaretz.com/egypt-muslim-sisters-rise-with-a-vision-1.5197442.

Avax. "Female Martyrs Train with Al-Aqsa Martyrs Brigade." *Avax News*. May 22, 2011. Accessed September 12, 2018. http://avax.news/sad/Female_Martyrs_Train_With_Al-Aqsa_Martyrs_Brigade.html.

Baker, Aryn. "How ISIS Is Recruiting Women from Around the World." *TIME*. September 6, 2014, accessed September 8, 2016. http://time.com/3276567/how-isis-is-recruiting-women-from-around-the-world/.

Banner, Francine. "Mothers, Bombers, Beauty Queens: Chechen Women's Roles in the Russo-Chechen Conflict." *Georgetown Journal of International Affairs* 9 (2) (Summer 2008): 77–88.

Barazangi, Nimat Hafez. *Women's Identity and the Qu'ran: A New Reading*. Gainesville: University of Florida Press, 2004.

Barlas, Asma. *"Believing Women" in Islam: Unreading Patriarchal Interpretations of the Qur'an*. Austin: University of Texas Press, 2002.

Bauer, Wolfgang. *Stolen Girls: Survivors of Boko Haram Tell Their Story*. New York: The New Press, 2016.

BBC News. "Hamas Woman Bomber Kills Israelis." *BBC News*. January 14, 2004. Accessed June 22, 2017. http://news.bbc.co.uk/2/hi/middle_east/3395973.stm.

Bergen, Peter L. *The Longest War: The Enduring Conflict between America and al-Qaeda*. New York: Free Press, 2011.

Bergen, Peter, Albert Ford, Alyssa Sims, and David Sterman. "Part II. Who Are the Terrorists?" *New America*. 2018. Accessed October 25, 2018. https://www.newamerica.org/in-depth/terrorism-in-america/who-are-terrorists/.

Berko, Anat. "Women in Terrorism: A Palestinian Feminist Revolution or Gender Oppression? *International-Institute for Counter-Terrorism*. June 12, 2006. Accessed February 5, 2018. https://www.ict.org.il/Article.aspx?ID=962#gsc.tab=0.

———. *The Path to Paradise: The Inner World of Suicide Bombers and Their Dispatchers*. Westport, CT: Praeger Security International, 2007.

Berko, Anat and Edna Erez. "Gender, Palestinian Women, and Terrorism: Women's Liberation or Oppression? *Studies in Conflict and Terrorism* 30 (6) (2007): 493–519.

Bianchi, Kendall. "Letters from Home: Hezbollah Mothers and the Culture of Martyrdom." *Combating Terrorism Center at West Point* 11 (2) (February 2018). Accessed July 31, 2018. https://ctc.usma.edu/letters-home-hezbollah-mothers-culture-martyrdom/.

Biography in Context. "How to Please Your Holy Warrior; Jihadist Chick Lit." *The Economist*. February 3, 2018. Accessed September 26, 2018. http://link.galegroup.com/apps/doc/A525895090/BIC?u=usclibs&sid=BIC&xid=24292283.

Blee, Kathlenn M. "Women in the 1920s' Ku Klux Klan Movement." *Feminist Studies* 17 (1) (Spring 1991): 55–77.

Bloom, Mia. *Bombshell*. Philadelphia: Penn State University Press, 2011.

Bodansky, Yossef. *Chechen Jihad*. New York: Harper Collins, 2007.

Bonn, Scott A. "White Females Are Rarely Murder Victims or Perpetrators." *Psychology Today*. October 12, 2015. Accessed September 25, 2018. https://www.psychologytoday.com/us/blog/wicked-deeds/201510/white-females-are-rarely-murder-victims-or-perpetrators.

Bonner, Michael. *Jihad in Islamic History*. Princeton: Princeton University Press, 2006.

Bronstein, Scott and Drew Griffin. "Young ISIS Recruit: I Was Blinded by Love." *CNN.* December 6, 2016. Accessed November 2, 2018. https://www.cnn.com/2016/12/02/us/mississippi-isis-muhammad-dakhlalla-interview/index.html.

Byman, Daniel L. and Jennifer R. Williams. "ISIS vs. Al Qaeda: Jihadism's Global Civil War." *The Brookings Institution*. February 24, 2015. Accessed July 31, 2018. https://www.brookings.edu/articles/isis-vs-al-qaeda-jihadisms-global-civil-war/.

Caiazza, Amy. "Why Gender Matters in Understanding September 11: Women, Militarism, and Violence." *IWPR Publication* 1908 (November 2001): 1–6.

Callimachi, Rukmini. "ISIS Enshrines a Theology of Rape." *New York Times*. August 13, 2015. Accessed June 23, 2017. https://www.nytimes.com/2015/08/14/world/middleeast/isis-enshrines-a-theology-of-rape.html?_r=0.

Caner, Ergun Mehmet and Emir Fethi Caner. *Unveiling Islam*. Grand Rapids, MI: Kregel Publications, 2002.

Cardi, Paula. *Hamas from Resistance to Government*. New York: Seven Stories Press, 2012.

Chastain, Mary. "List of Female Hezbollah Suicide Bombers Grows." *Breitbart.* August 18, 2013. Accessed June 23, 2017. http://www.breitbart.com/national-security/2013/08/18/women-rise-in-hezbollah-still-not-equal-to-men/.

———. "Women Volunteer for Sexual Jihad with Islamic State." *Breitbart.* August 27, 2014. Accessed January 31, 2018. http://www.breitbart.com/national-security/2014/08/27/women-volunteer-for-sexual-jihad-with-islamic-state/.

Chenoweth, Erica and Pauline Moore. *The Politics of Terror*. Oxford: Oxford University Press, 018.

Childress, Sarah and Joshua Baker. "American Mom Who Lived Under ISIS Charged with Lying to the FBI." *Frontline*. July 24, 2018. Accessed November 2, 2018. https://www.pbs.org/wgbh/frontline/article/american-woman-who-lived-under-isis-charged-with-lying-to-fbi/.

CNN Wire Staff. "Timeline: Osama bin Laden, Over the Years." *CNN*. May 2, 2011. Accessed December 30, 2015. http://www.cnn.com/2011/WORLD/asiapcf/05/02/bin.laden.timeline/.

Cohen, Ronen A. *The Rise and Fall of the Mojahedin Khalq 1987–1997*. Brighton, England: Sussex Academic Press, 2009.

Coleman, Christina and Veronica Hilbring. "Black Panther 50—Here Are The Women Of The Black Panther Party." *Essence*. October 21, 2016. Accessed November 7, 2018. https://www.essence.com/holidays/black-history-month/women-black-panther-party/.

Comolli, Virginia. *Boko Haram Nigeria's Islamist Insurgency*. London, Hurst & Company, 2015.

Connor, Tracy and Stephanie Seigel. "'Jihad Jane' Colleen LaRose Became a Terrorist for Love." *NBC News*. January 14, 2015. Accessed October 30, 2018. https://www.nbcnews.com/news/investigations/jihad-jane-colleen-larose-became-terrorist-love-n284636.

Cook, David. "Women Fighting in Jihad?" *Studies in Conflict and Terrorism* 28 (5) (2005): 375–84.

———. "Women Fighting in Jihad?" In *Female Terrorism and Militancy: Agency, Utility, and Organization*, edited by Cindy D. Ness, 37–48. New York: Routledge, 2008.

Cook, David and Olivia Allison. *Understanding and Addressing Attacks: The Faith and Politics of Martyrdom Operations*. Westport, CT: Praeger Security International, 2007.

Cooke, Miriam. "Women, Religion, and the Postcolonial Arab World." *Cultural Critique* 45 (Spring 2000): 150–84.

Cottee, Simon. "What ISIS Women Want." *Foreign Policy*. May 17, 2016. Accessed September 9, 2016. http://foreignpolicy.com/2016/05/17/what-isis-women-want-gendered-jihad/.

Counter Extremism Project. "Palestinian Islamic Jihad." *Counterextremism Project*. 2018. Accessed June 12, 2018. https://www.counterextremism.com/threat/palestinian-islamic-jihad.

———. "Tashfeen Malik." *Counter Extremism Project*. 2018. Accessed October 31, 2018. https://www.counterextremism.com/extremists/tashfeen-malik.

Cragin, R. Kim and Sara A. Daly. *Women as Terrorists*. Santa Barbara, CA: ABC-CLIO, 2009.

Cunningham, Karla. "Cross-Regional Trends in Female Terrorism." *Studies in Conflict and Terrorism*, 26 (3) (2003): 171–95.

Creswell, Robyn and Bernard Haykel. "Battle Lines: Want to Understand the jihadis? Read their Poetry." *The New Yorker*. June 8 & 15, 2015. Accessed August 20, 2018. https://www.newyorker.com/magazine/2015/06/08/battle-lines-jihad-creswell-and-haykel.

Dalton, Angela and Victor Asal. "Is it Ideology or Desperation: Why do Organizations Deploy Women in Violence Terrorist Attacks." *Studies in Conflict and Terrorism* 34 (10) (2011): 802–19.

Daraghmeh, Muhammad. "In Search of Stealthier Suicide Attackers: Islamic Jihad Encourages Women." *Associated Press*. 31 May 2003.

Davis, Jessica. "Women and Radical Islamic Terrorism: Planners, Perpetrators, Patrons? *The Canadian Institute of Strategic Studies*. May 2006. Accessed June 5, 2018. https://www.researchgate.net/publication/270959680_Women_and_rad ical_islamic_terrorism_planners_perpetrators_patrons.

———. *Women in Modern Terrorism: From Liberation Wars to Global Jihad and the Islamic State*. Lanham: Rowman & Littlefield, 2017.

Davis, Joyce M. *Martyrs: Innocence, Vengeance, and Despair in the Middle East*. New York: Palgrave Macmillan, 2003.

De Cataldo Neuberger, Luisella and Tiziana Valentini. *Women and Terrorism*. New York: St. Martin's Press, 1996.

Dearden, Lizzie. "ISIS Austrian Poster Girl Samra Kesinovic 'Used as Sex Slave' before Being Murdered for Trying to Escape." *The Independent*. December 31, 2015. Accessed November 5, 2018. https://www.independent.co.uk/news/world/ middle-east/isis-austrian-poster-girl-samra-kesinovic-used-as-sex-slave-before -being-murdered-for-trying-to-a6791736.html.

Dearing, Matthew P. "Agency and Structure as Determinants of Female Suicide Terrorism: A Comparative Study of Three Conflict Regions." MA Thesis, Naval Postgraduate School, 2012.

Della Porta, Donatella. "Left-wing Terrorism in Italy. In *Terrorism in Context,* edited by Martha W. Crenshaw, 105–59. State College, PA: Penn State University Press, 1994.

Department of Justice U.S Attorney's Office, District of Minnesota. "Minnesota Woman Charged with Stealing Passport to Travel to Syria." *United States Department of Defense*. December 2, 2014. Accessed October 30, 2018. https://www. justice.gov/usao-mn/pr/minnesota-woman-charged-stealing-passport-travel-syria.

Department of State. "Foreign Terrorist Organizations." *U.S. Department of State*. 2018. Accessed June 19, 2018. https://www.state.gov/j/ct/rls/other/des/123085.htm.

Di Giovanni, Janine. "Enter the Muslim Sisterhood." *Newsweek*. December 19, 2013. Accessed August 9, 2018. https://www.newsweek.com/2013/12/20/enter-muslim -sisterhood-244958.html.

Dickey, Christopher. "The Role of Women in al-Qaeda." *Newsweek*. January 2, 2010. Accessed August 9, 2018. https://www.newsweek.com/role-women-al -qaeda-70757.

Eager, Paige Whaley. *From Freedom Fighters to Terrorists: Women and Political Violence*. Burlington, Vermont: Ashgate, 2008.

Eickelman, Dale F. and James Piscatori. *Muslim Politics*. Princeton: Princeton University Press, 1996.

Emerson, Steven. *Jihad Incorporated*. Amherst, NY: Prometheus Books, 2006.

Encyclopedia Britannica. "Pancasila: Indonesian Political Philosophy." 2018. Accessed November 7, 2018. https://www.britannica.com/topic/Pancasila.

Epatko, Larissa. "Surviving Boko Haram: Kidnapped Girls Tell Their Stories." *PBS Newshour*. October 19, 2016. Accessed June 23, 2016. http://www.pbs.org/news hour/updates/surviving-boko-haram-kidnapped-girls-tell-stories/.

Eubank, William Lee and Leonard Weinberg. *The Rise and Fall of Italian Terrorism*. New York: Westview Press, 1987.

Evans, Ryan. "From Iraq to Yemen: Al-Qa'ida's Shifting Strategies." *Combating Terrorism Center at West Point*. October 1, 2010. Accessed January 12, 2016. https://www.ctc.usma.edu/posts/from-iraq-to-yemen-al-qaida%E2%80%99s-shifting-strategies.

Everywoman. "Women of Hezbollah." *Al Jazeera*. August 28, 2007. Accessed August 27, 2018. https://www.youtube.com/watch?v=vFCOFt24LLE.

Fair, Christine C. and Bryan Shepard. "Who Supports Terrorism? Evidence from Fourteen Muslim Countries." *Studies in Conflict and Terrorism* 29 (2006): 51–74.

Farahat, Cynthia. "The Muslim Brotherhood, Fountain of Islamist Violence." *Middle East Quarterly* (Spring 2017): 1–10.

Faridz, Devianti, Euan McKirdy, and Eliza Mackintosh. "Three Families Were Behind the ISIS-inspired Bombings in Indonesia's Surabaya, Police Said." CNN. May 15, 2018. Accessed September 19, 2018. https://edition.cnn.com/2018/05/13/asia/indonesia-attacks-surabaya-intl/index.html.

Fighel, Jonathan. "Palestinian Islamic Jihad and Female Suicide Bombers." *International Institute for Counter-Terrorism*. June 10, 2003. Accessed June 23, 2017. https://www.ict.org.il/Article/888/Palestinian%20Islamic%20Jihad%20and%20Female%20Suicide%20Bombers.

Firdaus, Febriana. "The Making of a Female ISIS Bomber." *New Naratif*. June 4, 2018. Accessed September 16, 2018. https://newnaratif.com/journalism/making-female-isis-bomber/.

Foden, Giles. "Death and Maidens." *The Guardian*. July 17, 2003. Accessed June 6, 2018. https://www.theguardian.com/world/2003/jul/18/gender.uk.

Forlitti, Amy. "Minneapolis Woman Gets Probation in Terrorism Case At Prosecution's Urging." *Twin Cities Pioneer Press*. April 27, 2017. Accessed October 30, 2018. https://www.twincities.com/2017/04/27/minneapolis-woman-gets-probtion-in-terrorism-case-at-prosecutions-urging/.

Fuller, Nicole. "Feds: Brentwood Woman Laundered Money to Support ISIS." *Newsday*. December 14, 2017. Accessed November 2, 2018. https://www.newsday.com/long-island/crime/brentwood-money-laundering-islamic-state-1.15455156.

Galvin, Deborah M. "The Female Terrorist: A Socio-Psychological Perspective." *Behavioral Sciences and the Law* 1 (2) (1983): 19–32.

Gardner, Frank. "The Crucial Role of Women within the Islamic State." *BBC News*. August 20, 2015. Accessed September 15, 2016. http://www.bbc.com/news/world-middle-east-33985441.

Georges-Abeyie, Daniel. "Women as Terrorists." In *Perspectives on Terrorism*, edited by Lawrence Freedman and Yonah Alexander, 71–84. Wilmington, DE: Scholarly Resources Inc., 1983.

Gerges, Fawaz A. *ISIS: A History*. Princeton: Princeton University Press, 2016.

Ghaddar, Hanin. "Hezbollah's Women Aren't Happy." *Tablet*. October 12, 2016. Accessed June 26, 2017. http://www.tabletmag.com/jewish-news-and-politics/215483/hezbollah-women.

Gigova, Radina. "Nigeria: Arrested Women Recruited for Boko Haram." *CNN*. July 5, 2014. Accessed August 8, 2018. https://www.cnn.com/2014/07/04/world/africa/nigeria-women-suspected-boko-haram/index.html.

Glover, Scott. "The FBI Translator Who Went Rogue and Married an ISIS Terrorist." *CNN*. May 1, 2017. Accessed November 1, 2018. https://www.cnn.com/2017/05/01/politics/investigates-fbi-syria-greene/index.html.

Golding, Bruce. "Female ISIS Captives Endure 'Brutal and Abnormal' Sex." *New York Post*. February 18, 2015. Accessed September 9, 2016. https://nypost.com/2015/02/18/female-isis-captives-endure-brutal-and-abnormal-sex/.

Gonzalez-Perez, Margaret. *Women and Terrorism: Female Activity in Domestic and International Terror Groups*. New York: Routledge, 2008.

Griset, Pamala and Sue Mahan, *Terrorism in Perspective*. Thousand Oaks, CA: Sage, 2003.

Groen, Janny and Annieke Kranenberg. *Women Warriors for Allah: An Islamist Network in the Netherlands*. Philadelphia: University of Pennsylvania Press, 2010.

Groskop, Viv. "Women at Heart of the Terror Cells." *The Guardian*. September 4, 2004. Accessed July 25, 2018. https://www.theguardian.com/world/2004/sep/05/russia.chechnya1.

Gunning, Jeroen. *Hamas in Politics*. New York: Columbia University Press, 2009.

Gürsoy-Naskali, Emine. "Women Mystics in Islam." In *Women in Islamic Societies: Social Attitudes and Historical Perspectives*, edited Bo Utas, 238-244. London: Curzon Press Ltd, 1983.

Habeck, Mary. *Knowing the Enemy, Jihadist Ideology and the War on Terror*. New Haven: Yale University Press, 2006.

Habiballah, Nahed. "Interviews with Mothers of Martyrs of the Aqsa Intifada." *Arab Studies Quarterly* 26 (1) (Winter 2004): 15–30.

Hahn, Gordon M. *Russia's Islamic Threat*. New Haven: Yale University Press, 2007.

Hamdan, Hanan. "Lebanese Women Determined to Continue Fight for More Political Representation." *Al-Monitor*. May 31, 2018. Accessed August 27, 2018. https://www.al-monitor.com/pulse/originals/2018/05/lebanon-2018-election-women-in-parliament-obstacles-quota.html.

Hamid, Shadi and Rashid Dar. "Islamism, Salafism, and jihadism: A Primer." *The Brookings Institution*. July 15, 2016. Accessed May 28, 2018. https://www.brookings.edu/blog/markaz/2016/07/15/islamism-salafism-and-jihadism-a-primer/.

Hammer, Chris. "The Women of Hamas." *SBS News*. August 23, 2013. Accessed August 27, 2018. https://www.sbs.com.au/news/the-women-of-hamas.

Harel, Amos. "First Known Female Hamas Bomb Maker Among Many Detainees." *Haaretz*. October 11, 2005. Accessed August 22, 2018. https://www.haaretz.com/1.4877573.

Harnden, Toby. "Hamas Mother's Suicide Bombing Kills 4." *The Telegraph*. January 15, 2004. Accessed July 30, 2018. https://www.telegraph.co.uk/news/worldnews/middleeast/israel/1451737/Hamas-mothers-suicide-bombing-kills-4.html.

Hasso, Frances S. "Discursive and Political Deployments by/of the 2002 Palestinian Women Suicide Bombers/Martyrs." *Feminist Review* 81 (2005): 23–51.

Hegghammer, Thomas. "The Soft Power of Militant Jihad." *The New York Times*. December 18, 2015. Accessed August 20, 2018. https://www.nytimes.com/2015/12/20/opinion/sunday/militant-jihads-softer-side.html.

Hekmat, Anwar. *Women and the Koran: The Status of Women in Islam*. New York: Prometheus Books, 1997.

Hendren, John and Clayton Sandell. "American Held in Ireland, No 'Jihad Jamie,' Is Released." *ABC News*. March 13, 2010. Accessed October 31, 2018. https://abcnews.go.com/WN/woman-released-arrest-terror-plot/story?id=10094548.

Hoffman, Valerie. "An Islamic Activist: Zaynab al-Ghazali." In *Women and the Family in the Middle East: New Voices of Change*, edited by Elizabeth W. Fernea, 233–54. Austin: University of Texas Press, 1985.

Hroub, Khaled. *HAMAS: A Beginner's Guide*, 2nd edition. New York: Pluto Press, 2010.

Huey, Laura, Inch, Rachel and Hillary Peladeau. "@ me if you need shoutout": Exploring Women's Roles in Islamic State Twitter Networks." *Studies in Conflict & Terrorism* (2017). Accessed November 5, 2018. https://www.tandfonline.com/doi/abs/10.1080/1057610X.2017.1393897.

Human Rights Watch. "V. Structures and Strategies of the Perpetrator Organizations." *Human Rights Watch*. 2002. Accessed June 19, 2018. https://www.hrw.org/reports/2002/isrl-pa/ISRAELPA1002-05.htm#P841_205536.

Hurdle, John. "10 Years for Plot to Murder Cartoonist." *New York Times*. January 6, 2014. Accessed October 31, 2018. https://www.nytimes.com/2014/01/07/us/jihad-jane-given-10-year-prison-sentence.html.

Hymowitz. Kay S. "Why Feminism is AWOL on Islam." *City Journal*. Winter 2003. Accessed January 8, 2018. https://www.city-journal.org/html/why-feminism-awol-islam-12395.html.

Insite Blog on Terrorism and Extremism. "Translated Message From Zawahiri's Wife To Muslim Women." *Insite Blog on Terrorism and Extremism*. 2008. Accessed September 19, 2018. http://news.siteintelgroup.com/blog/index.php/about-us/21-jihad/227-translated-message-from-zawahiris-wife-to-muslim-women.

Intelligence and Information Center. "As Part of the Gaza Strip Military Buildup, Women Are Trained for Combat and for Suicide Bombing Attacks." Israel Intelligence Heritage and Commemoration Center. September 7, 2008. Accessed September 28, 2018. https://www.terrorism-info.org.il/en/18419/.

"*ISIS: Sex Slaves*." YouTube documentary. 40:31. Posted by Ahlulbayt: Documentaries. June 14, 2016. https://www.youtube.com/watch?v=3A6-55TJNrl&t=148s.

Israel Ministry of Foreign Affairs. "Attack by Female Suicide Bomber Thwarted at Erez Crossing." *Israel Ministry of Foreign Affairs*. June 20, 2005. Accessed July 18, 2018. http://www.mfa.gov.il/mfa/foreignpolicy/terrorism/palestinian/pages/attack%20by%20female%20suicide%20bomber%20thwarted%20at%20erez%20crossing%2020-jun-2005.aspx.

Jacques, Karen and Paul J. Taylor. "Male and Female Suicide Bombers: Different Sexes, Different Reasons?" *Studies in Conflict and Terrorism* 31 (2008): 304–26.

Jones, David E. *Women Warriors: A History*. Lincoln, NE: Potomac Books, 2005.

Jones, Sophia. "The Sisters of the Muslim Brotherhood." *The Daily Beast*. July 9, 2013. Accessed August 9, 2018. https://www.thedailybeast.com/the-sisters-of-the -muslim-brotherhood?ref=scroll.

Kachroo, Rohit. "Bethnal Green Schoolgirl Kadiza Sultana Who Joined Islamic State 'Killed in Airstrike in Syria.'" ITV News Reveals. *ITV News*. August 11, 2016. Accessed November 5, 2018. https://www.itv.com/news/2016-08-11/bethnal-green -schoolgirl-kadiza-sultana-who-joined-islamic-state-killed-in-airstrike-in-syria/.

Kandil, Hazem. *Inside the Brotherhood.* Malden, MA: Polity Press, 2015.

Kassim, Abdulbasit and Michael Nwankpa. *The Boko Haram Reader*. London: Hurst & Company, 2018.

Keck, Zachary and Matthew Sparks. "The Shia Shift: Why Iran and Hezbollah Abandoned Martyrdom." *The National Interest*. May 28, 2018. Accessed August 14, 2018. https://nationalinterest.org/feature/the-shia-shift-why-iran-hezbollah -abandoned-martyrdom-25992.

Khaled, Leila. *My People Shall Live*. Raleigh, NC: NC Press, 1975.

Khaleeli, H. "The British Women Married to Jihad." *The Guardian*. September 6, 2014. Accessed November 5, 2018. https://www.theguardian.com/world/2014/ sep/06/british-women-married-to-jihad-isis-syria.

Khalil, Dalia. *Hizbullah: The Story from Within*. London: Saqi, 2005.

Khan, Muhammad Muhsin, ed. *The Translation of the Meaning of Sahih Bukhari*. Houston: Dar-us-Salam Publications, 1997.

Kramer, Martin. "The Moral Logic of Hezbollah." In *Origins of Terrorism*, edited by Walter Reich, 131–57. Washington, DC: Woodrow Wilson Center Press, 1998.

Laur, Nancy. "Terrorism: The Female Experience." Masters of Philosophy Thesis, The Irish School of Ecumenics, Center for Peace Studies, Trinity College, Dublin 1992.

Lawrence, Bruce B. *Shattering the Myth: Islam Beyond Violence*. Princeton: Princeton University Press, 1998.

Levitt, Matthew. *Targeting Terror U.S.: Policy Toward Middle Eastern State Sponsors and Terrorist Organizations, Post-September 11*. Washington, DC: The Washington Institute for Near East Policy, 2002.

Lister, Charles. "Profiling the Islamic State." *Brookings Doha Center Analysis Paper*. November 12, 2014. Accessed March 24, 2016. http://www.brookings.edu/~/ media/Research/Files/Reports/2014/11/profiling%20islamic%20state%20lister/ en_web_lister.pdf.

Løvlie, Frodie. "Questioning the Secular-Religious Cleavage in Palestinian Politics: Comparing Fatah and Hamas." *Politics and Religion* 7 (2014): 100–21.

MacDonald, Eileen. *Shoot the Women First*. New York: Random House, 1992.

Maclean, Ruth. "Dressed for Death: The Women Boko Haram Sent to Blow Themselves Up." *The Guardian*. May 5, 2017. Accessed August 8, 2018. https://www. theguardian.com/world/2017/may/05/dressed-for-death-the-women-boko-haram -sent-to-blow-themselves-up.

Margolin, Devorah. "A Palestinian Woman's Place in Terrorism: Organized Perpetrators or Individual Actors." *Studies in Conflict and Terrorism* 39 (10) (2016): 912–34.

Markus, Ben. "Arvada Teen Sentenced to 4 Years in Prison For ISIS Terror Plot." *Colorado Public Radio*. January 23, 2015. Accessed October 30, 2018. https://www.cpr.org/news/story/arvada-teen-faces-sentencing-over-terror-plot.

Martinez, Luis. "Number of ISIS Fighters in Iraq and Syria Drops, Increases in Libya, US Official Says." *ABC News*. February 4, 2016. Accessed March 24, 2016. http://abcnews.go.com/International/number-isis-fighters-iraq-syria-drops-increases-libya/story?id=36715635.

Martinez, Michael, Ana Cabrera, and Sara Weisfeldt. "Colorado Woman Gets 4 Years for Wanting to Join ISIS." *CNN*. January 24, 2015. Accessed October 30, 2018. https://www.cnn.com/2015/01/23/us/colorado-woman-isis-sentencing/index.html.

Marvasti, Jamshid A. and Susan Plese. "Female Suicide Warriors/Bombers." In *Psycho-Political Aspects of Suicide Warriors, Terrorism and Martyrdom, A Critical View from "Both Sides" in Regard to Cause and Cure,* edited by Jamshid A. Marvasti, 269–84. Springfield, IL: Charles C. Thomas, Publisher LTD, 2008.

Masters, Jonathan. "Mujahadeen-e-Khalq (MEK)." *Council on Foreign Relations*. July 28, 2014. Accessed November 7, 2018. https://www.cfr.org/backgrounder/mujahadeen-e-khalq-mek.

Masters, Sam. "Iraq Crisis: Starving, Desperate, but Safe from ISIS on Mount Sinjar." *Independent.* August 9, 2014. Accessed June 23, 2017. http://www.independent.co.uk/news/world/middle-east/iraq-crisis-starving-desperate-but-safe-from-isis-on-mount-sinjar-9659449.html.

Mastors, Elena and Alyssa Deffenbaugh. *The Lesser Jihad: Recruits and the Al-Qaida Network.* Lanham: Rowman & Littlefield Publishers, Inc., 2007.

Matfess, Hilary. *Women and the War on Boko Haram: Wives, Weapons, Witnesses*. London: Zed Books, 2017.

McCants, William. *The ISIS Apocalypse: The History, Strategy, and Doomsday Vision of the Islamic State*. New York: St. Martin's Press, 2015.

McCoy, Terrence. "'Lady al-Qaeda': The American-educated PHD the Islamic State Desperately Wants Freed." August 28, 2014. Accessed October 30, 2018. https://www.washingtonpost.com/news/morning-mix/wp/2014/08/28/lady-al-qaeda-the-american-educated-doctor-the-islamic-state-desperately-wants-freed/?utm_term=.b8b7ea4db9c4.

McGreal, Chris. "Women MPs Vow to Change Face of Hamas." *The Guardian*. February 17, 2006. Accessed August 27, 2018. https://www.theguardian.com/world/2006/feb/18/israel.islam.

Merari, Ariel. *Driven to Death*. Oxford: Oxford University Press, 2010.

Mernissi, Fatima. *Beyond the Veil: Male-Female Dynamics in Modern Muslim Society*. New York: John Wiley and Sons, 1975.

———. *The Veil and the Male Elite*. New York: Basic Books, 1991.

Mhajne, Anwar. "How the Muslim Brotherhood's women activists stepped up in Egypt." *Middle East Eye*. January 15, 2018. Accessed August 27, 2018. https://www.middleeasteye.net/essays/muslim-sisters-agents-resistance-2092726647.

Middle Eastern Forum. "U.S. Department of State: Marriage to Saudis." 2003. Accessed August 7, 2018. https://www.meforum.org/articles/other/u-s-department-of-state-marriage-to-saudis.

Milton-Edwards, Beverley and Stephen Farrell. *Hamas: The Islamic Resistance Movement*. Malden, MA: Polity Press, 2010.

Mitchell, Richard P. *The Society of the Muslim Brothers*. New York: Oxford University Press, 1969.

Murphy, Paul J. *The Wolves of Islam.* Washington, DC: Brassey's Inc., 2004.

Myers, Russell. "British Female Jihadis Running ISIS 'Brothels' Allowing Killers to Rape Kidnapped Yazidi Women." *Mirror*. September 10, 2014. Accessed June 23, 2017. http://www.mirror.co.uk/news/uk-news/british-female-jihadis-running -isis-4198165.

Naaman, Dorit. "Brides of Palestine/Angels of Death: Media, Gender, Performance in the Case of the Palestinian Female Suicide Bombers." *Signs* 32 (Summer 2007): 933–55.

Nacos, Brigitte. "The Portrayal of Female Terrorists in the Media: Similar Framing Patterns in the News Coverage of Women in Politics and Terrorism." *Studies in Conflict and Terrorism* 28 (5) (2005): 435–51.

Nance, Malcolm. *Defeating ISIS, Who They Are, How They Fight, What they Believe*. New York: Skyhorse Publishing, 2016.

Naskali, Esko. "Women of the Prophet's Family as They Feature in Popular Bazaar Literature." In *Women in Islamic Societies: Social Attitudes and Historical Perspectives*, edited by Bo Utas, 245–52. London: Curzon Press Ltd, 1983.

Ness, Cindy D. "In the Name of the Cause: Women's Work in Secular and Religious Terrorism." In *Female Terrorism and Militancy: Agency, Utility, and Organization*, edited by Cindy D. Ness, 11–36. New York: Routledge, 2008.

Nesser, Petter. *Islamist Terrorism in Europe: A History*. Oxford: Oxford University Press, 2015.

Neuberger, Luisella de Cataldo and Tiziana Valentini. *Women and Terrorism*. New York: St. Martin's Press, 1996.

Nivat, Anne. "The Black Widows: Chechen Women Join the Fight for Independence- and Allah." In *Female Terrorism and Militancy: Agency, Utility, and Organization* edited by Cindy D. Ness, 122–30. New York: Routledge, 2008.

Noueihed, Lin. "Sisters in the Vanguard as Egypt's Muslim Brotherhood Battles to Survive." *Reuters*. December 15, 2014. Accessed June 27, 2017. http://www. reuters.com/article/us-egypt-brotherhood-women-idUSKBN0JT1PD20141215.

Obaji, Philip. "Boko Haram's Rescued Sex Slaves Tell Their Horror Stories." *The Daily Beast*. May 6, 2015. Accessed July 19, 2018. https://www.thedailybeast. com/boko-harams-rescued-sex-slaves-tell-their-horror-stories?ref=scroll.

Oduah, Chika. "The Women Who Love Boko Haram." *Aljazeera*. September 22, 2016. Accessed July 19, 2018. https://www.aljazeera.com/indepth/features/2016/08/ women-love-loved-boko-haram-160823120617834.html.

O'Rourke, Lindsey. "What's Special about Female Suicide Terrorism?" *Security Studies,* 18 (4) (2009): 681–718.

Osborne, Samuel. "ISIS Starts Using Female Fighters and Suicide Bombers for the First Time." *Independent*. February 29, 2016. Accessed June 23, 2017. http://www. independent.co.uk/news/world/africa/isis-starts-using-female-fighters-and-suicide -bombers-for-the-first-time-a6903166.html.

Pape, Robert A. *Dying to Win.* New York: Random House, 2005.

Passmore, Leith. *Ulrike Meinhof and the Red Army Faction.* New York: Palgrave Macmillan, 2011.

Patkin, Terri Toles. "Explosive Baggage: Female Palestinian Suicide Bombers and the Rhetoric of Emotion." *Women and Language* 27 (2), (2004): 79–88.

Pedahzur, Ami. *Suicide Terrorism.* Malden, MA: Polity Press, 2005.

Peladeau, Hillary. "Support for Sisters Please"; Comparing the Online Roles of al-Qaeda Women and the Islamic State Counterparts." Master's Thesis, University of Western Ontario, 2016.

Perešin, Anita. "Fatal Attraction Western Muslimas and ISIS." *Perspectives on Terrorism* 9 (3) (June 2015): 21–38.

Perešin, Anita and Alberto Cervone. "The Western Muhajirat of ISIS." *Studies in Conflict and Terrorism* 38 (7) (2015): 495–509.

Pierce, Genevieve. "The Media's Gender Stereotype Framing of Chechen 'Black Widows' and Female Afghan Self-Immolators." Master's Thesis, Central European University, 2011.

Pokalova, Elena. *Chechnya's Terrorist Network: The Evolution of Terrorism in Russia's Northern Caucus.* Santa Barbara, CA: Praeger 2015.

Qazi, Farhana. "A Close Look at the Women in Al-Qaeda and ISIS." *FarhanaQazi. com.* January 31, 2015. Accessed August 9, 2018. http://farhanaqazi.com/a-close -look-at-the-women-in-al-qaeda-and-isis/.

Raghavan, S. V. and V. Balasubrmaniyan. "Evolving Role of Women in Terror Groups: Progression or Regression." *Journal of International Women's Studies,* 15 (2) (2017): 197–211.

Rajan, V. G. *Women Suicide Bombers: Narratives of Violence.* New York: Routledge, 2011.

Reuter, John. "Chechnya's Suicide Bombers: Desperate, Devout, or Deceived?" *The Jamestown Foundation.* August 23, 2004. Accessed July 25, 2018. https://james town.org/report/chechnyas-suicide-bombers-desperate-devout-or-deceived/.

Reuter, Krislyn. "Why Not Use Women?: An Examination of the Conditions Under Which an Islamic Terrorist Organization Will Employ Female Suicide Terrorism." MA Thesis, Georgetown University, 2011.

Roggio, Bill and Caleb Weiss. "Female Suicide Bombers Continue to Strike in West Africa." *FDD's Long War Journal.* December 4, 2015. Accessed June 23, 2017. http://www.longwarjournal.org/archives/2015/12/female-suicide-bombers -continue-to-strike-in-west-africa.php.

Rinehart, Christine Sixta. "Volatile Breeding Grounds: The Radicalization of the Egyptian Muslim Brotherhood," *Studies in Conflict and Terrorism* 32 (November 2009): 952–88.

———. *Volatile Social Movements and the Origins of Terrorism, The Radicalization of Change.* Lanham, MD: Lexington Books, 2014.

———. *Drones and Targeted Killing in the Middle East and Africa, An Appraisal of American Counterterrorism Policies.* Lanham, MD: Lexington Books, 2016.

Robin, Morgan. *The Demon Lover: The Roots of Terrorism.* New York: W.W. Norton & Company.

Roy, Sarah. *Engaging the Islamist Social Sector*. Princeton: Princeton University Press, 2011.

Russell, Charles A. and Bowman H. Miller. "Profile of a Terrorist." In *Perspectives on Terrorism,* edited by Lawrence Zelic Freedman and Yonah Alexander, 45–60. Wilmington, DE: Scholarly Resources, Inc., 1983.

Sageman, Marc. *Understanding Terror Networks*. Philadelphia: Pennsylvania University Press, 2004.

Salazar, Philippe-Joseph. *Words are Weapons*. New Haven: Yale University Press, 2017.

Saripi, Nur Irfani Binte. "Female Members of ISIS: A Greater Need for Rehabilitation." *Counter Terrorist Trends and Analyses* 7 (3) (April 2015): 26–31.

Schanzer, Jonathan. *Hamas vs. Fatah*. New York: Palgrave MacMillan, 2008.

Schenker, David. "The Women of Hezbollah." *The New Republic*. August 9, 2010. Accessed June 27, 2017. https://newrepublic.com/article/76826/the-women -hezbollah`.

Schmid, Alex P. "Public Opinion Survey Data to Measure Sympathy and Support for Islamist Terrorism." *International Centre For Counter-Terrorism—The Hague*. February 2017. Accessed November 8, 2018. https://icct.nl/wp-content/ uploads/2017/02/ICCT-Schmid-Muslim-Opinion-Polls-Jan2017-1.pdf.

Schweitzer, Yoram. "Introduction." In *Female Suicide Bombers: Dying for Equality,* edited by Yoram Schweitzer, 7–12. Tel Aviv: *Jaffee Center for Strategic Studies*, August 2006.

———. "Palestinian Female Suicide Bombers: Reality vs. Myth." In *Female Suicide Bombers: Dying for Equality*, edited by Yoram Schweitzer, 25–41. Tel Aviv: *Jaffee Center for Strategic Studies*, August 2006.

———, ed. *Female Suicide Terrorism*. Tel Aviv: Jaffe Center Publications, 2006.

Sciolino, Elaine and Souad Mekhennet. "Al Qaeda Warrior Uses Internet to Rally Women." *The New York Times*. May 28, 2008. Accessed November 5, 2018. https://www.nytimes.com/2008/05/28/world/europe/28terror.html.

Scribner, Charity. *After the Red Army Faction: Gender, Culture, and Militancy*. New York: Columbia University Press, 2015.

Searcey, Diane. "Boko Haram Strapped Suicide Bombs to Them. Somehow These Teenage Girls Survived." *The New Times*. October 25, 2017. Accessed August 8, 2018. https://www.nytimes.com/interactive/2017/10/25/world/africa/nigeria-boko -haram-suicide-bomb.html.

Selegny, Thomas. "Developments in the Modern Middle East: Gender & Revolutions: Re-thinking the "Woman Question" in the Modern Middle East." *Research Gate*. May 2014. Accessed July 31, 2018. https://www.researchgate.net/publica tion/303285448_Hezbollah_women%27s_motherhood.

Shakir, MH trans. *Qu'ran*. Elmhurst, NY: Tahrike Tarsile Qur'an, Inc., 2004.

Shehata, Said. "Profile: Egypt's Freedom and Justice Party." *BBC News*. November 25, 2011. Accessed August 27, 2018. https://www.bbc.com/news/world-middle -east-15899548.

Shevardnadze, Sophie. "ISIS Sex Slave Survivor: They Beat Me, Raped Me, Treated Me Like an Animal." *RT*. August 19, 2016. Accessed June 23, 2017. https://www.rt.com/shows/sophieco/336398-is-slave-horrors-crime/.

Shirazi, Faegheh. *Velvet Jihad: Muslim Women's Quiet Resistance to Islamic Fundamentalism*. Gainesville: University of Florida Press, 2009.

al-Shishani, Murad Batal. "Is the Role of Women in al-Qaeda Increasing?" *BBC News*. October 7, 2010. Accessed June 27, 2017. http://www.bbc.com/news/world-middle-east-11484672.

Sixta, Christine. "The Illusive Third Wave: Are Female Terrorists the New "New Women" in Developing Societies." *Journal of Women, Politics, and Policy* 29 (2) (2008): 261–88.

Skaine, Rosemarie. *Female Suicide Bombers*. Jeffferson, NC: McFarland & Company, Inc., Publishers, 2006.

Smith, Samuel. "Girl Impregnated by 3 Boko Haram Fighters Details Horrors of Sex Slavery." *Christian Post*. January 7, 2017. Accessed July 19, 2018. https://www.christianpost.com/news/girl-impregnated-by-3-boko-haram-fighters-details-horrors-of-sex-slavery-172653/page1.html.

Speckhard, Anne. "The Emergence of Female Suicide Terrorists." *Studies in Conflict and Terrorism*. 31 (11) (2008): 995–1023.

———. "Female Terrorists in ISIS, al Qaeda and 21rst Century Terrorism." *Trends Research: Inside the Mind of a Jihadist*. May 4, 2015. Accessed September 9, 2016. http://trendsinstitution.org/wp-content/uploads/2015/05/Female-Terrorists-in-ISIS-al-Qaeda-and-21rst-Century-Terrorism-Dr.-Anne-Speckhard11.pdf.

Speckhard, Anne and Khapta Akhmedova. "The New Chechen Jihad: Militant Wahhabism as a Radical Movement and a Source of Suicide Terrorism in Post-War Chechen Society." *Democracy and Security* 2 (2006): 103–55.

———. "Black Widows: The Chechen Female Suicide Terrorists." In *Female Suicide Bombers: Dying for Equality*, edited by Yoram Schweitzer, 63–80. Tel Aviv: Jaffee Center for Strategic Studies, August 2006.

———. "Black Widows and Beyond: Understanding the Motivations and Life Trajectories of Chechen Female Terrorists." In *Female Terrorism and Militancy: Agency, Utility, and Organization*, edited by Cindy D. Ness, 100–21. New York: Routledge, 2008.

Speckhard, Anne and Ardian Shajikovci. "The Roles of Women in Supporting, Joining, Intervening In, and Preventing Violent Extremism, in Sandjak." *International Center for the Study of Violent Extremism*. December 21, 2016. Accessed November 7, 2018. https://www.researchgate.net/publication/324900640_THE_ROLES_OF_WOMEN_IN_SUPPORTING_JOINING_INTERVENING_IN_AND_PRE VENTING_VIOLENT_EXTREMISM_IN_SANDJAK.

———. "Is ISIS Still Alive and Well on the Internet?" *International Center for the Study of Violent Extremism* (January 14, 2019).

Speckhard, Anne, Ardian Shajkovci, Claire Wooster, and Neima Izadi. "Mounting a Facebook Brand Awareness and Safety Ad Campaign to Break the ISIS Brand in Iraq." *Perspectives on Terrorism* 12 (3)(June 2018): 50–66.

Speckhard, Anne, Grace Wakim, and Ardian Shajkovci. "Ensuring a Long-term Win Against ISIS in Mosul: The Need for Rehabilitation and Reintegration Programs & Restoring Security and Justice." *International Center for the Study of Violent Extremism.* July 27, 2017. Accessed November 6, 2018. https://www.academia.edu/34049265/Ensuring_a_Long-term_Win_Against_ISIS_In_Mosul_The_Need_for_Rehabilitation_and_Reintegration_Programs_and_Restoring_Security_and_Justice.

Stack-O'Connor, Alisa. "Picked Last Women and Terrorism." *Joint Force Quarterly* 44 (1) (2007): 95–100.

Staff, Toi. "Encouraging our children to kill themselves for Palestine is a mother's most glorious duty, says wife of Hamas MP." *Times of Israel.* January 8, 2013. Accessed July 30, 2018. http://www.timesofisrael.com/encouraging-our-children-to-kill-themselves-for-palestine-is-a-mothers-most-glorious-duty-says-wife-of-hamas-mp/?fb_comment_id=128360617328786_170884#f3acb71d4e376aa.

Standish, Katerina. "Human Security and Gender: Female Suicide Bombers in Palestine and Chechnya." *Peace and Conflict Review* 1 (2) (2008): 1–39.

Starr, Harvey. *Approaches, Levels, and Methods of Analysis in International Politics: Crossing Boundaries (Advances in Foreign Policy Analysis).* London: Palgrave MacMillan, 2006.

Storey, Kate. "How Women Join ISIS: Women and Girls in Terrorism." *Maire Claire.* April 22, 2016. Accessed September 8, 2016. http://www.marieclaire.com/politics/a20011/western-women-who-join-isis/.

Stowasser, Barbara Freyer. *Women in the Qur'an: Traditions and Interpretation.* Oxford: Oxford University Press, 1994.

Sultan, Wafa. *A God Who Hates.* New York: St. Martin's Press, 2009.

Talbot, Rhiannon. "Myths in the Representation of Women Terrorists." Éire-Ireland 35 (3 and 4) (2000), 165–86.

Tehusijarana, Karina M. and Moses Ompusunggu. "What Is JAD? Terror Group behind Mako Brimob Riot." *The Jakarta Post.* May 14, 2018. Accessed November 7, 2018. http://www.thejakartapost.com/news/2018/05/14/what-is-jad-terror-group-behind-mako-brimob-riot-surabaya-bombings.html.

Third, Amanda. *Gender and the Political: Deconstructing the Female Terrorist.* New York: Palgrave MacMillan, 2014.

Tzoreff, Mira. "The Palestinian Shahida: National Patriotism, Islamic Feminism or Social Crisis." In *Female Suicide Terrorism*, edited by Yoram Schweitzer, 13–23. Tel Aviv: Jaffe Center Publications, 2005.

Victor, Barbara. *Army of Roses: Inside the World of Palestinian Women Suicide Bombers.* Emmaus, PA: Rodale, 2003.

Viner, Katherine. "I Made the Ring from a Bullet and the Pin of a Hand Grenade." *The Guardian.* January 25, 2001. Accessed September 15, 2016. https://www.theguardian.com/world/2001/jan/26/israel.

Von Knop, Katharina. "The Female Jihad: Al Qaeda's Women." *Studies in Conflict and Terrorism* 30 (5) (2007): 397–414.

Walther, Wiebke. *Women in Islam.* Princeton: Markus Wiener Publishing, 1992.

Warner, Jason and Hilary Matfess. "Exploding Stereotypes: Characteristics of Boko Haram's Suicide Bombers—The Unexpected Operational and Demographic." *Combating Terrorism at West Point.* August 17, 2017. Accessed July 18, 2018 https://ctc.usma.edu/app/uploads/2017/08/Exploding-Stereotypes-1.pdf.

Wasserstein, David J. *Black Banners of ISIS.* New Haven, CT: Yale University Press, 2017.

Webster, Benjamin. "Court to Hear New Reports on Pakistani Scientist's Fitness for Trial." *The New York Times.* July 5, 2009. Accessed October 30, 2018. https://www.nytimes.com/2009/07/06/nyregion/06competency.html.

Weinberg, Leonard. "The Violent Life: Left- and Right-Wing Terrorism in Italy." In *Political Violence and Terror, Motifs and Motivations,* edited by Peter Merkl, 145–68. Berkeley: University of California Press, 1986.

Weinberg, Leonard and William Lee Eubank. "Italian Women Terrorism." *Terrorism: an International Journal* 9 (1987).

The Rise and Fall of Italian Terrorism. Boulder, CO: Westview Press, 1987.

Weiss, Michael and Hassan Hassan. *ISIS: Inside the Army of Terror.* New York: Regan Arts, 2015.

Williams, David, Matthew Blake, Martin Robison, and David Martosko. "Yazidi 'Slave' Women Captured by ISIS Fanatics in Iraq." *Daily Mail.* August 8, 2014. Accessed September 8, 2016. http://www.dailymail.co.uk/news/article-2719698/President-Obama-authorises-airstrikes-Iraq-defend-civilians-Islamic-militants-swarming-country.html.

Zedalis, Debra D. *Female Suicide Bombers.* Honolulu: University Press of the Pacific, 2004.

Zollner, Barbara H. E. *The Muslim Brotherhood: Hasan al-Hudaybi and Ideology.* London: Routledge, 2009.

Index

About the Author

Christine Sixta Rinehart is an associate professor of political science at the University of South Carolina Palmetto College. She earned her PhD from the University of South Carolina in 2008. Her research interests include international terrorism, female terrorism, and security and counterterrorism. Her first book *Volatile Social Movements and the Origins of Terrorism: The Radicalization of Change* was published in December 2012 by Lexington Books. Her second book, *Drones and Targeted Killing in the Middle East and Africa: An Appraisal of American Counterterrorism Policies* was published by Lexington Books in December 2016.

www.ingramcontent.com/pod-product-compliance
Lightning Source LLC
Chambersburg PA
CBHW022312280326
41932CB00010B/1076